Narrative Processes in Emotion-Focused Therapy for Trauma

Narrative Processes in Emotion-Focused Therapy for Trauma

Sandra C. Paivio and Lynne E. Angus

American Psychological Association • Washington, DC

Published by
American Psychological Association
750 First Street, NE
Washington, DC 20002
www.apa.org

To order
APA Order Department
P.O. Box 92984
Washington, DC 20090-2984
Tel: (800) 374-2721; Direct: (202) 336-5510
Fax: (202) 336-5502; TDD/TTY: (202) 336-6123
Online: www.apa.org/pubs/books
E-mail: order@apa.org

In the U.K., Europe, Africa, and the Middle East, copies may be ordered from
American Psychological Association
3 Henrietta Street
Covent Garden, London
WC2E 8LU England

Typeset in Goudy by Circle Graphics, Inc., Columbia, MD

Printer: Sheridan Books, Chelsea, MI
Cover Designer: Mercury Publishing Services, Inc., Rockville, MD

The opinions and statements published are the responsibility of the authors, and such opinions and statements do not necessarily represent the policies of the American Psychological Association.

Library of Congress Cataloging-in-Publication Data

Names: Paivio, Sandra C., author. | Angus, Lynne E., author.
Title: Narrative processes in emotion-focused therapy for trauma / Sandra C. Paivio and Lynne E. Angus.
Description: Washington, DC : American Psychological Association, [2017] | Includes bibliographical references and index.
Identifiers: LCCN 2016058350 | ISBN 9781433827808 | ISBN 1433827808
Subjects: LCSH: Psychic trauma—Treatment. | Psychotherapy.
Classification: LCC RC552.T7 P35 2017 | DDC 616.89/14—dc23 LC record available at https://lccn.loc.gov/2016058350

British Library Cataloguing-in-Publication Data
A CIP record is available from the British Library.

Printed in the United States of America
First Edition

http://dx.doi.org/10.1037/0000041-000

In memory of Jerry Jellis (1951–2013), my partner and best friend
for 27 years, whose wisdom, intellect, strength of character,
and love continue to inspire and sustain me.
—*Sandra C. Paivio*

For Ken, Lauren, and Julia, whose love and support have been central
to the unfolding storyline of my life and work.
—*Lynne E. Angus*

CONTENTS

ACKNOWLEDGMENTS

We would like to acknowledge the dozens of clients who were willing to share their stories with us and who gave permission to have their therapy sessions recorded and used in future research and professional communications. Such access to real therapy sessions is invaluable to the clinical training of mental health professionals, who, in turn, have been able to help hundreds of clients and their families dealing with the devastating effects of child abuse trauma. These videos have also been an invaluable resource contributing to the development and refinement of EFT specifically tailored to meet the needs of complex trauma clients. This is evidenced in the development of the narrative-emotion process model described in this volume, and identification of interventions to support enhanced EFTT treatment outcomes.

We also would like to acknowledge the dedication and skill of the many therapists who have participated in these therapy sessions, and the many clinical graduate students who are cited in this book and who have made invaluable contributions to the development and refinement of the EFTT treatment model.

Narrative Processes in Emotion-Focused Therapy for Trauma

INTRODUCTION

What is complex trauma? Unlike single incident trauma, such as motor vehicle accidents or natural disasters, *complex trauma* refers to repeated exposure to traumatic events, usually at the hands of caregivers or loved ones. Therefore, complex trauma is almost always interpersonal in nature and involves betrayal and violations of trust often in attachment relationships. Examples include domestic violence and childhood abuse and neglect. The latter is the focus of emotion-focused therapy for trauma (EFTT) and this book.

How does it harm people in the long term? Exposure to the terror and horror of a single traumatic event involving threat of death or injury can result in symptoms of posttraumatic stress disorder (PTSD)—flashbacks, nightmares, avoidance of people and places that are reminders of the event (e.g., inability to drive in the case of a car accident), chronic irritability or difficulties sleeping, as well as feelings of guilt (i.e., the person feels that he or she is somehow responsible or should have done something to prevent the trauma)

http://dx.doi.org/10.1037/0000041-001
Narrative Processes in Emotion-Focused Therapy for Trauma, by S. C. Paivio and L. E. Angus

and alienation (i.e., no one can understand the person's experience). PTSD also is highly comorbid with other disorders such as anxiety and depression. Complex child abuse trauma additionally is associated not only with PTSD symptoms but also with a more complex array of disturbances. This is because of the repeated nature of the trauma exposure, the context of attachment relationships, and the age of the victim and the victim's core developmental tasks (i.e., consolidating a sense of self, relational capacities, and emotional competence). Children who are repeatedly terrorized by actual or threatened violence to themselves or loved ones, and who are sexually molested, harshly criticized, or completely ignored by those they depend on, develop enduring perceptions of self as worthless, unlovable, or negligible; difficulties with intimacy or trust; and deficits in emotional competence (i.e., awareness and regulation). Children in these environments typically do not receive appropriate emotion coaching and support from attachment figures and thus learn to rely on avoidance to cope with the intense negative feelings generated by abuse and neglect. These coping strategies can include suppression, numbing, and dissociation, as well as maladaptive behaviors such as substance abuse and self-harm. To cope, individuals can cycle between feeling overwhelmed and shutting down. Deficits in emotion awareness and regulation, in turn, have a profound negative impact on sense of self and interpersonal functioning. Disrupted affect and narrative processes are at the core of this constellation of disturbances.

What is the EFTT model? EFTT is an evidence-based, short-term, individual therapy for men and women dealing with different types of childhood maltreatment (emotional, physical, sexual abuse, and emotional neglect). A fundamental assumption underlying most trauma therapies, including EFTT, is that recovery requires emotional engagement with trauma memories for enhanced affect regulation and self-understanding. EFTT is based on the general principles of emotion-focused therapy (Greenberg and colleagues), and, as such, draws on years of programmatic research on the importance of emotion in psychotherapeutic change, as well as on a sophisticated technology for working directly with emotions and emotional processes in therapy. Thus EFTT is particularly well-suited to treating trauma-related disturbances. Clinical trials support the efficacy of EFTT (Paivio, Jarry, Chagigiorgis, Hall, & Ralston, 2010; Paivio & Nieuwenhuis, 2001), and process-outcome studies support the posited mechanisms of change and have contributed to development of the model (e.g., Holowaty & Paivio, 2012; Paivio, Hall, Holowaty, Jellis, & Tran, 2001). Additionally, results of these studies support the broad applicability of EFTT to both men and women with histories of different types of childhood maltreatment and symptom severity.

EFTT is designed for clients who are suitable for short-term, trauma-focused therapy with at least minimal capacity for emotion regulation and the capacity to focus on circumscribed issues from the past. Elements of EFTT can be integrated into a longer course of therapy for clients with more severe emotion regulation or behavior difficulties such as substance abuse or self-harm. EFTT focuses on helping clients to disclose their most painful personal stories and to express and work through feelings and unmet needs related to central attachment figures for the construction of new perspectives regarding self, others, and traumatic events. In some instances and where appropriate, EFTT therapists help clients to further explore, understand, and challenge cultural beliefs and issues of power and dominance that are often central to childhood trauma experiences.

One of the unique aspects of EFTT is that primary reexperiencing procedures are based on an empirically verified model of steps in the process of resolving such attachment injuries (Greenberg & Foerster, 1996) and ongoing intensive analyses of therapy sessions. The early phase of EFTT focuses on cultivating a safe and collaborative therapeutic alliance. Therapist empathic responding and compassion for suffering provides safety and support, and encourages client disclosure of painful memories and engagement in primary reexperiencing procedures (i.e., confronting imagined perpetrators in an empty chair or during interaction with the therapist) for the first time. During this phase, therapists also are attuned to client emotional processing difficulties that emerge in the context of their storytelling and engagement in reexperiencing procedures. For example, affect may be absent or overwhelmingly intense; content may be vague, externally focused, and lacking in insight or meaning; and content may reflect repetitive maladaptive patterns of feelings (e.g., fear, shame), beliefs about self and others, and behavior (e.g., inability to assert boundaries). These processing difficulties are the basis for case conceptualization and become the focus of explicit intervention during later phases of therapy.

The middle phase of EFTT focuses on reducing the intrapersonal difficulties that interfere with resolution of issues concerning perpetrators. A variety of interventions (e.g., two-chair dialogues, experiential focusing) are used in addition to confronting imagined perpetrators to address problems with emotion awareness and regulation, as well as chronic fear, avoidance, shame, and self-blame for the abuse. During client storytelling and these procedures, therapists support the emergence of healthy subdominant emotional responses (e.g., anger at violation, sadness at loss) and associated unmet needs (e.g., for respect, nurturance) for reflection and integration as part of a more adaptive self-narrative.

The late phase of EFTT is characterized by clients' full experience and expression of adaptive anger at violation and sadness about the many losses they have endured and feelings of entitlement to unmet attachment needs. Interventions facilitate the coconstruction of new meaning, that is, a view of self as more powerful, confident, and worthwhile and a view of abusive and neglectful others as more human, life-sized, and responsible for harm. It is important to note that for some clients, the new trauma narrative becomes one of understanding and forgiveness. Therapy termination focuses on integrating therapeutic experiences and bridging to the future.

What is the book's purpose? The present book uniquely integrates the theoretical, research, and clinical literature in the areas of emotion, narrative, and trauma to make a significant contribution to effective treatment practices for complex trauma. In light of the high prevalence of child abuse trauma in the community and especially in clinical samples, there is a need for effective treatments and intervention guidelines for the effects of complex trauma. As noted earlier, narrative and emotion processes are central to disturbances stemming from these childhood experiences. Although previous manuscripts on emotion-focused therapy (EFT) and EFT specifically for trauma have noted the importance of client narrative processes, explicit therapeutic strategies to enhance emotional transformation and new meaning making—in the context of client storytelling and self-narrative change—have not been fully addressed. This book moves narrative to the foreground ad makes explicit what therapists are implicitly responding to in client storytelling. The book also presents a system for identifying client problems using Transition and Change storytelling markers, which provides an additional tool to guide a moment-by-moment facilitation of narrative-emotion processes in EFTT sessions.

This book is intended for clinicians and graduate students across disciplines who are familiar with EFT, or not, and who are interested in learning more about working with narrative and emotion processes in therapy for complex trauma. For clinicians who work within a narrative therapy framework, this book provides an introduction to how to work with client emotional processes to enhance story change. Conversely, clinicians familiar with emotion-focused approaches will be provided a differentiated "process map" to enhance client narrative disclosure for deepened emotional processing, meaning transformation, and self-narrative change. Finally, we hope that our book will speak to a broad range of clinicians interested in working with complex trauma clients and will support future specialized training workshops both locally and internationally.

What will readers get from the book? The book provides a solid theoretical and research foundation, specific intervention guidelines, and richly illustrated clinical examples. Actual clients presented in this book have given their consent to participation in research and professional communication. Pseudonyms are used, and identifying information for these clients has been removed. Clinical material includes verbatim transcriptions as well as modified dialogue to better illustrate intervention principles. Some of these clients have been presented in previous volumes of EFT and EFTT (e.g., Angus & Greenberg, 2011; Greenberg & Paivio, 1997; Paivio & Pascual-Leone, 2010; Paivio & Shimp, 1998), and videotapes of their therapy sessions are presented in our workshops. Many other clinical examples are presented here for the first time and are interpreted and discussed from a narrative-informed, emotion-focused perspective that draws on key terms and clinical concepts, as listed in the Glossary.

Part I, Theory and Research, begins with an introduction to the nature of complex trauma (Chapter 1) and includes chapters addressing the unique contributions of the EFTT treatment model (Chapter 2) and the importance of narrative-emotion integration processes in human functioning and contributions to therapeutic change (Chapter 3). This is followed by presentation of a narrative-informed EFTT model for treating complex traumatic stress disorders (Chapter 4). Part II, Practice, includes chapters on assessment and process diagnosis (Chapter 5), intervention principles and guidelines (Chapter 6), and intervention specifically with narrative-emotion processes in the early, middle, and late phases of EFTT (Chapters 7, 9, and 11). Chapter 9 presents numerous case examples[1] to illustrate the diverse client narrative-emotion processing difficulties and EFTT interventions that are the focus of the middle phase of therapy in particular. Also, we follow two individual clients over the entire course of EFTT to illustrate how narrative-emotion processes change over time (Chapters 8, 10, and 12). These cases (a female client with a male therapist and a male client with a female therapist) were selected because they illustrate EFTT with and without the use of empty-chair dialogue and with different client processing and therapist intervention styles.

---

[1]Client identifiers have been disguised to protect patient confidentiality.

I

THEORY AND RESEARCH

1

THE NATURE OF COMPLEX TRAUMA

This chapter describes the essential features of complex trauma stemming from childhood maltreatment that are the focus of therapeutic intervention, including emotion-focused therapy for trauma (EFTT). Herein we discuss prevalence rates, sources of disturbance, and long-term effects, with an emphasis on disrupted narrative and emotion process.

DEFINITION

Features of trauma and posttraumatic stress disorder (PTSD) are similarly defined internationally (e.g., *Diagnostic and Statistical Manual of Mental Disorders*, fifth edition [*DSM–5*]; American Psychiatric Association, 2013). In the fourth edition text revision of the *Diagnostic and Statistical Manual of Mental Disorders* (*DSM–IV–TR*; American Psychiatric Association, 2000),

http://dx.doi.org/10.1037/0000041-002
Narrative Processes in Emotion-Focused Therapy for Trauma, by S. C. Paivio and L. E. Angus

trauma was defined by two criteria: (a) direct exposure to, or witnessing the death or serious injury of, another person; and (b) experiencing feelings of horror and helplessness at the time of the event. *DSM–5* (American Psychiatric Association, 2013) has eliminated the criterion of emotional reactions to the trauma because of evidence for the frequent occurrence of amnesia and dissociation at the time of the traumatic event. Therefore, emotional reactions of horror and helplessness are now considered risk factors for development of PTSD rather than criteria for trauma.

Although some experts identify three types of trauma (Courtois & Ford, 2013), most experts distinguish between two, on the basis of type, severity, or breadth of effects resulting in two main categories: Type I and Type II (Pelcovitz, Kaplan, DeRosa, Mandel, & Salzinger, 2000; Scoboria, Ford, Hsio-ju, & Frisman, 2006; van der Kolk & McFarlane, 1996).

Type I Trauma

Type I trauma involves a single traumatic incident that is sudden and that may or may not be interpersonal (e.g., assault), deliberate or accidental, or an "act of God" such as an earthquake or tsunami. Exposure to Type I trauma is most commonly associated with a single diagnosis of PTSD. Notably, a single traumatic event may occur within a more complex environment (Paivio & Pascual-Leone, 2010). For example, a child might experience the suicide of a caregiver, as well as having been previously subjected to prolonged neglect because of the caregiver's mental health problems. Moreover, as we see next, risk for developing PTSD after a traumatic event increases with previous exposures to trauma.

Type II Trauma

Type II or complex trauma, on the other hand, involves repeated exposure to traumatic events that are often insidious and always interpersonal and that include intentional acts or failure to act. Examples include combat trauma, domestic violence, and childhood maltreatment. Thus, complex trauma in childhood includes not only acts of commission but also acts of omission in the form of neglect, lack of protection, abandonment, and loss of an attachment figure through illness, divorce, or displacement. In such cases, it is common for victims to know their perpetrators; be subjected to ongoing abusive situations; and be further victimized by societal shortcomings that may be present in mental health, judicial, and social support systems (Paivio & Pascual-Leone, 2010).

Types of childhood maltreatment include physical, sexual, and emotional abuse; emotional and physical neglect; and exposure to family violence, frequently at the hands of attachment figures and caregivers. Bernstein and Fink (1998) defined and distinguished between several types of childhood abuse. Accordingly, *physical abuse* is defined as a bodily assault on a child by an adult that poses a risk of, or results in, an actual injury. Examples in EFTT clinical samples (Paivio, Jarry, Chagigiorgis, Hall, & Ralston, 2010; Paivio & Nieuwenhuis, 2001) ranged from severe physical discipline, which may include the use of objects such as belts, to injuries that required hospitalization. Some of these cases are presented in later chapters of this volume. *Sexual abuse* refers to the occurrence of sexual contact between a child and an older person that may include coercion. However, sexual abuse frequently does not take place during threatening or violent conditions. Rather, abusers may misuse their authority or relationship to the child, and the victim may recognize the presence of abuse only in retrospect. Additionally, sexual abuse includes a spectrum of inappropriate activities, ranging from penetration to no physical contact. Examples in EFTT clinical samples ranged from sexual fondling by a babysitter to the rape of a 3-year-old girl by her father.

The definitions of emotional abuse and neglect are less clear in the literature, but *emotional abuse* generally refers to instances of verbal assaults on a child by an adult that may include the threat of physical violence, witnessing violence, or degrading the child's sense of self-worth (Bernstein & Fink, 1998). In EFTT samples, these experiences ranged from verbal derogation by a parent to threats of violence using guns to witnessing severe beatings of a mother or sibling. *Emotional neglect* refers to the failure of caregivers to provide the child with basic psychological and emotional needs, and *physical neglect* refers to the failure to provide for basic physical needs (Bernstein & Fink, 1998). In EFTT samples, emotional neglect ranged from lack of attention and love to failure to protect a child from harm. These experiences typically are co-occurring because multiple forms of abuse and neglect frequently occur in the same family (Briere & Scott, 2006). Indeed, most clients in EFTT samples (76%; Paivio & Nieuwenhuis, 2001; 69%; Paivio et al., 2010) reported experiencing multiple types of abuse and neglect. Additionally, exposure to childhood trauma is cumulative, such that every instance of victimization increases vulnerability and the risk of repeated victimization. Research has also indicated that a history of childhood maltreatment is associated with an increased risk of developing PTSD in response to exposure to subsequent trauma, such as natural disaster, combat, or assault. The *DSM–5* (American Psychiatric Association, 2013), for example, lists several pretraumatic risk factors for developing PTSD, including exposure to prior trauma, especially during childhood, and childhood adversity such as economic deprivation, family dysfunction, and parental separation or death. Several clients in EFTT samples presented in later chapters of this volume were further victimized (e.g., emotionally neglected, sexually molested) following a separation or death of a parent. Sadly, the more vulnerable an individual is to begin with, the more vulnerable that individual is to being repeatedly victimized and to developing psychological disturbance. Moreover, multiple exposures to traumatic events are associated with a more complex array of disturbances, which are reviewed in the following sections.

PREVALENCE

Exposure to trauma is no longer considered rare (Foa, Keane, Friedman, & Cohen, 2009), and repeated exposure to violence in childhood is far more prevalent than exposure to single-incident trauma. Childhood maltreatment remains disturbingly common, despite the increased attention to these events in the media and on the part of mental health professionals. According to Finkelhor (1994), children are the most traumatized/victimized/exploited group around the world because of their small size, lack of maturity and power, and dependency.

Prevalence estimates of childhood abuse vary, partly because of differences in definitions and partly because of the methodology used across studies (Paivio & Cramer, 2004; Pilkington & Kremer, 1995). Retrospective self-reports of child abuse such as those cited in this chapter have been criticized as lacking accuracy compared with data obtained through prospective investigations. However, some literature has supported the reliability and value of retrospective studies (Hardt & Rutter, 2004; Paivio & Cramer, 2004). Despite the variability in estimates, studies consistently show that exposure to child abuse is common. Scher, Forde, McQuaid, and Stein (2004), for example, reported that approximately 30% of women and 40% of men experienced some form of childhood maltreatment, and 13% experienced multiple forms of maltreatment.

In terms of prevalence rates for different types of childhood maltreatment, a meta-analysis investigating the worldwide prevalence of self-reported child physical abuse indicated a rate of 22.6% with no variation in prevalence rates across genders, cultures, or geographic regions (Stoltenborgh, Bakermans-Kranenburg, van IJzendoorn, & Alink, 2013). The prevalence of childhood physical abuse ranged from 28% in Australia to 19% in England and the United States (Seedat, Nymai, Njenga, Vythilingum, & Stein, 2004).

Prevalence rates of self-reported child sexual abuse were 12.7% (Stoltenborgh, van IJzendoorn, Euser, & Bakermans-Kranenburg, 2011). Other studies of sexual abuse prevalence have reported 24% to 30% in Ireland, 3% to 17% in New Zealand, 18% in South Africa, and 14% in Kenya (Cawson, Wattam, Brooker, & Kelly, 2000; Fergusson, Horwood, & Lynskey, 1996; Seedat et al., 2004).

Fewer studies have investigated emotional abuse and neglect because of the lack of agreement in defining those less concrete forms of childhood maltreatment (Paivio & Cramer, 2004). However, a recent meta-analysis reported prevalence rates for self-reported emotional abuse of 36.3% (Stoltenborgh, Bakermans-Kranenburg, Alink, & van IJzendoorn, 2012). Another meta-analysis provided prevalence rates of 16.3% for physical neglect and 18.4% for emotional neglect. International self-report surveys are supported by corroborating evidence (witness, protection services, and police reports), and most experts agree that rates underestimate true prevalence because of underreporting due to shame and stigmatization.

Other studies have compared prevalence rates for males and females. For example, in Ontario, Canada, where the authors of this volume reside, the prevalence of child physical abuse was reported more frequently by males (33.7%) than females (28.2%; MacMillan, Tanaka, Duku, Vaillancourt, & Boyle, 2013). In contrast, sexual abuse was more common among females (22.1%) than males (8.3%). The high prevalence rates highlight that childhood abuse crosses cultural boundaries and is widespread across the world, in the United States, and in Canada. Experts have referred to child abuse as an epidemic. Therefore, it is essential to understand helpful treatment processes that address the difficulties experienced by survivors of childhood maltreatment that may include situating those experiences within the specific cultural context of clients' lives.

SOURCES OF DISTURBANCE AND LONG-TERM EFFECTS

The following sections identify three main interrelated sources of disturbance and the well-documented complex constellation of disturbances stemming from exposure to child abuse trauma.

Sources of Disturbance

Special considerations are required when victimization occurs in childhood because such trauma effects the development of core capacities—emotion regulation, sense of self, and interpersonal relations. Childhood maltreatment is a vulnerability factor implicated in almost every form of adult psychopathology (*DSM–5*; American Psychiatric Association, 2013; Ingram & Price, 2010). Experts have commonly identified three interrelated sources of disturbance underlying complex traumatic stress disorders stemming from childhood maltreatment (e.g., Courtois & Ford, 2013; Paivio & Pascual-Leone, 2010). These include repeated exposure to trauma and growing up in an environment of fear, negative attachment relationships, and chronic reliance on experiential avoidance. Although the means of intervention and emphases vary across approaches, treatments for complex PTSD stemming from childhood maltreatment address these sources.

Repeated Exposure to Trauma

Repeated exposure to trauma, the first source of disturbance, results in chronic PTSD, which was defined in *DSM–IV–TR* (American Psychiatric Association, 2000) by three symptom clusters. The first cluster is (a) avoidance of reminders of trauma, including situations, people, and associated feelings and memories of traumatic events; the second symptom cluster is (b) reexperiencing trauma feelings and memories, for example, in the form of nightmares or flashbacks when individuals feel like they are reliving the trauma in the present; and the third symptom cluster is (c) hyperarousal, which includes anger control problems, irritability, reckless behaviors, hypervigilance, and sleep disturbances. More recently, disruptions in cognition and mood as a fourth symptom cluster were added to *DSM–5* (American Psychiatric Association, 2013). These disruptions include memory gaps, negative beliefs and expectations concerning self and others, feelings of detachment or estrangement from others, and anhedonia.

There is considerable evidence that avoidance of trauma feelings and memories, characteristic of PTSD, perpetuates disturbance and interferes with healing and recovery (Foa, Huppert, & Cahill, 2006). This is because emotion structures formed at the time of the trauma are unavailable for modification and "emotional processing." Accordingly, the original feelings, negative beliefs, and fearful reactions—the lived story or experience of the trauma—remain unintegrated and disconnected from the unfolding narrative of the trauma event (the told story). In essence, the trauma remains "unfinished business" such that self and trauma narratives are characterized by repetitive maladaptive feelings, beliefs, and reactions formed during traumatic experiences—the Same Old Story. Avoidance symptoms can result in narratives that are devoid of emotion or are vague, superficial, and lacking in detail—empty and superficial stories. Thus, a major focus of intervention in EFTT, described in later chapters, involves helping clients to construct more specific, emotionally alive, and coherent narratives with more adaptive views of self, others, and traumatic events.

In terms of other PTSD symptom clusters, reexperiencing symptoms such as flashbacks and nightmares can be particularly debilitating. Exposure-based procedures involving principles of desensitization are typically used to address these symptoms, although these procedures can be stressful, and many clients decline participation in them (Scott & Stradling, 1997). Most treatment approaches, including EFTT, include an early phase focused on increasing emotion-regulation capacities to help clients tolerate these symptoms.

Psychotropic medication also is frequently recommended for re-experiencing as well as hyperarousal symptoms. Hyperarousal symptoms of PTSD are evident in client storytelling that involves dysregulated emotion with little meaning or coherence. Intervention with these "unstoried" emotions involves first enhancing emotion-regulation capacities to reduce arousal and distress and then helping clients to construct a coherent narrative concerning the meaning of their feelings. As noted in later chapters, accurately labeling and making sense of emotional experience reduces anxiety and aids in emotion regulation. Moreover, there also is evidence that dissociation at the time of trauma is particularly harmful and interferes with recovery because memory structures are inadequately developed. Self and trauma narratives are incoherent and dysregulating because the individual is unable to make sense of and thus process and recover from traumatic experiences. This has important implications for clinical practice, and experts have suggested the further differentiation of a separate dissociative subtype of PTSD (Lanius et al., 2004).

Negative Attachment Relationships and Childhood Maltreatment

The second major source of disturbance for victims of childhood maltreatment is negative experiences with attachment figures and thus insecure attachment. Children develop their sense of self and expectations of others (as well as emotion-regulation capacities discussed in the following section) in the context of attachment relationships. Experiences of abuse and neglect at the hands of attachment figures can result in enduring mental representations of self as incompetent, unlovable, or negligible and perceptions of intimate others as untrustworthy or dangerous. These mental representations continue to negatively influence current functioning and narrative-emotion processes. Individuals report problems with self-esteem, self-confidence, self-identity incoherence, and interpersonal functioning. The latter includes difficulties with intimacy, trust, assertiveness, interpersonal boundary definition, parenting, and transgenerational transmission of trauma.

Three insecure styles have been identified by adult attachment experts (Shaver & Mikulincer, 2007), and identifying clients' predominant (though not exclusive) adult attachment style is an important aspect of EFTT case conceptualization presented in later chapters of this volume. Client attachment style has implications for their engagement in core therapeutic tasks, particularly cultivating the therapeutic relationship. First, a fearful/avoidant attachment style is characterized by longing for but avoidance of close interpersonal relationships for fear of rejection. The content of client problem narratives, the Same Old Story, includes views of self as flawed, inadequate, or unlovable and views of significant others as critical and rejecting. Fearful/avoidant attachment may also include avoidance of painful or threatening internal experience, seen in empty storytelling, and thus interferes with the capacity to emotionally process and recover from trauma.

Second, a preoccupied attachment style is characterized by overdependency and clinging to others for fear of abandonment. This may be accompanied by the defensive anger and desperate attempts to avoid abandonment frequently observed in clients with features of borderline personality, for example. For clients with a history of childhood abuse and neglect, views of self and others that are evident in their narratives include self as powerless and weak and significant others as powerful and controlling. We see this in the client Charlize, whose case will be followed in later chapters on the phases of EFTT.

Third, a dismissing attachment style is characterized by extreme self-reliance and distrust of others. Client narratives include a view of self as independent and detached and significant others as unreliable, defective, and potentially hurtful. We see this in the case of the client Mark, who will be followed in later chapters. In addition to the aforementioned maladaptive views of self and others, many clients with histories of childhood maltreatment blame themselves for the abuse and experience confusion and self-doubt about their own internal experience and perceptions concerning the abuse. This results from invalidating and minimizing responses from caregivers (e.g., "You're exaggerating," "That never happened," or "You're crazy.") or pressure to keep the abuse a secret, including threats of harm or death to self and/or others, that may distort children's perceptions of the abuse experience (Pynoos, 1996). These maladaptive views of self and intimate others are evident in the repetitive narrative content of complex child abuse survivors, including EFTT clients we describe later in this volume.

Reliance on Experiential Avoidance

The third main source of disturbance is chronic reliance on experiential avoidance as a coping strategy. Children in abusive environments experience intensely negative feelings such as fear, anger, sadness, and shame and receive limited support in the form of "emotion coaching" (Gottman, 1997) and narrative processing to help them make sense of and cope with these feelings. Attachment theory states that along with perceptions of self and others, emotional competence is developed in the context of attachment relationships (Bowlby, 1988). Emotional competence includes an awareness of emotional states, as well as the emotional states of others, and the ability to verbally label these emotions (Saarni, 1999). Accurately labeling emotions helps an individual to elaborate; understand the meaning of personal memories and stories; and integrate emotional experiences as part of an emergent, coherent self-identity narrative. Emotional competence is central to healthy functioning, both in terms of self-awareness and interpersonal relations.

First, emotional competence is developed through emotion coaching and narrative processing of stressful events within attachment relationships. Emotion coaching consists of attending to and helping the child to label their feelings, in the context of evoking lived experiences, which assists in developing awareness and appropriate emotional expression. Emotion coaching also involves helping the child to make sense of stressful experiences through personal story disclosures in the dyadic context of caregiver conversations.

In terms of secure attachment, emotion and narrative processing are developed through parent–child dialogues regarding personal and emotional experiences (Etzion-Carasso & Oppenheim, 2000). Such conversations occur through the retelling of stories about past events, guided by caregivers, which serve to teach a child how to share, coregulate, and evaluate emotionally laden experiences (Koren-Karie, Oppenheim, Haimovich, & Etzion-Carasso, 2003). Parents teach children to create coherent stories by coconstructing a beginning, middle, and end of a narrative, along with the creation of meaning to understand the events within the narrative (Fivush, 2012). Caregivers validate a child's emotions associated with a stressful or traumatic event and help the child to reframe the experience in a healthy and constructive manner. Parents thus assist a child to understand negative feelings and experiences and teach coping strategies to use in stressful situations (Laible & Panfile, 2009).

Emotional competence and narrative processing capacities are central to an individual's psychological well-being. Emotions provide us with important information pertaining to our needs and the appropriate actions that are required to satisfy them (Damasio, 1999; Leahy, Tirch, & Napolitano, 2011). Furthermore, emotional competence is important for self-esteem and resilience when confronted with stressful situations (Saarni, 1999). It also plays a role in building connections with others and maintaining intimate relationships (Grewal, Brackett, & Salovey, 2006). The development of emotional competence and narrative processing skills contributes to the understanding of important emotional experiences, increases self-awareness, and forms the capacity to create meanings for events to form an integrated and coherent sense of self or self-narrative (Enosh & Buchbinder, 2005). During the creation of a coherent narrative about important events, images, memories, and implicit thoughts and feelings are transformed into language, making internal processes explicit and conscious (Brody & Park, 2004). Narratives become a means of organizing one's life experiences into a meaningful sequence (Fivush, 2012). When constructing a meaningful story of one's life through personal emotionally rich stories, one is able to form a coherent identity (Brody & Park, 2004), as well as to establish core values (Thorne & McLean, 2002, 2003).

When childhood maltreatment is combined with poor emotion coaching, there is an increased risk of impairment in the emotion system. The child does not learn to make sense of, or cope with, the intense negative feelings engendered by the trauma (Saarni, 1999). The child may thus rely on maladaptive coping strategies, including avoidance of painful, negative, or threatening internal experience, such as memories, emotions, and bodily sensations (Hayes, Wilson, Gifford, Follette, & Strosahl, 1996). Limited awareness of core emotions related to traumatic experiences, such as abuse and neglect (e.g., fear, shame, anger, grief), and associated meanings can negatively affect functioning throughout the lifespan because the meaning associated with these experiences has not been integrated into a coherent self-identity narrative.

Individuals with a history of childhood maltreatment can cycle between feeling overwhelmed and the emotional overcontrol observed in numbing, dissociation, and behaviors such as substance abuse and deliberate self-injurious behaviors (e.g., cutting, burning). Alexithymia, for example, is characterized by impaired emotion awareness, specifically difficulty identifying and labeling feelings, difficulty distinguishing feelings from bodily sensations, and being externally focused on behavior and events. Alexithymia, in turn, has been associated with numerous psychological disturbances, including depression, anxiety, PTSD, and limited social support (Taylor, Bagby, & Parker, 1997; Turner, 2001). Furthermore, research has supported alexithymia as mediating the relationship between childhood maltreatment and self-injury (Paivio & McCulloch, 2004). In other words, childhood maltreatment poses an increased risk for engaging in deliberate self-harm because of the individuals' difficulty identifying, labeling, and making sense of emotional experience to reduce distress. In the absence of these capacities, self-harm acts as an emotion-regulation strategy. Emotion awareness and regulation deficits are evident in the personal stories of trauma survivors, including the EFTT clients presented in later chapters, which can be devoid of emotion (empty stories) or intensely emotional but devoid of coherent meaning (unstoried emotion).

Additionally, avoiding specific negative but adaptive emotions, such as legitimate anger at violation and maltreatment of self and loved ones and sadness at the many deprivations and losses one has endured (e.g., for love, attention, encouragement, protection, innocence, joy), has specific negative effects on healthy functioning. According to emotion theory and research (Izard, 2002), anger at violation promotes self-empowerment and assertion of interpersonal boundaries, whereas sadness promotes grieving, acceptance of loss, and self-compassion. Specific information from these adaptive emotions is not available as a guide to adaptive functioning so the individual is disoriented. The individual may have an unclear sense of self and self-identity, lack clarity, and feel confused about core values, wants, and needs (along with feeling undeserving of having their needs met) so is unable to act in his or her own interest and get core needs met. Again, chronic reliance on experiential avoidance, especially experiences that are central to one's sense of self, in turn, is associated with a host of psychological difficulties (see Hayes et al., 1996, for a review).

Dissociation, discussed earlier, is an extreme form of avoidance both at the time of trauma and as a chronic coping strategy that is associated with development of PTSD and poor prognosis for recovery. Dissociation is understood as a strategy for coping with extreme fear or other intensely painful negative emotions that can have profound negative effects on adaptive functioning. For example, a husband and wife were in a large car pileup in which their car was on fire. The husband, who had no history of previous trauma, mobilized his coping resources and managed to help himself and his wife escape the fire. The wife, on the other hand, who had a history of child abuse trauma and dissociation, was completely immobilized and would have burned to death if her husband had not saved her.

Long-Term Effects

Childhood abuse and neglect are associated with different immediate and short-term effects depending on the age of the child (Courtois & Ford, 2013). Additionally, children at different developmental stages have different capacities to integrate distressing experiences into a coherent self-narrative. Adult clients in EFTT, for example, frequently reported childhood difficulties in school and in peer relationships, such as difficulties concentrating, ADHD, social anxiety, and behavior problems, including aggression. These early difficulties exacerbate the effects of maltreatment.

There is limited evidence for specific long-term effects of different types of childhood abuse, although exceptions are sexual dysfunction in cases of sexual abuse and aggression in cases of physical abuse and witnessing family violence. For example, Ford (2005) reported a link between early physical abuse and later anger control problems, and Wolfe (2007) reported strong links between early exposure to family violence and later dating aggression. There also is abundant evidence for the deleterious effects of childhood adversity on brain development (Lanius et al., 2004; Schore, 2003) and some evidence that the slow, insidious effects of chronic neglect may be more damaging than extreme violence. The most frequently observed profound long-term effects that are common across different subtypes of abuse include damage to self-esteem, self-confidence, and interpersonal trust that are evident in client personal stories about past and current events. These common long-term effects are the focus of EFTT.

The previously mentioned long-term effects involve specific interrelated domains of disturbance: (a) the first domain of disturbance includes various types of psychopathology, such as PTSD, social anxiety, depression, and personality disorders; (b) the second domain of disturbance involves emotion-regulation difficulties, including dysregulation and avoidance/overcontrol, as well as alexithymia; and (c) the third domain of disturbance involves self and relational difficulties, including negative self-esteem and self-confidence, unclear self-identity, interpersonal distrust, difficulties with intimacy, interpersonal boundaries, parenting, and repeated victimization. The latter is thought to be partly a function of emotion awareness deficits whereby children have not learned to identify or trust their perceptions involving threat or danger.

Recently, experts (Courtois & Ford, 2013) have proposed a model of complex PTSD consisting of five criteria that are in addition to those identified in the PTSD diagnosis as currently defined in the *DSM–5* (American Psychiatric Association, 2013). These additional criteria are (a) emotion-regulation difficulties, (b) disturbances in relational capacities, (c) alternations in attention and consciousness (e.g., dissociation), (d) adversely affected belief systems, and (e) somatic distress or disorganization. It is important to note that there also is evidence that all of these effects can be mitigated by the complex interactions of a number of factors. Mediating variables include age of onset, frequency, severity, relationship to perpetrator (betrayal of trust), and resilience (temperament and social support). It is essential to assess the presence of these mitigating factors in clients because they have implications for practice.

THE IMPORTANCE OF NARRATIVE AND EMOTION PROCESSES IN TRAUMA

Disruptions in affect and meaning are at the core of the constellation of disturbances stemming from child abuse trauma described previously. Moreover, individuals with unresolved child abuse trauma frequently produce impoverished trauma narratives, lacking in coherence and attention to associated feelings and meanings. As such, addressing maladaptive emotion and narrative processes, in the context of accessing and disclosing personal trauma memories, is central to therapy for complex trauma.

Survivors can have difficulty making sense of traumatic events partly because of the effects that trauma has on encoding and retrieving traumatic memories. There is evidence that trauma affects areas of the brain, such as the hippocampus, that are responsible for meaning creation and autobiographical memory (Siegel, 2003). In addition, PTSD is associated with memory gaps because the extreme physiological arousal experienced during traumatic events interferes with information processing (Foa, Molnar, & Cashman, 1995). Dissociation and avoidance of trauma feelings and autobiographical memories, another feature of PTSD, further compromises the capacity to make sense of these events as a coherent personal story. As described previously, children in abusive environments, without appropriate support, particularly learn to rely on avoidance of painful internal experience as a coping strategy (Paivio & Pascual-Leone, 2010). Additionally, invalidating and minimizing responses from caregivers, or pressure to keep the abuse a secret, may distort children's perceptions of the abuse experience (Pynoos, 1996). Thus, individuals with unresolved child abuse trauma frequently produce impoverished trauma narratives lacking in coherence and attention to associated feelings and meanings. As such, addressing maladaptive emotion and narrative processes is central to therapy for complex trauma.

Finally, several studies have found a number of features that characterize the narratives of individuals with unresolved trauma and PTSD. These features include narrative incoherence, fragmentation, incompleteness, past temporal orientation, absence of causal or "insight" words, and minimal references to internal experience, particularly use of feeling words. In the area of complex trauma, in particular, Mary Main's work with the Adult Attachment Interview (George, Kaplan, & Main, 1985; Main & Goldwyn, 1984) indicated that incoherent narrative quality of mothers with unresolved trauma predicted disorganized attachment in their infants, thus supporting the transgenerational transmission of trauma. Although research has consistently supported a link between unresolved trauma and impoverished narrative quality and psychological disturbance, most of this research artificially examines individual features in isolation of context. Such an analysis has limited clinical utility. In contrast, this book on EFTT addresses how to assess and work with narrative and emotional processes in actual EFTT therapy sessions with direct implications for effective treatment practices.

Margola, Facchin, Molgora, and Revenson (2010) examined the written narratives of students who experienced the sudden death of a classmate. Students who remained distressed 4 months poststudy demonstrated incomplete cognitive and emotional processing of the trauma—evident in a lack of reference to the deceased student, which suggests inhibition. However, students who were not distressed at the 4-month follow-up were able to explicitly refer to the death and confront the emotional response. This group also demonstrated evidence of insight, causation, and movement toward integrating the events into their worldview, which together suggest an attempt to make meaning of the emotional experience. Together, these studies suggest that the trauma narratives of children tend to be incoherent, avoid emotion, and lack meaning construction, especially among those exhibiting trauma-related distress.

The same characteristics of the written trauma narratives of childhood trauma survivors can be found among adult trauma survivors as well. For instance, Foa et al. (1995) found that the narratives of clients who did not benefit from cognitive–behavioral therapy for PTSD were more fragmented and focused more on the details of the events (actions and dialogue) than did the narratives of those who benefited the most from therapy. In contrast, the narratives of those who did benefit from therapy were found to focus less on the details of the events and demonstrated greater processing of the emotion and meaning associated with the trauma. In addition, the attempts to understand the meaning of the trauma were associated with a reduction in trauma-related symptoms.

Furthermore, several studies have found that poor mental health and PTSD severity are linked with narratives that contain more somatosensory detail, visceral symptoms of emotions, and negative feelings and bodily sensations (Beaudreau, 2007; Foa et al., 1995; Rubin, Feldman, & Beckham, 2004). Together the characteristics of trauma narratives identified by these studies suggest a separation of cognitive and visceral aspects of emotion and may indicate an absence of emotional processing among trauma survivors with PTSD (Foa et al., 1995; Rubin et al., 2004). The separation of cognitive and visceral aspects of emotion may also be understood as the detachment of narrative and emotion among trauma survivors contributing to trauma-related distress.

A lack of emotional processing and avoidance of emotion may disrupt the creation of new meaning and understanding of the trauma. Newman, Riggs, and Roth (1997) compared thematic disruption in narratives of individuals with simple PTSD, complex PTSD, and no PTSD. The authors defined *theme* as cognitive–affective representations of internal and external experiences, which influence how one understands the self, others, and the world. Results indicated that individuals with PTSD, with at least one traumatic event in their lifetime, experienced more thematic disruptions in narratives and demonstrated less trauma resolution than did those without PTSD. Moreover, those with complex PTSD had significantly more difficulty resolving trauma-related issues and creating adaptive meaning than did those with simple PTSD and no PTSD. This breakdown of thematic meaning may be followed by the disintegration of identity, as the individual struggles to assimilate the events into the system of constructs that previously organized their life story (Neimeyer, 2001). This study demonstrated that complex trauma can affect meaning construction over and above the disruptive effects of simple trauma.

The quality and lack of meaning in the narratives of trauma survivors may be linked to poor verbal expression of the trauma experience. A survey of medical center and university female employees with and without a history of rape found that employees with a history of rape were less likely to talk about their rape memories than were employees with unpleasant, nonrape memories (Tromp, Koss, Figueredo, & Tharan, 1995). In addition, the rape memories were less meaningful and contained higher ratings of negative affect than nonrape memories. The authors suggested that difficulty with verbally expressing the trauma may discourage participants from talking about the rape memories. This theory has been supported by several studies that have found a link between PTSD severity and poor verbal recall, verbal learning, and verbal fluency, and simpler language in trauma narratives (Amir, Stafford, Freshman, & Foa, 1998; Bustamante, Mellman, David, & Fins, 2001; Uddo, Vasterling, Brailey, & Sutker, 1993).

The sources of disturbance underlying complex traumatic stress disorders include repeated exposure to trauma, negative attachment relationships, and chronic reliance on avoidance. The constellation of disturbances resulting from these childhood experiences includes symptomatology (e.g., PTSD, social anxiety, depression, personality pathology), emotion-regulation difficulties (dysregulation and avoidance/overcontrol), self-narrative incoherence, and negative perceptions of self and others. Disruptions in affect and meaning are at the core of this constellation. Survivors can have difficulty making sense of traumatic events, partly because of the effects that trauma has on encoding and retrieving traumatic memories. PTSD is associated with memory gaps, dissociation, and avoidance of trauma memories and feelings, all of which interfere with emotional processing and recovery. Moreover, individuals with unresolved child abuse trauma frequently produce impoverished trauma narratives, lacking in coherence and attention to associated feelings and meanings. As such, addressing maladaptive emotion and narrative processes, in the context of accessing and disclosing personal trauma memories, is central to therapy for complex trauma.

Finally, numerous studies have examined narrative processes among trauma survivors (for a review, see O'Kearney & Perrott, 2006), and results consistently support a link between unresolved trauma and impoverished narrative quality. These studies report that trauma survivors that are distressed and struggle with trauma resolution may have difficulty disclosing and verbally describing the trauma memory. In fact, narrative disruption (Dimaggio & Semerari, 2004; Neimeyer, 1995) may take different forms, such as narratives reduced to a single dominant theme (blocking different more adjusted meanings), narrative dissociation (e.g., a personal relevant story emerges without any emotional resonance), or narrative disorganization (the client jumps from one topic to another, making it difficult for the therapist and the client to make meaning out of the account). Finally, narratives that are produced by trauma survivors are likely to be incoherent, contain more somatosensory and event details, and struggle to find meaning in the traumatic experiences.

NEED FOR EFFECTIVE TREATMENTS FOR COMPLEX TRAUMA

Unlike exposure to a single traumatic event, complex trauma stemming from child abuse typically entails repeated exposure to violence, often at the hands of loved ones and caregivers. Despite increased attention in the media and by mental health professionals, child abuse trauma remains disturbingly common, with prevalence estimates of 30% in the community and as high as 90% in clinical samples—likely because of the constellation of long-term effects associated with these childhood experiences. Accordingly, there is an urgent need for effective psychotherapy interventions that fully address client emotion-regulation difficulties, narrative incoherence, and attachment injuries in treatments for complex trauma clients. EFTT is one such effective treatment and is described in the following chapter.

2

THE UNIQUE CONTRIBUTIONS OF EFTT

This chapter describes common factors across effective treatments for trauma and features of emotion-focused therapy for trauma (EFTT) that distinguish it from other approaches to treating complex trauma, including a brief introduction to the general model of emotion-focused therapy (EFT) on which it is based. The chapter also describes fundamental tasks in EFTT and research supporting the EFTT treatment model, and concludes with a review of the benefits of narrative-emotion integration in EFTT.

EFTT is an effective treatment (Paivio, Jarry, Chagigiorgis, Hall, & Ralston, 2010; Paivio & Nieuwenhuis, 2001) for complex trauma, and the treatment model, described in *Emotion-Focused Therapy for Complex Trauma* (Paivio & Pascual-Leone, 2010), has been identified as making a unique and important contribution to the field of treatments for complex traumatic stress disorders (Courtois & Ford, 2013). EFTT is a short-term (16–20 sessions), individual therapy for men and women dealing with different types of childhood

http://dx.doi.org/10.1037/0000041-003
Narrative Processes in Emotion-Focused Therapy for Trauma, by S. C. Paivio and L. E. Angus

maltreatment (emotional, physical, sexual abuse, and emotional neglect). A fundamental assumption underlying most trauma therapies, including EFTT, is that recovery requires emotional engagement with trauma narratives for enhanced affect regulation and self-understanding. EFTT is particularly well-suited to enhancing emotional engagement because it is based on the general principles of EFT (Greenberg and colleagues), drawing on emotion theory and years of programmatic research on the importance of emotion processes for psychotherapeutic change, as well as on sophisticated intervention strategies for working directly with emotional processes. EFTT also integrates theory and research in the areas of attachment and trauma, described earlier, to explain emotion-regulation and narrative difficulties stemming from childhood maltreatment and to inform principles of recovery from these experiences.

COMMON FACTORS IN TRAUMA THERAPY

Best practice guidelines for treating complex traumatic stress disorders stemming from childhood maltreatment have been developed from a review of the literature across diverse therapeutic approaches (Courtois & Ford, 2013). These include the following principles:

1. Therapists need to ensure client safety *within* therapy sessions, for example, through provision of a safe therapeutic relationship as clients are disclosing details of abuse in their personal stories and principles of gradual exposure to painful trauma feelings and memories. Therapists also need to ensure that clients are safe *outside* of therapy sessions and that they have adequate resources and strategies for dealing with potential threats from self-harm as well as abusive relationships.

2. Therapists need to ensure that clients have adequate emotion-regulation capacities for dealing with painful feelings and PTSD symptoms before they can begin to focus on accessing and processing trauma feelings and memories in therapy. For clients with severe emotion dysregulation problems, this means that the early phase of therapy needs to focus on enhancing these capacities.

3. Effective therapies need to include some form of memory work to help clients to process traumatic experiences. Strategies can vary from encouraging the client to tell and retell the story of their traumatic experiences, to explicit exposure techniques, and to use imaginal confrontation (IC) as in EFTT. In all instances, clients are encouraged to reexperience traumatic events through

storytelling that includes references to external details of these events as well as their internal experience during the event—stories need to be sensory, personal, and affectively alive.

4. Effective therapies for complex PTSD involve strategies to help clients construct new, more adaptive meaning and coherent narratives regarding self, others, and traumatic events.

5. Effective treatment approaches are phase models, such that the early phase focuses on ensuring emotion-regulation capacities, the middle phase focuses on accessing and working through trauma feelings and memories, and the final phase focuses on consolidation of therapy experiences and bridging to the future.

Although the means of achieving these principles varies, these are common factors across different effective approaches to treating complex child abuse trauma, including EFTT. Features that distinguish EFTT from other approaches are reviewed next.

DISTINGUISHING FEATURES OF EFTT

In addition to the previously mentioned common elements, EFTT also is characterized by a number of features that distinguish it from other approaches to therapy for complex trauma (Paivio & Pascual-Leone, 2010). These distinguishing features are based on the general model of EFT and ongoing analyses of in-session therapy processes. We begin with a brief introduction to basic constructs and principles that characterize the general model of EFT and EFTT, which is based on the general model. These are elaborated with emphasis on constructs specifically related to narrative processes in Chapter 4.

First, the general model of EFT is based on recent emotion theory and research (Damasio, 1999; LeDoux, 1996), indicating that emotion is associated with a multimodal meaning system and a source of cognitive, affective, motivational, behavioral, and interpersonal information. This information is embedded in emotion structures or schemes that when activated in therapy, give access to the network of information. Particular discrete emotions, such as anger and sadness, are associated with specific adaptive information, and limited access to emotion impairs functioning because the associated information is not available for self-reflection or to guide functioning.

Second, EFT specifies a number of emotional change processes, including awareness, regulation, reflection, and transformation, that are relevant for different clients at different times in therapy. *Emotional transformation* refers to the process of changing one maladaptive emotion by accessing a more adaptive emotion and associated meaning. For example, accessing appropriate anger at violation can help to transform shame and self-blame for abuse.

Third, from a practice perspective, EFT uniquely integrates client-centered relationship principles (empathy, unconditional positive regard, genuineness) with gestalt and experiential interventions such as two-chair dialogues and experiential focusing.

Fourth, EFT theorists have specified a taxonomy of emotions and emotional processes that can be observed in therapy and guide appropriate intervention. Briefly, primary emotions are basic initial responses to external situations. Intervention with primary adaptive emotions, particularly negative emotions such as anger and sadness, involves accessing them for their adaptive information; primary maladaptive emotions are overgeneralized conditioned responses (e.g., trauma alarm) that need to be counterconditioned. A special case of primary emotion is emotional pain (e.g., at rejection) that needs to be experienced for its information about how one has been wounded. Secondary emotions are secondary to maladaptive cognitions (e.g., guilt generated by self-criticism) or primary emotion (e.g., anger covering shame). Intervention involves accessing and changing the maladaptive cognition or accessing the more primary emotion. Complex emotions such as depression and anxiety need to be explored for their cognitive–affective–behavioral components and modified. Instrumental emotions serve some instrumental function (e.g., anger to manipulate) and need to challenged, and clients should be taught more adaptive ways to get needs met.

Finally, EFT is characterized by process-diagnosis and marker-driven intervention. When markers or indicators of particular processing difficulties (e.g., self-criticism, "unfinished business" with significant others, lack of clarity or confusion about internal experience) emerge in session, particular interventions designed to address these difficulties are implemented.

EFT specifically for trauma is based on these principles and constructs as they apply to therapy for complex trauma difficulties. First, although EFTT can include standard emotion-regulation strategies—such as breathing, muscle relaxation, or mindfulness—therapist empathic responding, rather than skills training, is the primary intervention used to facilitate emotion regulation. Therapist empathic responding promotes emotion regulation by helping clients to accurately label and articulate the meaning of emotional experience, modulate the intensity of emotions (e.g., soothing responses reduce distress while evocative responses can activate overcontrolled emotion), and appropriately communicate feelings (Paivio & Laurent, 2001).

Second, a distinguishing feature of EFTT compared with other approaches is an emphasis on promoting client experiencing—the process of attending to and exploring the meaning of subjective internal experience and constructing new meaning from this process. This, rather than therapist-directed psychoeducation, challenging maladaptive cognitions—or interpretations—is the primary source of new information used in the construction of new meaning.

Promoting client experiencing is the basis of all procedures in EFTT, including reexperiencing procedures described next. The Client Experiencing Scale (Klein, Matthieu-Coughlan, & Kiesler, 1986) operationalizes the construct of experiencing. Accordingly, lower levels of experiencing are characterized by externalized, intellectual, or superficial description of events, with limited reference to internal experience. Moderate levels consist of personal accounts of events that include descriptions of emotional reactions and inner processes that provide a window into the client's inner world. At high levels of experiencing, connections and meanings are explored to understand problems or answer questions regarding the self. Interventions in EFTT are intended to deepen client experiencing, step-by-step.

A third distinguishing feature is that EFTT addresses both current client difficulties (e.g., with self-esteem, interpersonal relationships, and emotion regulation) and past issues. However, the main focus of EFTT is the resolution of past issues ("unfinished business") with particular perpetrators of abuse and neglect, usually attachment figures. This stems from the observation that clients are distressed not only by current self and relational difficulties, but also by unexpressed and constricted feelings and unmet attachment needs concerning these individuals.

Finally, EFTT is uniquely based on an empirically verified model of steps in the process of resolving these attachment injuries or unfinished business using a gestalt-derived, empty-chair dialogue intervention (Greenberg & Foerster, 1996). During this procedure the client is asked to imagine a perpetrator of abuse or neglect in an empty chair and express his or her thoughts and feelings about the abuse directly to this imagined other. Steps in the resolution process that discriminated clients who resolved issues from those who did not include full expression of previously constricted adaptive emotion (e.g., anger at violation, sadness at loss) and associated meanings; entitlement to unmet needs (e.g., for protection, love); and more adaptive perceptions of self and other, such that clients feel more self-affiliative and powerful and hold perpetrators, rather than self, appropriately responsible for harm.

Research and clinical observation of clients specifically dealing with childhood abuse in therapy using the empty-chair procedure resulted in modification of the previously described model of resolution specifically to meet the needs of this client group (Paivio et al., 2010; Paivio & Nieuwenhuis, 2001). This included more emphasis on memory work, reducing fear and experiential avoidance, understanding the empty-chair intervention as involving both interpersonal and exposure processes and thus reframing the procedure as IC, and developing an alternative less-stressful procedure for the significant minority of clients (25%) who decline to participate in IC (Paivio et al., 2001, 2010). The alternative empathic exploration (EE) procedure is based on the identical model of resolution and intervention principles as IC, except that clients are asked to imagine perpetrators in their "mind's eye," and all material is explored exclusively in interaction with the therapist. Research on these developments is presented later in this volume.

MECHANISMS OF CHANGE

Paivio and Pascual-Leone (2010) posited two main interrelated mechanisms of change in EFTT. First, the therapeutic relationship serves two primary functions: It provides (a) a safe and secure environment to reexperience traumatic events, and (b) an interpersonal relationship that helps to correct for past negative experiences with attachment figures. The second posited mechanism of change in EFTT is emotional processing of trauma memories. From the traditional behavioral perspective (Foa, Huppert, & Cavill, 2006), emotional processing involves modifying emotion structures through the admission of new information (e.g., by reexperiencing trauma feelings and memories in a safe therapeutic environment). From an EFTT perspective, emotional processing involves the process of emotional transformation described previously, whereby maladaptive feelings such as fear and shame are accessed, differentiated in the context of personal storytelling, and then transformed by accessing adaptive emotions such as anger and sadness and associated meanings.

PRIMARY TASKS AND CORRESPONDING
PHASES OF THERAPY

Markers of particular narrative and emotion processing difficulties are observed in therapy sessions, and these are associated with particular therapeutic tasks designed to address these difficulties. Specific interventions or procedures used to accomplish these tasks are presented in the Part II of this book. Alliance and experiencing tasks are the fundamentals of EFTT and the foundation of all phases and procedures.

Alliance Tasks

Cultivating the alliance is the primary focus of the first phase of therapy. A safe and empathically responsive relationship also is essential to disclosure of painful trauma stories and engagement in reexperiencing procedures. During IC of perpetrators in an empty chair, for example, clients need to feel sufficiently supported by the therapist to help them tolerate reduced contact with the therapist to engage in a dialogue with an imagined other. If they are unable to tolerate this, EE of trauma material is a better procedure because exploration takes place exclusively in the context of the therapeutic relationship. Cultivating a strong alliance also involves providing a rationale for and client agreement on the importance of emotional reexperiencing trauma memories as the means to trauma recovery and resolution of child abuse issues. This rationale is tailored to individual client stories and EFTT treatment goals. As well, alliance tasks take precedence over the course of therapy when client–therapist issues of distrust or control, disagreement or lack of clarity about goals and tasks, or ruptures in which the client feels seriously misunderstood, arise. Here, therapists must work with clients to resolve the difficulty before other tasks can be accomplished and therapy can proceed smoothly.

Experiencing Tasks

Deepening client experiential engagement in the context of a self-focused reflective storytelling mode is another fundamental task of EFT, including EFTT. As noted throughout this volume, attention to and exploration of subjective internal experience, particularly feelings and associated meanings and needs, is the primary source of new information and narrative coconstruction in EFT. Thus, deepening the experiencing is the basis of all phases, sessions, and procedures used in EFTT. In-session markers for problems with experiencing include superficial narratives that involve low-level experiencing with an external focus on behaviors and events; stories that indicate poor emotion awareness; clients' confusion or lack of clarity about their internal experience; or narratives in which clients are struggling to identify, label, or articulate the meaning of internal experience. Deeper levels of experiencing are characteristic of transitional narrative-emotion processes on the route to change.

The following emotion-regulation, intrapersonal conflict resolution, and reexperiencing tasks typically are the focus of the middle phase of EFTT, which focuses on reducing self-related difficulties. Strengthening a client's sense of self is a necessary precursor to resolving issues with perpetrators.

Emotion-Regulation Tasks

Emotion-regulation problems are typical of abuse survivors, including both underregulation and overcontrol. Because recovery depends on client capacity to emotionally engage with and process trauma narratives, these difficulties need to be identified and addressed. Markers for these problem narrative-emotion processes are evident in storytelling devoid of emotion, or emotional arousal indicating overcontrol or avoidance of emotion, or client discourse with overwhelming emotion that is devoid of narrative context. These are instances of unarticulated emotion observed in dissociative states, for example, that often lack connection with a specific memory narrative context.

Intrapersonal Conflict Tasks

Strengthening a client's sense of self also involves resolving intrapersonal conflicts. Markers for intrapersonal conflict tasks include self-criticism, self-interruption of emotional experience, self-doubt about perceptions or internal experience, or catastrophic expectations in which a dominant maladaptive part of the self negatively affects a less dominant but healthy "experiencing" part of self, that is, erodes self-esteem, squashes adaptive emerging experience, confuses or second guesses feelings and perceptions, or frightens the self. The task is to access, strengthen, and integrate emerging healthy resources (feelings, needs, perceptions) into a more adaptive and coherent self-narrative and view of self.

Reexperiencing Tasks

These tasks involve reprocessing past trauma or current distressing events by accessing details of the event as well as internal experience during the event. This is crucial because traumatic experiences and PTSD are associated with memory gaps, distorted perceptions, and incomplete processing such that victims often have difficulty making sense of these experiences. Markers for introducing reexperiencing tasks in EFTT include PTSD symptoms; stories about past situations in which the core maladaptive sense of self—for example, as defective or unlovable—developed; or stories of current situations in which the maladaptive pattern of thoughts, feelings, and behaviors was evoked.

Resolving Issues With Attachment Figures (Perpetrators)

Resolving issues with perpetrators is the primary task in EFT specifically for complex trauma. Markers for the midphase self-related tasks typically emerge in the context of exploring unresolved issues with perpetrators. Although this exploration occurs over the entire course of therapy, the task of resolving issues with perpetrators is the exclusive focus of the late phase of therapy. Markers include expressions of hurt, blame, and complaint toward a significant other, along with feelings of hopelessness about ever resolving issues—classic unfinished business. These markers are evident in the repetitive stories about the negative relationship with the other that developed from experiences of abuse and neglect.

RESEARCH SUPPORTING EFTT

Clinical trials support the efficacy of EFTT (Paivio & Nieuwenhuis, 2001; Paivio et al., 2010), and process-outcome studies support the posited mechanisms of change and have contributed to development of the model (e.g., Holowaty & Paivio, 2012; Paivio, Hall, Holowaty, Jellis, & Tran, 2001). Additionally, results of these studies support the broad applicability of EFTT to both men and women, with histories of different types of childhood maltreatment and with a range of symptom severity.

In terms of efficacy, Paivio and Nieuwenhuis (2001) examined the effectiveness of EFTT with the IC procedure. The study included 32 clients, and they were assigned to either immediate or delayed treatment conditions. Clients who immediately received EFTT showed significant improvement posttreatment and at 9-month follow-up in several areas of disturbance (i.e., symptomatology, target complaints related to abuse, interpersonal difficulties, and self-affiliation). In contrast, clients showed minimal improvement during the wait period, but after receiving EFTT they showed comparable improvements to the immediate therapy condition.

A more recent randomized clinical trial examined the efficacy of two versions of EFTT (Paivio et al., 2010) wherein clients were randomly assigned to one of two treatment conditions that implemented either the IC of perpetrators ($n = 20$) or EE ($n = 25$) of trauma issues, exclusively in interaction with the therapist. As noted previously, EE was designed to be a comparable but less stressful and less evocative procedure compared with IC. Results indicated significant improvements in symptomatology, interpersonal difficulties, and resolution of abuse issues for both treatment conditions and no significant differences between the two treatment conditions in terms of outcome. Thus outcome research on EFTT has identified two alternative effective treatment options for this vulnerable client group.

Furthermore, several process-outcome studies have supported the posited mechanisms of change in EFTT. Paivio and Patterson (1999), for example, examined the effect of different types of childhood abuse on the therapeutic alliance and treatment outcome. The study included 33 clients who were included in the Paivio and Nieuwenhuis (2001) outcome study described previously. Findings revealed that certain types of abuse interfered with alliance quality early in therapy, but those difficulties dissipated over the course of treatment and did not influence treatment outcome. Additionally, a stronger therapeutic alliance was associated with better outcome on several dimensions, including reduced symptoms of distress and resolution of issues with abusive/neglectful others. Results thus support the benefits of therapists' ongoing focus on maintaining a strong therapeutic alliance.

Paivio et al. (2001) examined emotional engagement with trauma experiences during the IC reexperiencing procedure. Paivio et al. (2001) defined engagement as including three main aspects: psychological contact with the imagined other, willing participation in the intervention, and expressing emotions. Research results indicated that higher quality engagement was associated with better outcome over and above contributions made by the therapeutic alliance. Outcome dimensions included greater resolution of abuse issues, reduction in symptoms, and decreased interpersonal problems. Additionally, lower levels of client engagement were associated with higher dropout rates. It is important to note that results of this study also indicated that a significant minority of clients (25%) were unwilling or unable to participate in IC over the course of therapy, either because of performance anxiety or because it was too evocative. This was the impetus for developing the less stressful and less evocative EE procedure described previously.

Several studies also have found positive associations between emotional arousal and depth of experiencing during reexperiencing procedures and therapeutic outcomes in EFTT. For example, Holowaty and Paivio (2012) found that clients in the Paivio and Nieuwenhuis (2001) outcome study identified events with higher emotional arousal as more helpful compared with control events. These clients also reported that experiencing the depth of their pain during the first IC was one of the most helpful events in therapy. Robichaud (2004) found that greater depth of experiencing during early sessions involving trauma narratives predicted better outcome for the same clients. Ralston (2006) examined processes for clients in the Paivio et al. (2010) randomized controlled trial and found that deeper experiencing during both the IC and EE reexperiencing procedures predicted better outcome in both EFTT conditions, and higher levels of arousal during the less evocative EE procedure predicted better outcome in EFTT with EE. In terms of therapist factors, a recent study (Mlotek, 2015) found that higher quality of therapist-expressed empathy during Session 1 of EFTT predicted higher quality of client engagement in reexperiencing procedures over the course of therapy, as well as better outcome in terms of reduced trauma symptoms and resolution of issues with particular perpetrators.

In sum, the previously described findings from process-outcome research on EFTT identify in-session procedures and processes that contribute to client change. These findings thus increase confidence in the treatment model and are what is most relevant to clinical practice with this client group.

BENEFITS OF NARRATIVE-EMOTION INTEGRATION IN EFTT

One of the fundamental assumptions of emotion theory and research (e.g., Damasio, 1999; Izard, 2002; LeDoux, 1996) is that emotions are a rich source of information. This information is embedded in protonarrative action structures (Angus & Greenberg, 2011), also referred to as *emotion schemes* (Greenberg & Paivio, 1997). These are in effect multimodal meaning systems that entail a rapid synthesis of autobiographical memory-based actions, situational cues, emotional responses, and cognitive appraisals. Emotions can provide important intrapersonal information about thoughts, beliefs, needs, values, and desires as well as prepare us to take action in our relationships with others. Moreover, primary adaptive emotions, such as anger at violation or sadness about the loss of a loved one, are associated with specific relational "plotlines" and action tendencies that guide adaptive functioning for the fulfillment of core needs. Accessing and disclosing emotionally salient, autobiographical memory narratives provides access to this complex information network, making it available for further exploration and emotional change that is the basis for the construction of coherent, self-narrative accounts.

A large body of literature also supports the benefits of translating traumatic autobiographical memories and emotions into language (e.g., Angus & Bouffard, 2004; Pennebaker & Seagal, 1999) for enhanced narrative coherence and meaning making. Angus (2012), for example, pointed out that it is the interplay between narrative construction and meaning-making processes that allows clients to organize and symbolize emotional experiences as an integrated, coherent story. Greenberg and Angus (2004) suggested that the meaning of an emotion is understood when it is organized within a coherent narrative framework that identifies what is felt, about whom, in relation to what need or issue. In turn, when clients symbolize their emotions in narrative form, they can more easily regulate their emotional responses to cope effectively both intra- and interpersonally.

Finally, narrative and emotion integration in trauma has been an important area of theoretical and clinical work. The perseverative, intense, and intrusive quality of trauma memories and associated emotion may reflect failure to organize, contain, and integrate the emotional trauma material through narrative structure, which in turn may perpetuate trauma disturbances and break down one's sense of continuity, self-coherence, and emotional control (Amir, Stafford, Freshman, & Foa, 1998; Angus & Greenberg, 2011; Foa, Molnar, & Cashman, 1995; Wigren, 1994). As noted earlier, trauma survivors who remain unresolved and symptomatic tend to have trauma memories that have yet to be translated into language, resulting in impoverished narratives, emotional dysregulation, and poor understanding of the meaning of the events and associated emotions (Paivio & Pascual-Leone, 2010). The verbal symbolization of emotions is crucial for the regulation of emotion and development of narrative coherence among trauma survivors, which in turn may be associated with the alleviation of trauma-related distress.

Trauma therapies involve stories that reflect how clients understand self, others, and traumatic events. There are both content (what is told) and qualitative (how it is told) aspects of client narratives. In terms of content, dominant problematic narratives include views of self and others that are negative and overgeneralized and views of traumatic events that are vague, lacking in detail, and impersonal. In terms of quality, problematic narratives can be devoid of affect or overly emotional and incoherent and lacking in meaning (Carpenter, Angus, Paivio, & Bryntwick, 2016). Thus a key goal in the treatment of trauma is facilitating the exploration and articulation of the fragmented and emotionally vivid trauma memories, with the aim of producing a coherent and complete narrative that, in turn, orders events, contains and regulates affect, and infuses meaning to events. Also, the influence of implicit cultural, societal, and familial beliefs about childhood abuse can now be more fully explored, and critically challenged, with perpetrators of the abuse held accountable for their actions. Traumatic experiences are thus more fully integrated into a client's sense of self and a coherent life story.

Research specifically addressing narrative and emotion processes in EFTT, and the importance of narrative in healthy development and therapeutic change, are presented in the following chapter.

3

WHY CLIENT STORYTELLING MATTERS

In this chapter we first review the contributions of coconstructive story sharing in childhood to the development of a coherent self-narrative by adolescence and enhanced emotional self-regulation and self-reflective capacities, as a function of attachment style, in adulthood. We then discuss implications of the developmental theoretical and research literature regarding narrative expression, coherence, and emotional self-regulation for effective psychotherapy practice, especially in relation to working with complex trauma. We begin with a general perspective on why stories matter.

Representing a wide range of specialty areas within psychology (Bruner, 2004; Polkinghorne, 2004; Sarbin, 1986; White, 2007), clinicians and psychotherapy researchers alike have increasingly drawn on the concept of narrative to identify the processes entailed in generating explanations of everyday events and organizing these experiences into a coherent view of self as an unfolding life story. As personal stories organize and represent the complex

http://dx.doi.org/10.1037/0000041-004
Narrative Processes in Emotion-Focused Therapy for Trauma, by S. C. Paivio and L. E. Angus

interplay of embodied feelings, actions, beliefs, and intentions that have been directly experienced by a narrator, they provide a kind of evidential "truth" that fictional accounts simply cannot supply. As such, we draw on personal stories and the emotions, intentions, and beliefs they represent as evidence of who we are to form impressions of others and, as McKee (1997) suggested, to engage and maintain human contact (Angus, 2012).

We have grown into the storytelling universe of our language and our culture since early childhood and use its resources in the same familiar and spontaneous way as language in general. Searching for meaning is in fact a form of happiness, and there is no lasting pleasure unless it is pleasure steeped in meaning (Goldman & Greenberg, 1997). Experience itself, however, does not simply carry meaning within it, fully formed. Rather, we pattern our experience into personal stories that enable reflection and the articulation of intelligible frames of meaning. These frames of meaning, and the language in which they are expressed, are not the private property of any particular individual but belong to the larger social context of shared forms of intelligibility. We learn to make sense of life events in forms that fit our culture, and the meanings we make are sustained in our most important interpersonal relationships.

For a life experience to be interpersonally meaningful, its story must be retold or enacted with others. Jerome Bruner (1986) argued that the sense of self-identity actually originates in the embodied act of *storying* our experiences in the world such that they can be shared with others and reflected on for new self-understanding. For Bruner, the construction of selfhood cannot proceed without a capacity to narrate as it is in the act of articulating a situated point of view, in relation to actions and events, that storytelling gives expression to human agency and self-identity. When we become narrators of our own stories, we produce a selfhood that joins us with others and that permits us to look back selectively to our past and shape ourselves for the possibilities of an imagined future. We are, in essence, narrative beings.

Stories are of essential importance as they shape our understanding of the world and are the foundation for the construction of personal identity and views of the self. Our understanding of self through time influences the way in which the past is constructed, which in turn shapes the way in which the self is conceptualized in an ongoing dialectical fashion. Emerging from a dialectic of discovery and construction, we live out or enact our autobiographies as we compose them. *Narrative* is the name for a special repertoire of instructions and norms of what is to be done, and not to be done, in life and how individual experience is to be integrated into a generalized and culturally established set of rules of acceptable ways to be. As noted by Feldman, Bruner, Kalmar, and Renderer (1993), "mastery of narrative models must be one of the central tasks of cognitive development in any culture" (p. 340).

NARRATIVE EXPRESSION:
A DEVELOPMENTAL PERSPECTIVE

Stern (1985) outlined how our narrative sense of self and capacity for narrating our experience emerge to form the final stage of a rapid developmental sequence through infancy and early childhood. It begins with the *emerging self*, a nascent organization of the world as apprehended through sensation. Then comes the *core self*, which features a sense of agency (will), affect, and temporal continuity (memory). Next, the *intersubjective self* emerges as a sense of being in relationship. Through mirroring interactions with a caregiver, the capacity for mental representation of affective experience—the basic building block of emotion regulation—develops. The *verbal self* emerges soon after the intersubjective self. New language capacity at this stage permits an expansion of the self, by providing a new way to share experience and mutually create meaning. At the same time, however, language fragments the self because the immediate wholeness of experience is imperfectly coded in representational form. Words, according to Stern (1985), "isolate experience from the a-modal flux in which it was originally experienced. Language can thus fracture the a-modal global experience. A discontinuity is introduced" (p. 176). This can be especially true for emotional experience.

Story is the way human beings make sense out of the chaotic and seemingly unrelated events of their lives, and it has been argued that the act of externalizing lived experiences as personal stories—or autobiographical reasoning—is an essential self-organizing process that facilitates an increased understanding of self and others. Supporting this view is a growing body of research suggesting that people understand and make meaning of their lives in a storied form (Angus, Levitt, & Hardtke, 1999; Bruner, 1986; McAdams, 1993; Polkinghorne, 2004; White & Epston, 1990), and a considerable amount of research has been conducted on how narrative capacities develop in early caregiving relationships.

Daiute and Nelson (1997) argued that making sense of the world is a major cognitive challenge for children of all ages, essential to meeting basic physical, emotional, and social needs and desires. From the child's perspective, making sense involves figuring out "what is going on here," predicting "what will happen next," and addressing the key relational question, "where do I fit in?" These key orienting questions help the child infuse the world with personal meaning and an increasing awareness of self as intentional, valuable, and connected to persons and events in her environment. Daiute and Nelson also noted that scripts—the skeletal general action sequences that compose events—incorporate the ways of culture and provide a referential "core" for personal narratives that is the developmental starting point of stories.

As scripts represent what happens in general, they do not require an internal evaluative component. In contrast, personal stories are narrated from a situated point of view that incorporates an implicit or explicit evaluative component that assesses the emotional, interpersonal, and/or physiological impact of unexpected outcomes for the self. Accordingly, Daiute and Nelson (1997) identified two important characteristics that differentiate stories from scripts. First, stories individuate a canonical general script by comparing it with the unexpected happening that is the impetus to tell a story. Second, stories evaluate the unexpected happenings from the specific point of view of the narrator, who has experienced the unanticipated event. As such, it may be the case that scripts function as predictable, cultural frames that provide a context for children to learn how to not only individuate their unique self-experiences but also bring meaning to them through the narration of salient life events.

Narrative form also captures the notion that human lives are "becomings" or journeys, in which actions and happenings occur before, after, and at the same time as other actions and happenings. As noted by Nelson (1996) and other developmental researchers, the capacity to narrate personal experiences in terms of human intentions, purposes, and goals is foundational to the development of the capacity to adopt the perspective of another, in relation to the self, and to articulate new personal meanings from this vantage point. In fact, it is the very act of articulating a specific point of view—including intentions, purposes, and goals—in relation to a set of actions and unfolding events that gives expression to human agency in personal narrative accounts. Addressing the complex relationship between telling stories and intentionality, Bruner (1986) suggested that a narrative mode of knowing can be conceptualized as simultaneously representing two different levels or "landscapes" of meaning, the landscape of action—which involves the states, actions, and events that occur in the physical world—whereas the landscape of consciousness involves an interpretation of the states, actions, and events that are experienced by the characters.

Narrative Expression, Identity, and Self-Coherence in Adolescence

Narratives provide a type of temporal gestalt in which the meanings of individual life events and actions are not determined by individual characteristics or abilities but by their relationship to the whole of the unfolding story, within a particular plot or theme. The story renders the experiences and memories of the client into a meaningful coherent story. The way in which events are structured or ordered, according to the narrative form, results in the person's view of reality and its truth or distortion. It is important to note that it is not being suggested that narrative provides especially privileged access to truth, but rather it is one discourse among others that is both historically and culturally embedded. But ultimately, human events are understood as parts of a whole story with a temporal structure of beginning, middle, and end. The self then is understood as a unified or continuous entity, and this is not clearly prior to the operations of reflection but engendered by them.

Developmental researchers (Stern, 1985) identified the construction of a coherent self-narrative representation as an important cognitive marker of young adulthood. Whereas children recall single events that have had a particular significance in their lives (Habermas & Bluck, 2000; McAdams & Janis, 2004), it is young adults who develop the capacity to make causal connections between events in their life, unrelated in immediate time. By symbolizing patterns emerging in situations, self-narrative representations help to create a sense of coherence and stability over time and provide discursive explanations for the sometimes inconsistent meanings and aspects of self that emerge in challenging situations and relationships (Angus & McLeod, 2004b).

Conversations that help children to interpret, reminisce, and recount experiences are also central to the development of a child's beginning personal narrative (Nelson, 1996) that structures an emergent sense of a unique self-identity. Initially, children recall single events that have had a particular significance in their lives (Habermas & Bluck, 2000; McAdams & Janis, 2004) and eventually develop the capacity to make causal connections between events in their life unrelated in immediate time (Bruner, 1986). Memories are no longer simply referenced according to markers in time, but also to the emotions, motivations, goals, and attempts captured in the memory (Nelson & Fivush, 2004). The narrative construction of a shared familial past provides a perspective on how to evaluate, interpret, and morally evaluate important life events.

McAdams and Janis (2004) suggested that during adolescence, core themes emerge that connect different life episodes together and serve as a coherent interpretive lens for understanding self and others (Habermas & Bluck, 2000). Autobiographical memories organized according to self-defining themes also provide us with a sense of who we were and who we are, and give us a sense of purpose, unity, and identify. Accordingly, the capacity to narrativize, understand, and integrate our most important life stories is key to adaptive identity development and the establishment of a differentiated, coherent view of self. Specifically, the articulation of more coherent, emotionally differentiated account of self and others that facilitates heightened self-reflection, agency, and new interpersonal outcomes is a corrective emotional experience of self.

The terms *self-narrative* and *macronarrative* (Baumeister & Newman, 1994) have also been used by personality researchers and clinicians to refer to the individual's development of an overall perspective, or view of self or selves and personal identity, in which discrete events are placed in a temporal sequence and are meaningfully organized along a set of intrapersonal and interpersonal themes (Angus, Levitt, & Hardtke, 1999; Baumeister & Newman, 1994; Bruner, 1986; Howard, 1991; McAdams & Janis, 2004; Polkinghorne, 2004; Sarbin, 1986; Singer & Blagov, 2004; Spence, 1982; White, 2004). For Bruner (2004), the sense of self originates in the embodied act of storying our lived experiences of the world. As such, it is the integration of emotionally salient, lived stories that is the foundation for personal identity and enables a sense of self-coherence and continuity over time. Once organized and externalized as a story, our subjective world of emotions, beliefs, and intentions can be shared with others, a storied "past" can be returned to for further self-understanding, and the hopes and dreams for an imagined future can be articulated. The term self-narrative or macronarrative (Angus, Levitt, & Hardtke, 1999) has been used to refer to the overall "story," which meaningfully organizes or schematizes, in a temporal sequence, the events of one's life (White, 2004).

Addressing the relationship between identity and personality, McAdams and Janis (2004) argued that personality itself consists of three levels of individuality—dispositional traits (e.g., depressiveness, neuroticism, extraversion), characteristic adaptations (e.g., motives and goals, coping strategies, defenses), and integrative life narratives (e.g., identity). For these authors, identity itself takes the form of an inner story, complete with setting, scenes, character, plot, and themes. They suggested that in late adolescence and young adulthood, people living in modern societies begin to reconstruct the personal past, perceive the present, and anticipate the future in terms of an internalized and evolving self-story, an integrative narrative of self that provides modern life with some modicum of psychosocial unity and purpose. In terms of psychotherapy, McAdams and Janis suggested that no form of psychotherapy is likely to have a big impact on basic temperament traits, but clients' specific strategies, their adaptations, and their internalized life narratives have as much impact on behavior as do dispositional traits. In changing people's goals and strategies, and in providing new stories to use in making sense of their lives, therapists affect the personalities of individuals as much as they are changing the dynamics in families and other social relationships.

Narrative Self-Coherence and Enhanced Emotion Regulation: Attachment Theory

As noted by Sonkin (2005), Bowlby (1997) coined the term *attachment* to describe four defining markers of infant/child attachment status-proximity maintenance (wanting to be physically close to the attachment figure), separation distress, safe haven (retreating to caregiver when sensing danger or feeling anxious), and secure base (exploration of the world knowing that the attachment figure will protect the infant from danger). Sonkin, citing Sroufe (2005), suggested that early attachment relationships are vitally important because they function as a kind of early, dyadic emotion regulation, and that as children become better at expressing their needs and emotions, they learn effective self-regulation skills. In particular, it is essential that parents have the capacity to not only be sensitive or "attuned" to the verbal and nonverbal cues of a child (Stern, 1985) but also to communicate that understanding in the context of empathic responses and coherent story development. As such, attachment appears to be central to the capacity for emotion regulation and coherent narrative expression, in the context of significant interpersonal relationships. Finally, in terms of adult attachment status, Sonkin (2005) identified three key findings emerging from the research literature: (a) the attachment status of a prospective parent will predict the attachment status of their child to that parent-with as high as 80% predictability (Fonagy, Gergely, Jurist, & Target, 2002); (b) although changes over time can influence the attachment status of a child, there is a strong continuity between infant attachment patterns, child and adolescent patterns, and adult attachment patterns; and (c) adults assessed as having an insecure state of mind with regard to attachment have greater difficulties in managing problems in life generally, and interpersonal relationships specifically, than those assessed as securely attached (Shaver & Mikulincer, 2007).

As noted previously, adult attachment patterns or styles are developmentally formed ways of regulating affect and processing information and autobiographical memory narratives with respect to close interpersonal relationships. Because adult attachment patterns are related to attitudes toward seeking and receiving help and to distinct ways of engaging in emotionally significant relationships, client attachment patterns are likely to affect psychotherapeutic processes. One of the key approaches to measuring adult attachment patterns is the Adult Attachment Interview (AAI; George, Kaplan, & Main, 1985; Main & Goldwyn, 1984). The AAI operationalizes adult "states of mind with respect to attachment" in terms of different patterns of coherence and collaboration in narrating about attachment-related experiences. Secure attachment interviews are identified as balanced, emotionally differentiated, and open, and demonstrate narrative coherence. In contrast, dismissing interviews are overly brief, lack emotional expression, and are often marked by inherent contradictions between overgeneral, positive evaluations of childhood experiences and lack of convincing autobiographical evidence. Finally, preoccupied interviews contain long-winded and confusing accounts that are marked by continued emotional entanglement. Each of these different narrative "surface structures," which differ in the capacity to narrate a coherent and emotionally differentiated story, are also thought to be related to particular ways of regulating attention and emotion that have their roots in childhood experiences (George et al., 1985; Main, 1991).

What is it about the coherence of a life story that reflects the attachment status of the subject? When disclosing and narrating a lived event to another, it is likely to generate both subtle and not so subtle emotions about the experience of "what happened." How emerging emotions are regulated is going to, in part, determine the way the story is told. Accordingly, individuals with *secure* states of mind shift their attention flexibly between attachment and nonattachment related domains, recognize their need for attachment relationships, and at the same time remain psychologically separate from significant others. Individuals with *dismissing* states of mind direct their attention away from attachment-related experiences and the emotional attachment-related feelings of being in close interpersonal relationships to try and *deactivate* feelings of needing or longing for comfort. In contrast, individuals with *preoccupied* states of mind are continually caught up in attachment-related experiences and *hyperactivate* the emotional responses related to the attachment relationships. Accordingly, significant variations in attention, emotion-regulation, and narrative coherence are clearly of relevance to psychotherapy, which requires clients to engage in a collaborative dialogue about emotionally difficult topics and to provide a reasonably clear account of their situation for the therapist to empathize and intervene with precision (Daniel, 2011).

Reflective Functioning and Narrative Processes

Fonagy et al. (1995) argued that a hallmark of secure attachment is the capacity to access, narrate, and reflect on one's internal emotional experience, while at the same time reflect on the mind of another. The terms *reflective functioning* (RF) and *mentalization* are used interchangeably to refer to the sociocognitive capacity to think about oneself and others as psychological beings and to consider underlying mental states and motivations when interpreting behaviors. This occurs in the context of both moment-to-moment interpersonal interactions (Ensink, Berthelot, Bernazzani, Normandin, & Fonagy, 2014) and the disclosure of attachment-based autobiographical memory narratives (George, Kaplan, & Main, 1985).

As noted by Macaulay, Angus, Carpenter, Bryntwick, and Khattra (2016), RF (self-directed and interpersonal) is intrinsically tied to mentalization and narrative processes. Storying a personal experience entails stepping out of it, in all its somatosensory and affective richness, to reflect on and make sense of the event—including the mental states and emotions underlying the behavior of the story's key players. Bateman and Fonagy (2013) argued that mentalizing is dynamic and fluctuates according to interpersonal patterning as well as context: Secure attachments lay the groundwork for mentalizing even when under stress, whereas insecure attachments may lead to interruptions in mentalization under certain stressful contexts. Mentalization may be likened to "security in mental exploration," a sense of freedom and interest in accessing and symbolizing inner life, including distressing experiences and painful memories (Bateman & Fonagy, 2013, p. 596). This reciprocally promotes security of attachment by making it possible to connect to others for support when under distress.

RF refers to mentalization about attachment relationships and experiences, and even more specifically, to mentalization in the context of constructing narrative accounts of attachment-related memories and experiences (Fonagy, Steele, Steele, Moran, & Higgitt, 1991). When adults are interviewed about their childhood attachment experiences using the AAI (George et al., 1985), the ensuing narrative can be used to categorize the interviewee's mental representations of attachment. As noted earlier, AAI narratives' structural and processing features (e.g., how it is told), rather than content, determines the classification of attachment representations. The emphasis on narrative process rather than content highlights the dynamic nature of mentalization, as an interviewee experiences fluctuating safety exploring the inner life of his or her attachment memories and experiences. The AAI can be coded for RF, the extent to which interviewees reflect on their own and their caregivers' supposed mental states as they narrate attachment memories and experience (Fonagy, Gergely, Jurist, & Target, 2002). Parental RF is a robust predictor of their child's attachment security (Fonagy & Target, 2005; Meins, Fernyhough, Fradley, & Tuckey, 2001; Slade, Grienenberger, Bernbach, Levy, & Locker, 2005) and promotes attunement and responsivity to the intentions behind the child's actions and emotional needs. Clearly, the capacity for reflectivity and the resultant narrative organization of emotionally salient attachment experiences are significant for adaptive interpersonal behavior and may have direct implications for productive client engagement in psychotherapy sessions.

Psychotherapy often focuses directly or indirectly on attachment relationships and experiences; the therapeutic relationship itself might activate a client's attachment representations (Daniel, 2011). As stated previously, reflectivity is crucial for accessing and storying personal experiences and may be thought of as fluid, fluctuating "security in mental exploration" of inner life (Bateman & Fonagy, 2013). When seen from this perspective, reflectivity in a client's in-session narrative has potential clinical utility—as a lens for attending to the client's moment-to-moment security in mental exploration and as a guide for intervening to increase security and mental exploration.

Evidence is emerging that it may be possible to facilitate client movement in the direction of secure states of mind, and strengthened RF capacity, through psychotherapy interventions (Fonagy et al., 1991; Levy et al., 2006;

Toth, Rogosch, & Cicchetti, 2008). Given the differences between the dismissing and the preoccupied categories, it is likely that the "road" to security differs for these clients, and this may have important implications for psycho-therapeutic technique (Holmes, 2001). Later chapters of this volume present cases that exemplify emotion-focused therapy for trauma (EFTT) with each of these attachment types. Jeremy Holmes (2001) talked about the narratives of insecurely attached individuals and coined the terms *story-making* and *story-breaking* as the narrative focus for effective therapeutic interventions. In the case of dismissing attachment (e.g., the case of Mark), where the story is so restricted as to reduce the possibility of painful or distressing emotion, the therapist is helping the client create a story that is coherent, full of memory and manageable feelings. In the case of preoccupied attachment (e.g., the case of Charlize), where anxiety overruns the client's story and it becomes convoluted and saturated with anger or sadness, the therapist's role is to help break the negative cycle of the stuck narrative, regulate emotional expression more effectively, and create and reflect on a personal story that is more balanced and coherent.

CLIENT NARRATIVE AND EMOTION EXPRESSION IN PSYCHOTHERAPY

Addressing the functions of client narrative expression in psychotherapy, Angus, Lewin, Bouffard, and Rotondi-Trevisan (2004) argued that personal story disclosures are fundamental to the development of a shared context of meaning and understanding between clients and therapists. In particular, Angus and Kagan (2007) suggested that a client's willingness or capacity to disclose emotionally salient personal stories—in a detailed, evocative, and specific manner—enhances therapist empathic attunement and facilitates the development of a secure relational bond in the therapy relationship.

Schank (2000) in fact argued that the capacity to narrate personal stories to others is the essential basis of autobiographical memory: "We need to tell someone else a story that describes our experiences because the process of creating the story also creates the memory structure that will contain the gist of the story for the rest of our lives" (p. 115). For Schank, telling a story is not a rehearsal but an interpersonal act of creation that is, in turn, a memorable relational experience itself. Accordingly, clients' disclosure of emotionally salient life experiences is not only an act of personal memory (re)construction, but it also entails the creation of a new interpersonal experience with the person of the therapist.

Additionally, when clients provide narrative accounts of past personal experiences in psychotherapy, they disclose information related to the self that plays an important role in identity, emotion, behavior, and personality change processes (Singer & Blagov, 2004; Singer & Salovey, 1993). As such, client autobiographical memory narratives, or personal stories, also help psychotherapists to understand client complaints and current modes of adjustment and to discern key conflictual themes (Luborsky & Crits-Christoph, 1990) that shape maladaptive interpersonal patterns (Goldman & Greenberg, 1997; Greenberg, 2002).

Overgeneral Autobiographical Memory, Emotional Avoidance, and Self-Incoherence

Emerging research evidence from both the cognitive experimental (Williams et al., 2007) and psychotherapy research literature (Boritz et al., 2011, 2014) has indicated that a key cognitive marker of clinical depression is a preference for overgeneral autobiographical memory (ABM) representations and difficulty accessing and disclosing specific, or episodic, ABM narratives of personal life events. This is important because the inability to access and integrate specific episodic ABM has been associated with reduced self-coherence, increased rumination and worry, impairment in social problem solving, and a reduced capacity to imagine future events (Conway & Pleydell-Pearce, 2000). Interestingly, cognitive researchers such as Teasdale (1999) have suggested that overgeneral memory representations may function as an effective emotion avoidance strategy (Boritz, Angus, Monette, Hollis-Walker, & Warwar, 2011) that results in impaired specific autobiographical memory recall that is essential for effective problem-solving and the articulation of new personal meanings. Taken together, these findings suggest that therapists' ability to help clients move to more specific autobiographical memory disclosures in therapy sessions may be a key emotion processing step—and change event—in effective treatments of depression.

Self-Narrative Incoherence and Complex Trauma

From a narrative process model (Angus, Boritz, & Carpenter, 2013; Angus, Levitt, & Hardtke, 1999) perspective, accessing and articulating the client's world of emotions, beliefs, expectations, needs, and goals—what Bruner (1991) termed the "landscape of consciousness"—is critical for the resolution of complex trauma. The reflexive decentering from, and then reengagement with, traumatic experiences, from different relational vantage points, facilitates the articulation of new understandings about the self in relation to others (Angus & Bouffard, 2004). It is the reflexive processing of emotions, beliefs, hopes, needs, motives, intentions and goals—and their inclusion in the events of the trauma narrative—that enables the experience to be more fully understood, accepted, and integrated as part of the life story. In essence, it is the integration of the sequential, linear unfolding actions and feelings, intentions, and responses evoked over the course of the event that enables the construction of a coherent and meaning-filled narrative account of our interpersonal experiences with others in the world.

To facilitate a coherent account of key life experiences, it is essential that clients elaborate and differentiate emotional meanings in the context of a detailed narrative account of the traumatic events and their impact on the client's life. Angus (2012; Angus et al., 2012) argued that client and therapist achieve this goal by collaboratively engaging in three distinct modes of inquiry: (a) *external narrative mode*, which entails the description and elaboration of the traumatic autobiographical memories in which the question of what happened is addressed/landscape of consciousness; (b) *internal narrative mode*, which entails the description and elaboration of painful emotions and bodily experience connected with the traumatic memory and addresses the question of what was felt during the episode as well as what is felt now in the person's life and/or the therapy session in response to remembering the experience; and finally, (c) *reflexive narrative mode*, which entails the reflexive analyses of issues attendant to what happened in the event (external) and what was felt (internal) in which the question of what does it mean is addressed and contributes to the articulation of the landscape of consciousness. In essence, the narrative process modes are viewed as essential components of a distinctive mode of human meaning making that creates; maintains; and, when needed, revises our sense of self in the world.

Angus (2012) suggested that it is the interplay between narrative construction and meaning-making processes that allows a client to organize and symbolize emotional experiences as an integrated, coherent story. However, the overwhelming experience of trauma may impede the integration of emotion, cognition, and memory, as well as disrupt emotional and narrative coherence (Freer, Whitt-Woosley, & Sprang, 2010; Herman, 1992; Newman, Riggs, & Roth, 1997; Wigren, 1994). Narrative incoherence can include disorganized temporal order, lack of detail, repetition, and unfinished thoughts (Halligan, Michael, Clark, & Ehlers, 2003; Jelinek et al., 2010; Mundorf & Paivio, 2011). This incoherence may be due to the disorganized quality of trauma memories, which are often relived as intrusive fragments of bodily sensations, negative affect, and images that, for unresolved clients, tend to be detached from linguistic form and lack personal significance (Amir, Stafford, Freshman, & Foa, 1998; Angus & Bouffard, 2004; Beaudreau, 2007; Rubin, Feldman, & Beckham, 2004; Tuval-Mashiach et al., 2004; van der Kolk, Hopper, & Osterman, 2001). Exposure to trauma appears to disrupt the interrelationship of narrative and emotion, which may contribute to trauma symptom development.

Angus and Greenberg (2011) postulated that narratives are given significance and salience when fused with emotions, and emotions are given meaning when placed in their narrative context. It is through the construction of a coherent narrative that human beings organize, contain, and regulate affect, and make connections between the mind and body. The intense and intrusive quality of trauma memories and associated emotions may reflect a failure to organize, contain, and integrate the emotional trauma material through narrative structure (Amir et al., 1998; Angus & Greenberg, 2011; Foa, Molnar, & Cashman, 1995; Wigren, 1994). This lack of narrative structure may perpetuate trauma disturbances and break down one's sense of self-coherence and emotional control (Angus & Bouffard, 2004). Angus (2012) suggested that in the context of effective therapy practice, it is important to highlight that clients often communicate their most important concerns through storytelling and as such, a central task for therapists is to help clients engage and revise the negative plotlines of their "same old" storytelling for the coconstruction of a more relevant, coherent, and emotionally integrated self-narrative. It is important to note that the ability to form a coherent self-narrative that meaningfully connects event and emotions has been associated with positive mental health outcomes (Pennebaker & Seagal, 1999), whereas clients whose stories are unavailable, incoherent, or incomplete reported significant psychological and emotional difficulties (Tuval-Mashiach et al., 2004).

Additionally, several studies have examined the contributions of narrative and emotion integration in therapy (e.g., Angus, 2012; Boritz, Angus, Monette, Hollis-Walker, & Warwar, 2011; Boritz et al., 2014; Carpenter et al., 2016; Greenberg, Auszra, & Herrmann, 2007). Results of these studies have suggested that it is not simply the expression of emotion or emotional arousal in session that is important, but rather it is the reflective processing of emergent, adaptive emotions, arising in the context of personal storytelling and/or emotion-focused therapy (EFT) interventions, that is associated with change.

Taken together, there is broad agreement among neuroscience (Damasio, 1999; Schank, 2000), cognitive developmental (Bruner, 2004; Nelson, 1996), attachment (Bowlby, 1988; Siegel, 2003; Trevarthen & Hubley, 1987), and psychotherapy researchers (Angus & McLeod, 2004a; Gonçalves & Stiles, 2011) that narrative and emotional expression are key elements of human consciousness that shape lived experiences into personal stories for enhanced self-reflection and interpersonal communication. Specifically, the research literature reviewed in this book has suggested that a client's fluctuating "security in exploring inner life," especially in the context of complex trauma, may be enhanced by attending to narrative and emotion processes during therapy sessions.

As seen through this interpersonal lens of working with both narrative and emotion processes, a therapist's task is twofold. The first task is to empathically attune to a client's personal storytelling in such a way that the client becomes increasingly secure in his or her exploration of inner life and is able to disclose and experientially enter painful, specific ABM narratives for heightened narrative coherence and emotional differentiation. The second key therapeutic task is to attune to indicators of the client's narrative and emotion processing for markers of secure reflectivity and opportunities to further enhance emotional regulation, new meaning making, and positive self-narrative change.

The narrative-emotion process (NEP) model (Angus, 2012) and Narrative-Emotion Process Coding System (Angus Narrative-Emotion Marker Lab, 2015) were developed to provide EFT therapists with a moment-to-moment process map for the identification of key narrative-emotion storytelling markers for the implementation of effective treatment strategies and interventions. A full description of the NEP model and its integration with an EFT approach to complex trauma is elaborated in Chapter 4. Additionally, descriptions of Problem, Transition and Change subgroups, and individual marker subtypes, are provided in Chapters 5 and 6 to present a process map to guide the facilitation of client narrative and emotion change processes in early-, middle-, and late-phase EFTT sessions, addressed in subsequent chapters.

4

A NARRATIVE-INFORMED APPROACH TO EFTT

In this chapter we first introduce the narrative-emotion process (NEP) practice model, key assumptions, and research support in the context of emotion-focused therapy for trauma (EFTT). Next we provide an overview of fundamental assumptions and key practice principles that guided the development of an integrative model of working with narrative and emotion processes in EFTT.

INTEGRATING NARRATIVE AND EMOTION PROCESSES IN THE GENERAL MODEL OF EMOTION-FOCUSED THERAPY

Greenberg and Paivio (1997) stated that a central task for emotion-focused therapy (EFT) psychotherapists is the facilitation of client emotional processes such that primary adaptive emotional responses can be accessed,

http://dx.doi.org/10.1037/0000041-005
Narrative Processes in Emotion-Focused Therapy for Trauma, by S. C. Paivio and L. E. Angus

symbolized, and meaningfully understood in the context of client personal storytelling and chair task interventions. The articulation of personal meaning unfolds through an ongoing dialectic between automatic, immediate, sensorimotor, and affective experience and the cognitive/narrative symbolization and organization of components of that experience in consciousness. From a narrative processes perspective (Angus & Greenberg 2011), it is the client's disclosure of emotionally salient, autobiographical memory narrative that is often the experiential starting point for this reflective processing of evoked emotion. As such, facilitating client reflection on accessing and symbolizing primary adaptive emotional experiences, in the context of salient personal stories, is a key EFTT intervention strategy that is predicated on the assumption that the ability to meaningfully integrate one's narrative and emotional lives is a vehicle for therapeutic change.

Angus (2012) suggested that it is the interplay between narrative, emotion, and meaning-making processes that enables therapy clients to organize and symbolize emotional experiences as an integrated, coherent self-identity narrative. Accordingly, we suggest that it is the exploration and differentiation of emotions, in the context of emotionally salient narrative disclosures and EFT interventions, such as role-play dialogues, that facilitates the emergence of a new view of self and new outcome stories (White, 2004). This is for the articulation of a more coherent, agentic self–narrative (Angus & Kagan, 2013) and the achievement of productive EFT outcomes (Angus & Greenberg, 2011; Paivio, 2013).

Emerging from a systematic review of narrative process research studies in EFT (Angus, 2012), Angus and Greenberg (2011) identified a multistage, dialectical–constructivist model of NEP that culminates in successful client self-narrative reconstruction in EFT. Originally conceptualized by Greenberg and Pascual-Leone (1997), and then further elaborated from a narrative process perspective by Angus and Greenberg, dialectical constructivism proposes that a person generates meaning through the narrative organization of emotional experience. Additionally, rather than viewing the client as independently constructing meaning, EFT's dialectical constructive perspective sees effective psychotherapy as a coconstructive enterprise wherein the therapist is an important contributor to the meaning-making process. EFT thus involves an interpersonal, *dialectical* process involving a synthesis of biology, culture, emotion, and reason that situates the client in a less radically independent, interior position vis-à-vis the *construction* of new story meanings and self-understanding.

According to narrative-informed and experiential–humanistic approaches to psychotherapy, clients' seek therapy when they experience a distressing discrepancy or incoherence between felt emotions, actions, cultural norms, and an autobiographical sense of self or self-narrative (Angus,

2012; Angus & Bouffard, 2004). In a similar vein, making sense of a life experience begins by reflecting on, and then verbally symbolizing, an internal, implicit "bodily felt sense" of the lived experience within a narrative context. The organization of emotional experience as a told story not only enhances a personal understanding of the event but also functions as an effective mode of emotional self-regulation.

Consistent with Damasio's (1999) contention that the first impetus to story a lived experience is the awareness of an inner bodily felt feeling, Angus and Greenberg (2011) argued that it is often the expression of an emotional feeling that is a key indicator of the personal significance of a story. Furthermore, the narrative scaffolding of emotional experiences provides a framework for the organization and integration of felt emotions with unfolding action sequences. For Angus and Greenberg, core emotional experiences such as pain, hurt, sadness, or loving compassion need to be situated and symbolized in the context of personal stories so that important information about a client's needs and goals, and the personal and cultural meanings of what happened, can be further articulated and understood. As such, EFT therapists are encouraged to help clients vividly experience bodily felt feelings, through either the disclosure of emotionally salient personal stories and/or participation in specific EFT interventions.

Angus and Greenberg (2011) also suggested that reflection on emotions and feelings, emerging in the context of client story disclosures, is critical for enhanced self-understanding and self-narrative coherence. For instance, reflective inquiry into emotionally salient personal stories can provide clients and therapists with an opportunity to deconstruct limiting cultural and social norms (White, 2004) and heighten the client's sense of personal agency (Polkinghorne, 2004). This is for the purpose of constructing new personal meanings, discovering new views of self and self-narrative reconstruction (Angus & Kagan, 2013). Polkinghorne (2004) argued that it is a client's enhanced sense of personal agency that is the essential ground for the production of unique, unexpected outcome stories (White, 2004) that profoundly challenge and destabilize a client's Same Old Story (Angus & Greenberg, 2011). This leads to the emergence of a new self-narrative account that instantiates a more compassionate and proactive view of self (Mendes et al., 2010, 2011). Finally, the contributions of narrative and emotion processes for the development of heightened client reflection in psychotherapy have also been highlighted in the developmental/attachment literature (Macaulay, Angus, Carpenter, Bryntwick, & Khattra, 2016), as well as the psychotherapy research literature more broadly (Angus, 2012; Angus, Watson, Elliott, Schneider, & Timulak, 2015; Bucci, 1995; Mergenthaler, 2008).

It is important to note that it is the triadic nature of narrative disclosure— integrating action, emotion, and meaning—that provides an organizing framework to reflectively link actions and consequences and enables us to infer the intentions of others. The capacity to accurately understand the intentions of others is viewed by attachment researchers as essential for establishing and maintaining secure interpersonal relationships and as a key reflective functioning capacity. A sensitive, empathic attunement to the inner intentions of others is also essential for empathic connections with others wherein the motives of self and others are simultaneously acknowledged and experienced as equally valid but distinct. Understanding another's intentions also helps us to predict future courses of actions and to adjust or change our expectations accordingly. Through narrative expression, we can come to understand our own emotional responses in combination with the intentions that shape the actions of others and, as such, develop a deeper, reflective understanding of ourselves and others as social beings.

The following sections review basic principles of clinical theory and practice in the general model of EFT (Greenberg & Paivio, 1997; Greenberg, Rice, & Elliott, 1993) related to narrative-emotion integration processes (Angus & Greenberg, 2011) that are the basis for an integrative, narrative-informed model of EFT for complex trauma (EFTT) and a summary of research findings investigating narrative and emotion process markers in EFTT.

Dialectical Construction of Self

The fundamental task in psychotherapy is the construction of new personal meanings. EFT draws on dialectical–constructivist theory to understand this process. From this perspective (Greenberg & Pascual-Leone, 1997; Greenberg et al., 1993; Pascual-Leone, 1987, 1990a, 1990b, 1991), the reflexive construction of new personal meanings involves self-narrative organization and articulation of felt emotional experiences. The following core assumptions have been identified as crucial for the emergence of new personal meanings in psychotherapy: (a) client agency; (b) human reflexivity and meaning-making processes; (c) accessing emotion schemes, autobiographical memory narratives, and emotional processing for the facilitation of self-narrative identity change; and (d) the coconstructive nature of the client–therapist dialogue (Angus & Greenberg, 2011).

Within a dialectical–constructivist framework, the narrative framing of emotional processes, at both tacit and conscious levels of awareness, contributes to promoting personal change experiences in therapy (Angus & Greenberg, 2011; Greenberg & Angus, 2004). Drawing on recent developments in the study of human consciousness, Damasio (1999) argued that human beings essentially live and breathe in a world that is ordered and experienced as an unfolding story, in time.

More specifically, Damasio (1999) suggested that human consciousness comes into being with the creation of a tacit narrative account and that it is manifested in the feeling of knowing. As such, both narrative and emotion processes, operating at tacit levels of consciousness, are fundamental to the generation of an emotional felt sense or experience. In turn, the awareness of a bodily felt referent, so central to experiential therapy (Gendlin, 1997), is symbolized within the context of an unfolding external (environmental) or internal (autobiographical memory-based) narrative scene. It is the interaction of this bodily felt sense within the external or internal narrated scene that leads to emergent emotional responses and meaning being carried forward for the articulation of new views of self and others and self-narrative change. To better understand themselves, people continually symbolize, story, and explain themselves to themselves—and in so doing construct an ongoing, emergent self-narrative that provides a sense of self coherence. In essence, this is a combination of head and heart that entails an embodied integration of emotion, storytelling, and reflective processes.

A narrative-informed, dialectical–constructivist approach to self-awareness and human meaning making (Angus & Greenberg, 2011) identifies four key stages in which narrative, emotion, and reflective processes are at play in EFT therapy sessions. The first stage involves the rapid *synthesis* of affective responses from sensations and tacit autobiographical memories—organized as emotion schemes—that evoke inner bodily feelings in current situations. EFTT strategies help clients to translate tacit live stories and painful emotion schemes into told stories.

The second stage entails the allocation of attention to the bodily felt sense to *symbolize*—reflexively differentiate and name the feeling state—to create a known subjective reality as a told story. In essence, emotions are put into narrative form, and narratives are given significance by fusing them with emotion. Without access to bodily felt experience, particularly emotion, client storytelling becomes a chronicle of events devoid of emotional content and personal meaning. Without narrative context and elaboration, clients tend to become lost in a swamp of undifferentiated emotion and confusing action sequences (Macaulay et al., 2016). As such, effective EFT therapists help clients to focus their reflective awareness on emergent felt feelings in the context of personal story disclosure for enriched self-reflection and new meaning making.

The third stage entails the *conscious articulation of new meaning*. New personal meanings are articulated in relation to the experiences of both self and others. At this stage, a conscious, causal explanation of experienced emotions is provided in the form of an explicit narrative account.

The fourth and final stage entails the *consolidation of an identity self-narrative*. This final stage addresses the role of emotion and narrative processes at the level of self-identity construction or macronarrative change. This occurs either by the integration of the new narrative and personal meanings into preexisting views of self or others, or the inception of a radical reorganization of the self-narrative and the articulation of new emotionally significant ways of viewing and understanding the self. It is the combination of all four stages—synthesis, symbolization, meaning making, and identity consolidation—that is key to significant client shifts and self-change. Each of these stages, in turn, offers different opportunities for therapeutic interventions as described in Part II of this book.

Self-Identity Narrative

There is broad agreement among neuroscience (Damasio, 1999; Schank, 2000), cognitive-developmental (Bruner, 2004), and psychotherapy researchers (Angus & McLeod, 2004a; Gonçalves & Stiles, 2011) that narrative schema is a core organizing principle of human consciousness that shapes lived experiences into personal stories that can then be shared with others for enhanced social bonds and self-understanding. When we become narrators of our own stories, we produce a selfhood that can be shared with others and that permits us to look back selectively to our past and shape ourselves for the possibilities of an imagined future. It is in the act of articulating a situated point of view, in relation to actions, events, and cultural norms, that storytelling gives expression to human agency and self-identity.

According to cognitive and developmental researchers (Bruner, 2004; Habermas & Bluck, 2000; McAdams & Janis, 2004; Singer & Blagov, 2004), the capacity to narrate, understand, and integrate our most important life stories—as a coherent self-narrative—is key to adaptive identity development and the establishment of a more differentiated, flexible view of self. As noted in earlier chapters, McAdams and Janis (2004) concluded that our internalized self–narratives may have as much impact on guiding actions and behavior as dispositional traits, and as such, when therapists help their clients to construct new self-narrative representations, they are in fact impacting the personalities of their clients and supporting enduring change.

Research on Narrative and Emotion Processes in EFT

Similar to the concept of EFT microprocess markers (Elliott, Watson, Goldman, & Greenberg, 2004), NEP markers are intended to provide empathically attuned therapists with a process-diagnostic map to help guide the implementation of effective moment-to-moment interventions. Each marker represents an opportunity for specific process-guiding intervention to facilitate productive engagement in personal autobiographical memory disclosure, emotional differentiation, and reflective meaning making.

Narrative-emotion storytelling markers are intended to provide EFT therapists with a practical process-diagnostic map to guide the implementation of effective therapeutic strategies that address clients' difficulties disclosing painful autobiographical memories, accessing emotions, and engaging in enriched meaning making. Marker-guided therapist responses help clients to further access, express, and reflect on emergent emotions and construct a more coherent and agentic self-narrative that challenges the maladaptive relational patterns of clients' Same Old Stories. It is important to note that key process dimensions related to depth of client experiencing and emotional arousal are integrated within distinct client storytelling markers to provide therapists with a simplified process-diagnostic map for the implementation of effective marker-guided interventions. Each marker differs in the degree to which clients disclose specific autobiographical memories; symbolize bodily felt experience; express emotion; reflect on their own or others' minds and behaviors; coherently integrate actions, emotions, and personal meaning; and articulate change. As such, individual Narrative-Emotion Process Coding System (NEPCS; Angus et al., 2016) markers, described in later chapters of this volume, also point to opportunities for specific EFT interventions that enhance narrative-emotion integration and self-coherence. The moment-by-moment facilitation of narrative and emotion integration processes, for emotional transformation and new story outcomes, is consistent with core assumption of the EFT model (Angus & Greenberg, 2011) and has the added advantage of providing EFT therapists with an in-depth understanding of how client emotional processes are linked to different kinds of storytelling and can serve as key indicators of client readiness for change and participation in specific EFT interventions.

Evolving from their theoretical conceptualization of narrative-emotion integration markers in EFT, the NEP model (Angus, 2012) and NEPCS (Angus Narrative-Emotion Marker Lab, 2015) identifies 10 distinct client process markers that capture different ways in which clients engage with and story about personal experiences across diverse treatment modalities. Extensive empirical evaluation and testing (Angus et al., 2016; Angus, Gonçalves, Boritz, & Mendes, in press; Boritz, Barnhart, Angus, & Constantino, 2016; Boritz, Bryntwick, Angus, Greenberg, & Constantino, 2014; Carpenter, Angus, Paivio, & Bryntwick, 2016; Friedlander et al., 2016) have resulted in the identification of 10 empirically validated narrative-emotion process subtypes operationalized using the NEPCS. The 10-marker subtypes are clustered into Problem (e.g., stuckness in repetitive story patterns, overcontrolled or dysregulated emotion, lack of reflectivity), Transition (e.g., reflective, access to adaptive emotions and new emotional plotlines, heightened narrative and emotion integration), and Change (e.g., new story outcomes and self-narrative discovery, and coconstruction and reconceptualization) subgroups.

More specifically, NEP Problem markers identify underregulated, over-regulated, undifferentiated emotional states that are often expressed through incoherent, rigid, repetitive, and maladaptive self-narratives. Problem markers are thought to reflect underlying processes that may be involved in the maintenance of the presenting clinical problem and that are unproductive toward therapeutic change. There are four distinct Problem markers, including Same Old Storytelling, Empty Storytelling, Unstoried Emotion, and Superficial Storytelling.

NEP Transition markers represent client movement toward greater integration, through heightened reflectivity; the expression of differentiated emotional responses; and narration of more specific, exploratory personal stories. Transition markers highlight opportunities for therapists to enhance client reflection on emerging bodily felt experience, significant episodic memories, emerging alternative or conflicting action tendencies and views of the self, and important intra- or interpersonal patterns and themes. There are four distinct Transition markers, including Reflective Storytelling, Experiential Storytelling, Competing Plotlines Storytelling, and Inchoate Storytelling.

NEP Change markers indicate the generation and integration of new understanding, meaning, and action tendencies and capture client storytelling about experiences of change in action. The two Change markers—Unexpected Outcome and Discovery Storytelling—represent the descriptions of actual adaptive change; reports of new emotional or cognitive responses and action tendencies; or the emergence of a more coherent, adaptive understanding of the self and relationships. The Unexpected Outcome Storytelling marker is informed by Michael White's (2007) contributions to narrative therapy theory and practice and identifies when clients disclose positive emotional, interpersonal, and behavioral change stories in therapy sessions. Discovery Storytelling represents the explicit articulation of a more emotionally integrated and coherent self-identity narrative that instantiates new, more adaptive and satisfying ways of being in the world. Furthermore, Discovery Storytelling is the basis for clients' self-narrative reconstruction or reconceptualization, a category identified in the Innovative Moments Coding System (Gonçalves, Mendes, Ribeiro, Angus, & Greenberg, 2010) to capture when clients explicitly reframe their problematic Same Old Stories as belonging to a difficult past and begin to anticipate positive emotional and interpersonal changes evidenced in the present as defining plotlines for new views of self and future story outcomes.

To date, research using the NEP coding system has identified client narrative-emotion subgroups in EFT, client-centered (CC) therapy, and cognitive therapy (CT) for major depression (Boritz et al., 2016; Boritz et al., 2014); motivational interviewing (MI) plus cognitive–behavioral therapy (CBT) for generalized anxiety disorder (Macaulay, Angus, Khattra, Westra, & Ip, 2017); and EFTT (Bryntwick, Angus, Paivio, Carpenter, & Macaulay, 2014; Carpenter et al., 2016). Results have consistently identified significantly higher proportions of NEP Transition and Change markers in mid- and late-phase sessions for clients who achieved recovery by treatment termination, irrespective of therapy approach.

More specifically, when compared with clients who recover by treatment termination, unchanged clients evidenced significantly higher, overall proportion of NEPCS Problem markers (Same Old Storytelling, Empty Storytelling, Unstoried Emotion, and Superficial Storytelling), irrespective of client diagnostic sample (major depressive disorder, generalized anxiety disorder, complex trauma) or treatment approach (CC, CT, EFT, EFTT, MI+CBT; Angus et al., 2016). In terms of specific NEPCS Problem markers, unchanged depressed, anxious, and complex trauma clients evidenced significantly higher proportions of Superficial and Empty Storytelling in particular, when compared with clients who recovered by treatment termination. In turn, these clinical findings suggest that it may be important for therapists to pay particular attention to helping clients access and disclose specific, autobiographical memory narratives for deepened emotional engagement and reflection in early-phase therapy sessions.

Additionally, NEPCS findings also provide evidence that unchanged clients, across therapy approaches, have difficulty sustaining engagement in Transition markers for enhanced self-reflectivity, accessing new emotion, or the articulation of Competing Plotline Storytelling that may function as a sensitive indicator of client readiness for change in early- and mid-phase therapy sessions. Two EFT clinical studies (Boritz et al., 2016; Bryntwick, Angus, Paivio, Carpenter, & Macaulay, 2014) have also established that unchanged EFT clients evidence significantly less narrative flexibility (shift from one NEPCS marker to another) when compared with recovered EFT clients. More specifically, unchanged clients engaged in significantly fewer Transition and Change marker shifts when compared with recovered clients, and they showed a preference for shifts to Problem marker such as Superficial, Empty, and Same Old Storytelling. As such, therapist empathic, process-guided responses that consistently help clients to (a) articulate the underlying emotional plotlines of their Empty Storytelling, (b) access and disclose specific autobiographical memories for heightened experiential engagement in the context of Superficial storytelling, (c) increase awareness of the painful costs of remaining stuck in the grip of the Same Old Story, and (d) identify the emergence of Competing Plotline Storytelling markers will result in more frequent, productive narrative-emotion process shifts.

Conversely, recovered clients consistently evidenced significantly higher proportions of NEP Transition (e.g., Competing Plotlines Storytelling, Inchoate Storytelling, Experiential Storytelling, and Reflective Storytelling) and Change (e.g., Unexpected Outcome Storytelling and Discovery Storytelling) when compared with unchanged clients. Moreover, although unchanged clients showed high levels of emotional avoidance in their storytelling throughout their treatment sessions, NEP analyses has indicated that recovered clients, irrespective of client diagnostic sample or treatment modality, became less emotionally guarded (e.g., Inchoate Storytelling) and more willing and able to access and disclose their most painful specific autobiographical memories (Boritz, Angus, Monette, & Hollis-Walker, 2008; Boritz, Angus, Monette, Hollis-Walker, & Warwar, 2011) and emotions (i.e., Experiential Storytelling, Inchoate Storytelling, Competing Plotline Storytelling), for new meaning making (Reflective Storytelling), in mid- and late-phase sessions (Boritz et al., 2014).

In terms of EFTT specifically, clients who had recovered from complex trauma by treatment termination were found to spend significantly more time in NEP Transitional markers—Reflective, Experiential, Competing Plotline, Inchoate Storytelling—at the early and middle stages of therapy when compared with unchanged clients (Bryntwick, Angus, Paivio, Carpenter, & Macaulay, 2014; Carpenter et al., 2016). NEP Transition markers were also found to have a distinct pattern of occurrence when compared with Change markers—in particular Discovery Storytelling—that were more frequent at the late stage of therapy for the recovered client subgroup. Taken together, these findings suggest that Transition markers comprise productive processes toward *potential* change in EFTT, rather than indicating change as a fait accompli. The surprisingly consistent identification of higher proportions of NEP Change markers for recovered clients (Angus et al., 2016; Angus et al., in press), particularly Discovery Storytelling in later stage sessions, suggests that the articulation of a new view of self, in the form of self-narrative integration and change, may be essential to trauma recovery by treatment termination. As such, it may be the case that NEP Transitional and Change markers are able to capture key EFTT processing steps that result in autobiographical memory reconsolidation (Lane, Ryan, Nadel, & Greenberg, 2015), a process wherein clients' maladaptive emotion schemes and autobiographical trauma narratives are reengaged and updated with new, more adaptive emotional outcomes and positive self-narrative change (Angus & Kagan, 2013; Angus et al., in press). Lane et al. (2015) argued that autobiographical memory reconsolidation may in fact be a core principle of change that is evidenced in a broad range of effective approaches, including EFTT.

It is important to note that in addition to identifying and validating productive processing patterns in EFTT psychotherapy sessions, the articulation of NEP Problem, Transition, and Change markers have contributed to the further elaboration of EFTT in informing the implementation of marker guided therapist interventions in EFTT sessions, as described next.

WORKING WITH NARRATIVE-EMOTION PROCESSES IN EFTT

EFTT focuses on helping clients disclose their most painful personal stories, to express and work through feelings and unmet needs related to central attachment figures, for the construction of more adaptive affectively rich narratives containing new perspectives regarding self, others, and traumatic events. As noted in Chapter 2, a distinguishing feature of EFTT is a focus on resolving issues with particular perpetrators of abuse and neglect. Other approaches to treating complex trauma focus mainly on current self-related and interpersonal difficulties (e.g., Chard, 2005; Cloitre, Koenen, Cohen, & Han, 2002). Clients, however, not only have current difficulties but also continue to feel disturbed by unmet needs and longings with particular attachment figures. Accordingly, EFTT is based on an empirically verified model for resolving "unfinished business" or attachment injuries using a gestalt-derived, empty-chair intervention (Greenberg & Foerster, 1996). An early-outcome study supported the effectiveness of treatment based on this model with general clinical sample (Paivio & Greenberg, 1995). EFTT involves a refined treatment model that was based on observation of clients in the Paivio and Greenberg (1995) sample who were dealing with child abuse trauma. Modifications included more work with self-related difficulties, such as fear/avoidance and shame; a longer course of therapy to accommodate these processes; and reframing the empty-chair technique as IC to emphasize the traumatic nature of these experiences. IC was viewed as involving both interpersonal and exposure processes. An early-outcome study supported the effectiveness of EFTT (Paivio & Nieuwenhuis, 2001) with the IC procedure. A recent clinical trial involved the development and evaluation of an alternative less stressful version of EFTT with EE of trauma material. EE is based on the identical model of resolution and intervention principles as IC-only clients are encouraged to imagine perpetrators in their "mind's eye," and evoked trauma feelings and memories are explored exclusively in interaction with the therapist (Paivio, Jarry, Chagigiorgis, Hall, & Ralston, 2010).

Most recently, NEPCS Problem, Transition, and Change markers have been theoretically and empirically linked with process-guiding interventions that enhance productive client engagement in autobiographical memory disclosures, emotional differentiation, and reflective meaning making in EFTT sessions (Angus et al., 2016). More specifically, Problem markers, such as

Superficial or emotionally Empty Storytelling, provide therapists with a parsimonious, process-diagnostic map for the identification of client emotional and narrative processing difficulties in EFTT sessions. When emotion is inhibited, restricted, or remains unsymbolized and unintegrated, there is less exposure to distressing or threatening emotional experiencing. This undercuts the possibility of new emotional awareness, transformation, and self-narrative change. Accordingly, in the middle phase of EFTT, movement toward productive narrative-emotion processing involves shifts from emotional avoidance, and stuckness in maladaptive patterns and repetitive storytelling, to accessing, exploring, symbolizing, and reflecting on emergent emotional experiencing for enhanced narrative-emotion coherence and storytelling reflecting self-discovery, transformation, and new outcomes.

In the context of working with emotions in EFTT, it is the enhanced expression of new emergent emotional responses for further symbolization, reflection, and narrative integration that appears to challenge the basic pattern and premises of a client's maladaptive Same Old Story for the emergence of storytelling with more adaptive feelings, needs, and beliefs in middle- or working-stage EFTT sessions. This is evident in the shift from NEPCS Problem to Transitional storytelling markers. Not surprisingly, it is also during the working phase that clients are encouraged to engage in two-chair and imaginal confrontation (IC)/empathic exploration (EE) interventions for the resolution of "unfinished business" and intrapersonal conflict splits (e.g., self-criticism, self-interruption) that are definitive of Transitional narrative-emotion storytelling markers.

It is important to note that detection of Change narrative-emotion storytelling markers indicating client discoveries about self or actual new behaviors or interactions can help EFTT therapists to notice, and further elaborate on, clients' expression of surprise, excitement, contentment, or inner peace in response to experiencing new emotional responses and/or taking positive action to fulfill personal needs and goals. It is when clients begin to break free of the maladaptive patterns, which have defined their Same Old Stories, and experience and report new, more adaptive emotions and action tendencies that EFTT therapists can help them to articulate a new view of self that highlights their role as agents of present and future change and preferred story outcomes (Angus et al., in press; Cunha et al., 2016). In a nutshell, the goal of therapist narrative-emotion process-guiding intervention is to shift clients from Problem storytelling to sustained, productive emotional and reflective engagement in Transition storytelling. This, in turn, invites clients' reflection on experiences of emotional and narrative change—in the context of storytelling reflecting Change—for heightened self-narrative coherence and/or reconstruction.

We now elaborate on key narrative and emotion practice principles and fundamental assumptions that have guided the development of a narrative-informed approach to EFTT that is the focus of this book.

Basic Assumptions

The following are basic assumptions about the nature of emotion, trauma and trauma recovery, narrative coherence, and attachment that underlie the EFTT treatment model.

1. Emotions are (a) a rich source of information about thoughts, feelings, motivation, action tendencies, goals, and beliefs embedded in personal story disclosures; (b) particular discrete emotions, such as anger, fear, and sadness, provide specific information that guides adaptive actions embedded in tacit emotion schemes; and (c) the entire self-identity narrative or meaning system is accessed and available for modification when emotion schemes are activated in the context of EFTT IC/EE interventions and two-chair dialogues.

2. Basic assumptions concerning the nature of trauma and trauma recovery are that (a) traumatic experiences are encoded in experiential memory (emotion structure or scheme) and activated in current similar situations; (b) avoidance perpetuates disturbance; and (c) reexperiencing or "unlocking the emotional brain," and articulating a coherent trauma narrative, is required for emotional processing and recovery.

3. Accordingly, basic assumptions about narrative self-coherence include the importance of clients' disclosures of specific, emotionally salient autobiographical memories for (a) heightened therapist empathic attunement and access to underlying maladaptive emotion schemes and (b) the development of a more coherent, emotionally differentiated self-identity narrative in which painful "untold" trauma memories can be organized and told as a coherent story for further emotional integration and the emergence of a new view of self.

4. Basic assumptions regarding narrative and attachment are: (a) trauma experiences are encoded in memory as internal, autobiographical memory-based representations of self and others that continue to influence current perceptions and views of self; (b) abuse and neglect frequently results in a core sense of self or self-narrative as inferior, worthless, unlovable, and negligible and

a sense of others as neglectful, untrustworthy, and dangerous; and (c) traumatic internal autobiographical memory-based representations of self and other negatively impact the capacity to disclose, reflect, and coherently integrate painful emotions and trauma narratives, resulting in emotional dysregulation, self-incoherence, and disrupted interpersonal relationships with others.

Key Practice Principles

The following are fundamental principles that guide the practice of narrative-informed approaches to EFT and EFTT.

Emotion Schematic Processing and Repetitive Storytelling

An *emotion scheme* is the basic autobiographical memory unit that shapes clients dominant maladaptive repetitive storytelling in therapy sessions. This is similar to but distinct from the terms *emotion structure* or *relational structure* because it is not a static representation but involves an action plan contextualized within a prototype narrative scene. In some instances these terms will be used interchangeably in this book. The terms refer to the network of action tendencies and interpersonal narrative scenes as a meaning system associated with particular emotions. The entire meaning system can be activated in particular situations, and components include thoughts, beliefs, concerns, memories, feelings, bodily experience, and behavior.

For example, a client described in later chapters begins the session sharing a personal story in which her mother once again made unreasonable demands on her, and once again, she acquiesced instead of standing up for herself (the "same old" pattern or story). This interpersonal situation or scene evoked the core maladaptive emotion scheme with feelings of anxiety and underlying anger and sadness, autobiographical memories of her mother's emotional abuse and neglect, perceptions of her mother as selfish and controlling and herself as powerless victim, conflict between wanting to push her mother away and to please her, a tension headache, and behaviorally withdrawing. Embodied in narrative form, emotion schemes quickly connect our emotional responses with the events happening in our lives. They function rapidly and implicitly to automatically produce felt experience and action tendencies and, as such, are the foundations of the experiencing self.

Although emotion schemes are not directly available to awareness, their output in the context of client storytelling is. Emotion schemes are, in essence, emotionally salient autobiographical memory narratives that when activated produce affective experiences and nonverbal responses and provide a script for how to be in situations. This is why clients' disclosures of emotionally salient autobiographical memory narratives (personal stories) are so fundamental to facilitating emotional and self-identity change in EFTT. Emotion schemes need to be activated, articulated in language, and reflected on to form the narratives that guide our conscious lives.

Depth of Experiencing and Enhancing Reflective Storytelling

As noted previously, one of the distinguishing features of EFT and EFFT is that client experiencing—rather than the therapist challenging cognitions, psychoeducation, or interpretations—is the primary source of new information used in the construction of new meaning in EFTT. The construct of experiencing refers to the process of attending to and exploring subjective internal experience (usually feelings and meanings) and constructing new meaning from this process. The Client Experiencing Scale (Klein, Mathieu-Coughlan, & Kiesler, 1986) defines levels of experiencing, and Chapter 5 of this volume presents markers for identifying the various levels. In brief, low levels of experiencing are externally oriented with a focus on behavior and events. Moderate levels of experiencing are more personal and affective. Higher levels of experiencing include some exploration of meaning, questions about self, and ultimately construction of new meaning.

Emotional Transformation and Self-Narrative Change

Emotional transformation involves changing emotion with emotion rather than cognition. Greenberg and Pascual-Leone (1997) identified several subprocesses involved in emotional processing that have implications for intervention. These include awareness, regulation, reflection, and transformation. Each one of these may be a change processes with particular clients and at particular moments in time. For example, awareness of emotion is an important change process in and of itself for clients who are avoidant or alexithymic, which leads to further change once emotional experience is reflected on and its meaning understood. Regulation is an important change process for clients who are avoidant of or overwhelmed by intense negative feelings because it allows access to the meaning associated with emotional experience. Reflection on meaning results in greater narrative coherence and understanding. Transformation involves accessing the information associated with adaptive emotion, as a new emotional plotline, to help modify the meaning associated with maladaptive emotions embedded in clients repetitive maladaptive patterns or stories (NEP Problem markers) and thus shifting the dominant maladaptive pattern (NEP Transitional markers) for the emergence of new views of self and self-narrative change (NEP Change markers).

As described earlier, anger can help modify shame and self-blame as well as fear, and sadness can shift maladaptive blaming and rejecting anger. The information associated with these emotional plotlines is incompatible.

Once these maladaptive emotions are activated in therapy, simultaneously activating the adaptive alternative so that adaptive information can be integrated into the meaning system or self-narrative, something new is created—assertiveness or self-compassion, for example.

The Role of Therapist Empathy in Trauma Disclosure and Emotional Processing

Therapist-expressed empathy is a multidimensional construct consisting of verbal and nonverbal factors, including warmth, concern, and understanding of both affective and cognitive aspects of the client's inner world. According to Paivio and Laurent (2001), soothing empathic responses can reduce arousal and distress, and evocative responses can heighten arousal to activate emotion schemes. Accurate empathic responses can help clients accurately label feelings and explore the meaning of emotional experience. Understanding and making sense of feelings, in turn, promotes regulation. Empathic responses also can help clients communicate emotional experience. Overall, empathic responding helps clients construct coherent, affectively rich, and meaningful personal narratives that in turn contribute to self-identity and interpersonal functioning.

It is the therapeutic capacity to empathically attune to clients' emerging emotional experiences that provides clients with a safe, secure interpersonal space for accessing, disclosing and reexperiencing painful personal memories. Additionally, EFTT therapists can help clients narrate and organize painful emotions by actively identifying specific situational contexts and cues that help contain and explain emotional experiences, as a told story. As Angus and Greenberg (2011) suggested, therapists can use scaffolding questions such as "Where do you feel that emotion in your body? When you do recall sensing that feeling inside you? Where were you when you felt that?" to help clients identify a narrative context for undifferentiated emotional experiences that, in turn, make those feelings more understandable, specific, and controllable.

Alternatively, a therapist's empathic attunement to clients' overgeneralized, autobiographical memory narrative representations of self and others devoid or "empty" of emotional feeling or tone can help clients to access and symbolize previously avoided emotional responses that help bring new meaning to the events under discussion. Translating lived experience into told stories thus helps clients regulate their emotion, and the empathic relationship provides a secure base in which this is achieved and helps develop a basic sense of security.

A Narrative-Informed Model of Resolution in EFTT

The narrative-informed model of resolution in EFTT acts as a "process map" to guide intervention session by session. Accordingly, clients enter therapy with current self-related difficulties and relational problems as well as unresolved issues, pain and bad feelings, longings concerning early abuse, betrayals, and abandonment at the hands of loved ones. This is classic "unfinished business" in which the client has not been able to clearly express feelings and understand, make sense of, and come to terms with these experiences. Client Problem storytelling reflects views of self as worthless, powerless, or victimized and views of perpetrators as all-powerful, insensitive, uncaring, dangerous, malicious, neglectful, or evil. Despite their best efforts, clients have been unable to come to terms with these experiences, as these feelings and beliefs are embedded in maladaptive emotion structures or schemes that get activated again and again in current situations and relationships, and nothing shifts because they are stuck in the past. The purpose of the IC (see Figure 4.1) is to help the story evolve and cause a shift in the old pattern, and the catalyst for change is accessing and expressing previously inhibited adaptive emotions (anger at violation, sadness at loss) and associated meanings.

In this procedure, the client is asked to imagine and possibly enact an abusive/neglectful other (the relationship[s] that causes the most distress and is the focus of therapy) in an empty chair and to attend to and express evoked thoughts and feelings to the imagined other. There is back-and-forth interaction between the client and the imagined other. The top of Figure 4.1 represents steps in the process for the imagined or enacted other; the bottom of Figure 4.1 represents steps in the client's process.

Imagining the perpetrator in the empty chair typically will evoke a reaction of global upset or distress in the client (bottom of Figure 4.1), which may be followed by collapse into resignation or powerless, "What's the point—nothing will ever change." The therapist's job is to help differentiate these global feelings into clear expressions of adaptive anger and sadness, again directed at the imagined other. Adaptive information from these emotions will be used to shift the Same Old Story and construct more adaptive narratives concerning self and other.

However, before this can happen, we have observed that in EFTT this procedure frequently activates highly painful and disturbing trauma memories that evoke extreme distress and fear, avoidance, and collapse into shame and self-blame. Client Problem and Transitional storytelling reflects intrapersonal difficulties, struggles, or conflicts, and clients are unable to move forward in the process (clear expression of anger, sadness, and associated needs) until these conflicts are worked through. Thus, in the middle or working phase of EFTT, the IC procedure typically is used in conjunction with a variety of other procedures designed to address these self-related issues or blocks to resolution. These are described in detail in Chapter 9 on the middle phase of therapy.

As clients move forward in the resolution process, both the content and quality of their narratives shift to include more adaptive views of self and

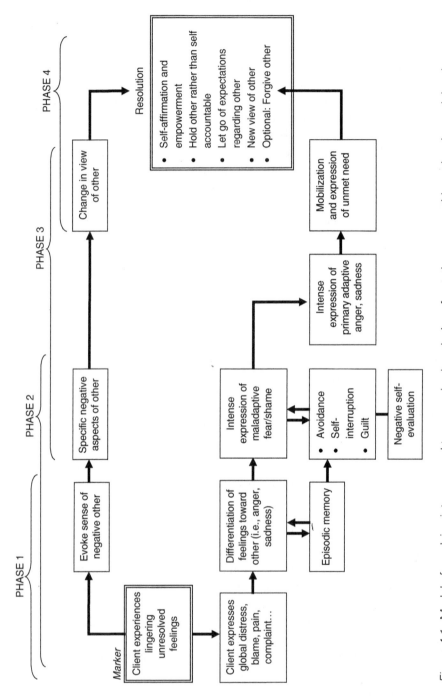

Figure 4.1. Model of resolving interpersonal trauma using imaginal confrontation or empathic exploration and the phases of emotion-focused therapy for trauma. From *Facilitating Emotional Change: The Moment-By-Moment Process* (p. 248), by L. S. Greenberg, L. N. Rice, and R. K. Elliott, 1993, New York, NY: Guilford. Copyright 1993 by Guilford. Adapted with permission.

other, increased access to emotional experience and reflection, and coherent storytelling. As clients begin to feel more self-aware, worthwhile, and confident, they are better able to confront perpetrators and fully express anger at violation and sadness at loss and reflect on associated meaning, including the effects of unmet needs. Clients also begin to feel more entitled to and deserving of these needs being met. In clearly and assertively expressing themselves to the imagined other for the first time, perceptions of the other also begin to shift. These are evident in Change storytelling markers. They are seen as less powerful, more human, and life-sized; clients also may begin to imagine that the other would regret having caused harm and be repentant, or they may see the other as pathetic rather than all-powerful. In any case, clients become more autonomous, separate from the other, and are able to let go of expectations from the other, for example, that they will change or apologize.

Resolution consists of clients feeling more self-aware, affiliative, confident, and autonomous and having a more differentiated view of the other, possibly one of forgiveness, yet always holding the other, rather than self, accountable for harm. The client feels finished and able to reflect on the meaning of achieving a new trauma story outcome—holding the perpetrator responsible—that also supports a new view of self as agentic, courageous, empowered, and deserving of having critical interpersonal needs met. As such, an important impact of resolving trauma-based unfinished business is the emergence of a new view of self and self-narrative change in final-phase EFTT sessions.

Narrative Processes and Mechanisms of Change in EFTT

The basic change process in the general model of EFT (Greenberg & Paivio, 1997) starts with secondary distress (helplessness, powerlessness) that is often expressed in the context of the client's disclosure of painful memories or engagement in Same Old Storytelling during early-phase sessions. This is differentiated into primary maladaptive emotions (fear, shame, sadness) in the context of reprocessing specific autobiographical memories or chair dialogues, which are then further explored for meaning (e.g., maladaptive beliefs, unmet needs). Next, the client shifts from identifying unmet needs to feeling deserving or entitled to these needs. This increased sense of entitlement to unmet needs helps challenge negative self-evaluations of the Same Old Story, and thus accesses alternative primary adaptive emotion (anger at maltreatment, sadness at loss) and associated meanings as a new, more agentic emotional plotline. This occurs in the context of a safe therapeutic relationship.

In terms of EFTT, in particular, there are two posited interrelated mechanisms of change: the therapeutic relationship and narrative-emotional processing of trauma events. The therapeutic relationship has two functions. First, a safe, empathically responsive, and collaborative therapeutic relationship helps clients to disclose and explore painful autobiographical memory narratives to facilitate heightened narrative coherence and emotional self-regulation. Second, this relational experience helps to correct early experiences of insecurity and invalidation in attachment relationships.

The second mechanism of change also involves two elements. First, maladaptive emotion schemes evident in clients' Same Old Stories reflecting maladaptive patterns of feelings (e.g., fear, shame), beliefs, and behaviors, and/or associated trauma-based autobiographical memories are accessed, narrated, and explored so these can be modified. These are modified through exposure to new information, such as the emergence of more adaptive emotional responses or a coherent trauma narrative. In particular, the exploration and differentiation of emotions in the context of specific autobiographical memory storytelling supports adaptive, autobiographical memory reconsolidation (Lane, Ryan, Nadel, & Greenberg, 2015) that supports the emergence of new perspectives of the self, or self-narrative change, that have been predictive of treatment outcomes in a range of therapy approaches and clinical disorders, including EFTT (Angus & Greenberg, 2011; Angus et al., 2016, in press; Carpenter et al., 2016).

The second element involves accessing previously inhibited adaptive emotion (e.g., anger at maltreatment, sadness at loss), or new emotional plotlines, so that associated adaptive resources can be used to help modify maladaptive meaning for the construction of more coherent, agentic, identity self-narratives. Again, this focus on the process of emotional transformation (changing emotion with emotion) for new outcome story change is unique to EFT and EFTT. For example, adaptive anger at violation helps to change maladaptive fear, shame, and self-blame, and adaptive sadness at loss accesses compassion for self and self-soothing responses that again help to counteract maladaptive shame and self-blame. This fundamentally changes the meaning of clients' most important stories and, in so doing, their view of self and adaptive self-narrative reconstruction.

Building on the key assumptions provided in this chapter, the following chapters present process-diagnostic assessment guidelines (Chapter 5) for the implementation of effective marker-guided interventions (Chapter 6). Chapters 7 through 12 provide a comprehensive description of key narrative and emotion intervention strategies in early-, middle-, and late-phase EFTT sessions.

II
PRACTICE

5

ASSESSING NARRATIVE-EMOTION PROCESSES IN EFTT

This chapter first elaborates on the emotion typology developed by Greenberg and colleagues (Greenberg & Paivio, 1997; Greenberg, Rice, & Elliott, 1993) that was introduced in Chapter 2. This is a useful heuristic in guiding the intervention process in emotion-focused therapy (EFT), including EFT for trauma (EFTT). These emotion subtypes are the basic units of therapeutic attention that facilitate emotion transformation for new reflective meaning making and self-narrative change. Sections that follow describe how to access and assess basic discrete emotions in the context of client storytelling and interventions, which are the focus of therapeutic work. These are followed by more macrolevel process maps that guide intervention over the course of sessions and the entire course of EFTT. These include the Degree of Resolution Scale (DRS; Singh, 1994), the Client Experiencing Scale (EXP; Klein, Mathieu-Coughlan, & Kiesler, 1986), and the Narrative-Emotion Process Coding System (NEPCS; Angus Narrative-Emotion Marker Lab, 2015).

http://dx.doi.org/10.1037/0000041-006
Narrative Processes in Emotion-Focused Therapy for Trauma, by S. C. Paivio and L. E. Angus

First, there is a consensus that repeated exposure to trauma fundamentally involves disruptions in emotional and narrative processes. Clients who have not resolved or come to terms with traumatic experiences have impaired emotion awareness and regulation capacities and are unable to make sense of these experiences and integrate them into a coherent narrative. Self-narrative incoherence, wherein actions and emotions resist integration for further reflection and meaning making, is disturbing and extremely dysregulating. Accordingly, there is consensus regarding the essential role of emotion and narrative integration in recovery from complex trauma. As such, most trauma treatments involve interventions that facilitate an emotional reexperiencing of trauma memories for enhanced narrative coherence and new meaning making.

EFTT is based on the general principles of EFT, which highlight the essential role of emotion in dysfunction and change. These principles have been previously presented in other treatment manuals on the general model of EFT (e.g., Elliott, Watson, Goldman, & Greenberg, 2004; Greenberg et al., 1993; Greenberg & Paivio, 1997). Emotional processing of trauma autobiographical memories first involves having clients access and disclose maladaptive patterns of feelings, beliefs, and behaviors evidenced in narratives about interpersonal concerns and trauma events. These maladaptive emotion schemes are now available for empathic validation, exploration, and emotion and narrative change. Although the strategies differ, a focus on accessing and changing maladaptive patterns of thoughts, feelings, and reactions is common to most trauma therapy approaches (Briere & Scott, 2006; Foa, Keane, Friedman, & Cohen, 2009).

The second aspect of emotional processing is a distinguishing feature of emotion-focused approaches. This involves accessing adaptive emotion and associated new meaning to modify maladaptive feelings, beliefs, and expectations for emotional transformation and narrative reconstruction. Accurate emotion and narrative/storytelling assessment (process diagnosis) is essential to appropriate intervention. The following sections first outline the emotion typology, which is the basis for intervention, and then address guidelines for assessing narrative-emotion integration processes for further intervention in therapy sessions. Examples of therapeutic work with each of these types of narrative-emotion processes are presented in the chapters that follow on the phases of EFTT.

EMOTION TYPOLOGY

The following emotion typology that is fundamental to EFT (Greenberg et al., 1993; Greenberg & Paivio, 1997) helps the clinician distinguish between adaptive and maladaptive emotions and to distinguish among different subtypes of these broad categories.

Primary Adaptive Emotion

Emotion theorists have identified a core set of emotions that are universal across cultures, that appear to be biologically based, and that guide adaptive functioning (Izard, 2002). These are direct responses to the environment and are unmediated by cognition or socialization processes; socialization affects the expression but not the experience of these emotions. For example, anger at violation serves to empower, self-protect, and establish interpersonal boundaries and distance in threatening situations; sadness at significant intra- or interpersonal loss promotes grieving, withdrawal, or seeking contact and comfort to heal; fear is a response to immediate threat of harm and serves to self-protect through escape or sometimes immobilization or freezing. Problems with these emotions concern their intensity or avoidance so that adaptive information is not available. Client storytelling is either stripped of emotional content and/or arousal (empty story) and associated meaning or is dysregulated and lacks the context of a coherent autobiographical memory narrative account ("unstoried" emotion). Intervention with these emotional processing difficulties involves regulation—reducing or intensifying arousal to activate the emotion structure or scheme. We present numerous examples of intervention with these processing difficulties in the chapters that follow.

An important subtype of primary adaptive emotion that is frequently observed in complex trauma survivors is emotional pain—for example, the pain associated with rejection by an attachment figure. For some clients, therapy involves the profound difficulty of accepting, at a heartfelt level, the fact that they were not loved. Although it is understandable that a client might avoid the disclosure of such a very painful, specific personal memory of rejection, the translation of that lived experience to an affectively alive narrated told story provides both client and therapist with essential information to further understand how the client was so deeply wounded and why it was so meaningful to him or her. This is essential to healing. Intervention involves helping clients to approach and narrate previously avoided painful and often traumatic memories to construct more emotionally coherent and compassionate self-narratives.

Maladaptive Emotion

Problems with maladaptive emotion concern the frequency and/or intensity of experience and expression, the lack of narrative context, the masking of adaptive emotion and associated adaptive information, and experience and expression that are inappropriate to the situation so that the emotional experience does not guide adaptive functioning.

Primary Maladaptive Emotion

Primary maladaptive emotions are immediate and direct responses to the situational context of lived events, just as in primary adaptive emotion, but these are conditioned and overgeneralized and not appropriate to the situation. Typical examples include the overgeneralized fear to a range of cues and stimuli that are characteristic of posttraumatic stress disorder (PTSD) or reactive anger in response to touch observed in clients who have been assaulted. Intervention involves in vivo or imaginal exposure and counterconditioning. Examples of this are presented in the following chapters when the introduction of the imaginal confrontation (IC) procedure in EFTT activates trauma memories and fear. In these instances, effective intervention involves gradual exposure and use of less evocative strategies, such as empathic exploration (EE), in the context of a safe and empathic therapeutic relationship.

Another subtype of primary maladaptive emotion is more complex core self-organization that can be activated in current situations. Although this is a complex meaning system comprising feelings, beliefs, and memories, this is a direct and holistic response to the environment that, unlike secondary emotions described next, is not generated or mediated by cognition or other emotion. Clients, for example, may state, "I know my husband loves me, but I can't understand why, I feel unlovable" or "I know I am not stupid, I have a PhD for God's sake, but I feel stupid." This is comparable to the core maladaptive emotion schemes, evidenced as clients' Same Old Stories involving repeated patterns of maladaptive feelings (e.g., fear, shame, sadness), beliefs about self and others, and behaviors. Client self-narratives at the beginning of therapy are dominated by a core sense of self as vulnerable and insecure and needing safety; worthless and unlovable and needing acceptance and self-esteem; or sad, alone, and abandoned and needing connection. Effective intervention involves accessing and restructuring the core emotion structure or self-organization, typically through autobiographical memory narrative work—disclosure, narration, and exploration of recent or distal personal memories in which the core sense of self was activated or developed and alternate healthy adult resources (adaptive feelings, needs, perceptions) are simultaneously activated.

Secondary Emotion

Secondary emotions, unlike primary (mal)adaptive emotional responses, are reactions to and mediated by maladaptive cognitions or other emotions. They are the end product of a sequence of other feelings and cognitions. For example, EFTT clients presented in the following chapters feel guilt or shame in reaction to self-criticism (e.g., "I should have been able to stop him.")

or anxiety in reaction to catastrophic expectations (e.g., "If I start crying, I will never be able to stop."). Intervention involves accessing the maladaptive cognition as well as acknowledging and expressing subdominant alternate healthy emotional responses (e.g., protest against unfair criticism, need for self-respect) to challenge and change the client's repetitive maladaptive narratives. Alternately, emotions can be secondary to another primary and often vulnerable emotion experienced in a threatening situation—for example, anger in response to feelings of fear or shame in childhood sexual abuse, or shame in response to feelings of vulnerability in situations of bullying and unfair victimization. This is similar to the concept of defensive emotions whereby the secondary emotion serves a protective function. The problem in most of these instances is that the client is avoiding recollecting, disclosing, and reexperiencing painful autobiographical memories, and primary adaptive emotional responses, that evoked the secondary emotional reactions in the first place. For example, the client Mark, who is presented in a later chapter, initially expressed defensive anger toward his mother that covered more vulnerable, primary adaptive feelings of sadness, fear of rejection, and not being loved. Intervention in these instances first involves recalling and narrating early childhood memories of emotional and physical abuse to access underlying primary emotions and associated adaptive feelings and needs for the coconstruction of a more integrated, coherent self-narrative.

Emotions, such as anxiety or depression, involve complex cognitive–affective–behavioral–motivational processes. Depression, for example, can involve feelings of sadness, shame, anger, and powerlessness; maladaptive beliefs about self as weak or bad; malevolent expectations of others; and behavioral withdrawal. Both depression and anxiety, particularly social anxiety, are highly comorbid with complex PTSD. Intervention involves exploring emotionally salient personal memory disclosures to access new, more adaptive primary adaptive emotion and action tendencies for the articulation of a more agentic, compassionate view of self.

Instrumental Emotion

Instrumental emotions are conscious or unconscious attempts to get needs met in interpersonal relationships, such as anger to control others or sadness to elicit support. Instrumental emotions are less often the focus of EFTT intervention but are observed in clients with anger control problems and in borderline personality disorder, both of which are comorbid with complex PTSD. EFTT intervention involves confronting and understanding the instrumental nature of the emotion, identifying the underlying unmet needs that provoke the expression of the emotion, and teaching more appropriate ways to get needs met.

How to Identify the Different Emotion Types

As highlighted throughout this manuscript, the narratives of clients with histories of complex trauma can be devoid of emotion or devoid of coherent narrative context so that different specific emotions are not always obvious in their personal stories. Nonetheless, accurate assessment is essential to appropriate intervention. There are several sources of information the clinician can use to guide accurate assessment of different types of emotional experience in the context of client personal disclosures and narratives.

The first is information about normal human functioning and universal emotional responses to circumstances. Here we are referring to emotional experience rather than expression, which can differ depending on culture (Izard, 2002). For example, anger is a universal response to maltreatment, violation, unfairness, and injustice, whereas sadness is about loss and what was missed.

Second, virtually all forms of psychopathology have affective components, and specific diagnoses are frequently associated with specific emotional responses. For example, the recollections and personal stories of clients who are depressed will frequently involve feelings of powerlessness and shame (weak/bad self), whereas those of clients diagnosed with posttraumatic stress disorder (PTSD) will frequently involve feelings of fear and alienation and problems with emotion dysregulation.

The third source of information used to guide accurate emotion assessment is knowledge about client issues and clients' typical ways of responding that are revealed in the context of their personal disclosures and storytelling across sessions.

The fourth and most important source of information is empathic attunement to client moment-by-moment experience observed in their verbal and nonverbal expressions, in both the content and quality of their narrative disclosures. As emphasized throughout this volume, empathic attunement—the ability to sense into the inner world of another—is a precondition for process diagnosis and intervention and a hallmark of EFT.

Finally, for more experienced therapists, a related source of information to guide emotion assessment is their own internal reactions to client expressions. For example, clients' tears in the context of stories concerning unmet needs for love or appreciation may elicit a desire to comfort them or compassion for their emotional suffering and pain, suggesting primary adaptive sadness. Alternately, this story might elicit a desire to protect or stand up for the client, suggesting vulnerability and fear. More distancing reactions on the part of the therapist would suggest maladaptive emotional experience, such as powerlessness and victimization. An important caveat here is that the trustworthiness of therapist internal reactions as an emotion assessment tool is entirely dependent on the therapist's emotional self-awareness. For this reason, we always recommend that EFT therapists receive their own therapy.

The Nature of Adaptive Anger and Sadness

Typically, the adaptive emotions we are trying to access and encourage in EFTT are previously suppressed anger at violation and sadness at loss and their associated adaptive meanings. Anger is associated with an erect body posture (anger gives us "backbone"), energy, eyes wide open and often looking directly at the other, and a vocal quality that is externally focused and firm. In terms of action tendencies, adaptive anger promotes distance from the other and wanting to push the other away, a need to protect or stand up for oneself, and a need to assert one's limits and interpersonal boundaries. In terms of content, anger is associated with words such as *hate, resent, annoyed, dislike, ripped off,* or *cheated,* which can be used in empathically responding to client personal stories concerning issues of violation, fairness, and justice.

Adaptive Anger

The following features outlined by Greenberg and Paivio (1997) distinguish adaptive from maladaptive anger expression: (a) it is fleeting rather than chronic; (b) it is externally directed at a specific other, rather than self, for specific harm; (c) it is assertively expressed using I–you language, rather than aggressive blaming, fingerpointing, and hurling insults, or passive, cold rejection (rejecting anger); (d) there is some exploration of meaning in terms of reasons for the anger and negative effects, rather than simple statements such as "I hate you"; (e) it is differentiated from other emotions so the associated information is available; and (f) the intensity is appropriate to the situation. Research using these criteria has found that healthy anger expression during the IC procedure of EFTT was associated with interpersonal dimensions of change and abuse resolution (Paivio & Carriere, 2007). Maladaptive anger, on the other hand, is too intense, chronic, covering up more vulnerable experience, or generated by maladaptive cognitions such as unrealistic expectations of entitlement. The latter are the focus of intervention in many anger-management strategies (e.g., Novaco, 2007).

Contempt and disgust are similar to anger. Contempt involves haughtiness, rejection, and with an air of superiority, looking down one's nose at the other; disgust is more bodily rejection (e.g., "You make me sick."). Adaptive expressions are directed at specific others—for example, during IC or EE, typically regarding reprehensible and immoral behavior or sexual abuse and coercion. Maladaptive expressions are frequently observed in client self-narratives involving self-criticism and in two-chair dialogues in which these emotions are directed at the self and involve a struggle between two parts of self—the dominant part that criticizes or squashes experience, for example, and the part that reacts with guilt or shame or suppression. In these instances, the goal is to access and support healthy rebellion against the dominant maladaptive emotional plotline.

Adaptive Sadness

Primary adaptive sadness, on the other hand, is associated with withdrawal and "turning the lights down" or seeking contact and comfort. Bodily experience includes low energy; curling up or lying down; and a soft, inwardly focused, wistful voice. Adaptive sadness promotes grieving, acceptance, and healing from loss, and elicits compassion for self and others. The same criteria for adaptive anger expression outlined earlier apply to sadness, except that adaptive sadness can be directed at the self and can be used to elicit self-compassion. Maladaptive sadness, on the other hand, is not fleeting and related to specific losses or unmet needs. Rather, client self-narratives are dominated by the chronic sad mood associated with depression, for example, or a core sense of self as lonely and abandoned and longing for connection. These recurring and repetitive themes are observed in the same old story the client wants to change.

The Nature of Fear and Shame

Fear and shame are typically the maladaptive emotions that are the focus of therapeutic attention and change in EFTT. Fear and shame are thought to be functionally equivalent (Paivio & Pascual-Leone, 2010) as both involve hiding and withdrawal and are difficult to work with in therapy because they are difficult for clients to tolerate and explore. As an adaptive emotion, fear is in response to and protects against a specific environmental threat. Problems associated with adaptive fear for some abuse survivors can be their difficulty in recognizing threat or trusting their own perceptions because of invalidating environments. This is thought to contribute to the revictimization frequently observed in complex trauma survivors.

Adaptive shame, on the other hand, serves to maintain social standards. For example, sexual abuse survivors are aware of having violated social standards, and this maintains the secret and protects them from possible rejection and isolation. Victims also can be perpetrators, and their shame is appropriate although better reframed as guilt and regret with the potential to make amends. An example of adaptive shame is presented in later chapters in the case of Mark, who acknowledged embarrassment and shame at treating his wife badly. Most often fear and shame are observed as the core maladaptive emotion scheme that emerges in client self-narratives involving negative beliefs about self, avoidance, and unmet needs for self-esteem and confidence. As well, these can be observed in narratives involving struggles between parts of self as secondary emotions resulting from catastrophic expectations or self-criticism.

PROCESS-DIAGNOSTIC MAPS TO GUIDE EFTT INTERVENTIONS

The process maps presented next are assessment tools that guide intervention over the entire course of therapy. We begin with the EXP (Klein et al., 1986) and the Emotional Arousal Scale (EAS; Machado, Beutler, & Greenberg, 1999) because assessing the quality of these processes is a part of all tasks and procedures in EFTT. This is followed by the revised model of resolution and the DRS (Paivio & Pascual-Leone, 2010), on which EFTT is based, and the NEPCS (Angus et al., 2016), which is the basis of the narrative-informed approach to EFTT that is the focus of this volume. Process maps that are more specifically relevant to self-development in the middle phase of therapy, such as steps in the processes of experiential focusing, two-chair dialogues, allowing emotional pain, and accessing self-soothing are presented in Chapter 9.

Assessing Client Depth of Experiencing

Assessing client depth of experiencing is an essential part of process diagnosis that guides effective moment-by-moment intervention regardless of tasks or procedures. Depth of experiencing also is one dimension of the narrative-emotion process (NEP) markers, especially Reflective Storytelling that is presented in later sections of this chapter. The following summarizes broad clinically recognizable categories of experiencing taken from the EXP (Klein et al., 1986).

Low-Level Experiencing

At low levels of experiencing (Levels 1 and 2 on the EXP), client narratives are externally oriented with a focus on behavior (often the behavior of others), situations, and events. Vocal quality is external as if the client were talking *at* you or giving a lecture. The story has a rehearsed quality. For example, a client might tell the following story: "I heard my father come home, I knew he was drunk. I grabbed my little brother and hid under the bed until he left." Here the therapist might imagine the clients' experience, but no clues are given in the narrative; it is strictly the facts—a chronicle of events.

Moderate-Level Experiencing

At moderate levels of experiencing (Levels 3 and 4 on the EXP), client narratives are more personal and affective and include references to self and use of emotion words or metaphors that provide a window onto the client's internal experience. Vocal quality is more emotional and alive. For example, the same story told in the previous example would sound more like the following: "I heard my father come home, I was terrified because I knew he was drunk, I grabbed my little brother and we hid under the bed. I was so afraid he would make a noise and Dad would find us." Here the client communicates what it was like in the situation, his or her internal experience at the time, but there is no attempt to understand the experience, place it in context, or explore its meaning.

High-Level Experiencing

Higher levels of experiencing in storytelling (Levels 5–7 on the EXP) include some attempt to understand, interpret, explore, or reflect on the meaning of experience. Clients may pose questions and problems about self. For example, the same story as in the previous examples might include: "Why can't I get over it, I feel like I'm still this little kid, always on edge, waiting for my father to walk in that door." At the highest levels, client narratives include attempts to answer these questions and solve these problems. The voice is internally focused and has a searching quality. Ultimately, the client arrives at new meaning—a new understanding of self, others, and the situation—and a new Discovery narrative emerges: "Now I see how much he is still in me, in my head, all that childhood fear still ruling my life. Now, when I feel scared, I can step back, look at it from my adult self, and calm the little girl inside."

Assessing Client Level of Emotional Arousal

The level of emotional arousal in client narratives is another important process-diagnostic dimension. As noted throughout this volume, assessing client difficulties with emotional expression and arousal in the context of their trauma and personal storytelling has obvious implications for appropriate intervention. Level of arousal is one dimension of the specific NEP Problem markers that are presented next. The following summarizes clinically recognizable levels of emotional arousal originally described in the EAS (Machado et al., 1999) and used in EFTT process research.

Low Emotional Arousal

At the lowest levels of emotional arousal, client narratives contain no emotion words, and there is no evidence of arousal in vocal quality, facial expression, or gestures in their storytelling. At somewhat higher levels, clients may use some emotion words in their storytelling, but there is no evidence of emotional arousal. Vocal quality is external, as if they are talking *at* you. This is Empty Storytelling described next. Clients whose storytelling involves the lowest levels of emotional arousal are difficult for therapists to read and empathically respond to because the significance of the story is unclear. We see this in the case of Mark, who is presented in later chapters.

Moderate Emotional Arousal

At moderate levels of emotional arousal, client narratives contain references to feelings, either through the use of emotion words or metaphors, phrases, and action tendencies that have clear references to feelings (e.g., "I wanted to crawl in a hole and die."). There are indicators of arousal in a more modulated vocal quality, facial expression, and gestures as well. For example, the client's voice may quiver in sadness or be raised in anger, vocal quality is more internally focused, tears may well up in the eyes, gestures could include clenched fists, and so on. The client may still be holding back from full expression, or the moderate level of emotional arousal is appropriate to the narrative content and the client is able to continue with storytelling. Therapists are readily able to perceive, identify, and empathically respond to the client's emotional reactions.

High Emotional Arousal

At the highest levels, emotions are fully expressed with no holding back. Clients may sob or pound pillows with their fists or a plastic bat. Emotions are either clearly identified using the most intense words (e.g., *hate, rage, anguish, despair*), or distress is undifferentiated and the client is unable to articulate his or her emotional experience. This is Unstoried Emotion, described next.

Relationship Between Experiencing and Arousal

Research has found that higher levels of observer-rated experiencing and expressed emotional arousal are associated with successful therapeutic outcome (Goldman, Greenberg, & Pos, 2005; Holowaty & Paivio, 2012; Pos, Greenberg, Goldman, & Korman, 2003; Ralston, 2006).

There also appears to be an important empirical relationship between client-expressed emotional arousal and depth of experiencing in EFTT sessions (Paivio & Pascual-Leone, 2010). For example, Ralston (2006) found that higher levels of emotional arousal in EFTT were associated with moderate levels of client experiencing, whereas higher experiencing levels were associated with relatively lower levels of expressed emotional arousal. High arousal, such as deep sobbing, activates emotion schemes, but arousal level needs to diminish to explore the meaning of feelings, the pain or loss. Although the EXP (Klein et al., 1986) has been an important measure of client change processes in EFT research, key dimensions identified by the measure are too molar to provide clinicians with specific information regarding how and when to effectively implement therapeutic interventions on a moment-to-moment basis. Additionally, the EXP provides only minimal criteria addressing the quality/degree of client emotional arousal and narrative expression in therapy sessions. For example, clinicians cannot begin to deepen experiencing when client storytelling is overly general, abstract, and devoid of specific episodic memory detail. As such, NEP Problem, Transition, and Change markers that represent key indicators of client emotional arousal, narrative coherence, and self-reflection may address an important gap for enhanced therapist training in EFT treatment approaches.

Model of Resolution

EFTT is based on a model of resolving interpersonal trauma as shown in Figure 4.1. Specific steps in the process are described in a modified version of the DRS (Greenberg & Hirscheimer, 1994) presented next and in the Appendix. Following every session, the therapist should identify client progress in the resolution process, which will establish the short-term goal for the following session. This model applies to the entire course of therapy as well as to therapeutic work specifically during IC and EE intervention procedures. Description of each level also addresses client storytelling characteristics.

Stuck in the Same Old Story (DRS Level 1)

Levels 1 and 2 of the DRS represent the early phase of therapy and the IC/EE procedures. These levels are characterized by Problem narrative-emotion storytelling markers, which are presented in later sections of this chapter. At Level 1, when clients begin therapy, they tell stories of past and current situations in which the core maladaptive emotion scheme was developed and is activated. They are stuck in the Same Old Story consisting of global negative views of significant others and maladaptive views of self and repeated patterns of maladaptive behavior. By definition, clients are stuck in "unfinished business" because they have been unable to experience and express authentic feelings and needs. The client Charlize, for example, whose case we present in later chapters, sees her mother (past and present) as selfish, controlling, and manipulative and herself as unloved, negligible, and unable to stand up to her mother. She experiences similar feelings and beliefs in her relationship with her husband. At this stage, the therapist is assessing the client's emotional processing difficulties that emerge in the context of storytelling—the presence and type of emotion words used, degree of emotional arousal, and the client's capacity for experiencing and reflection. This assessment refers to not only the client's modal way of operating, but also peak—what they are capable of in terms of depth of experiencing and emotion-regulation capacities. The therapist is attuned to the presence of client healthy resources evident in Transitional narrative-emotion subtypes—stories indicating access to adaptive feelings, needs, and action tendencies; depth of experiencing; and reflectivity. This assessment involves observation of client narrative quality as it spontaneously emerges in storytelling, as well as how responsive clients are to therapist interventions (empathic responses, questions, directives) that direct attention to and promote exploration and reflection on internal experience— the dyadic coconstruction of narrative.

Emotional Reaction to Trauma Memories (DRS Level 2)

At Level 2 of the DRS, an emotional reaction is evoked in response to recalling autobiographical trauma memories and imagining abusive or neglectful others in the IC or EE procedures. Initially the emotional reaction is typically undifferentiated global distress, hurt, blame, and complaint about the other and the collapse into resignation and hopelessness that things will ever change. Again this is indicative of Problem narrative-emotion storytelling subtypes, indicating a sense of being stuck in maladaptive patterns and emotion awareness and regulation difficulties—both dysregulation and overcontrol.

Working Through Self-Related Difficulties (DRS Level 3)

Level 3 of the DRS marks the middle or working phase of therapy. Clients' stories concerning self, perpetrators, and trauma memories typically are dominated by repeated collapse into fear/avoidance, self-doubt, guilt, shame, and self-blame. These are self-related or intrapersonal rather than interpersonal difficulties that again include problems with emotion awareness and regulation evident in Problem narratives. These narratives are devoid of affect or narrative context, superficial and abstract, or focused on external behavior and events (low-level experiencing). These narratives also indicate the persistent activation in current situations of a core maladaptive sense of self evident in repetitive storytelling. However, at this stage in the resolution process, clients also begin to access healthy internal resources (feelings, needs, perceptions of self and others) evident in Transitional narrative-emotion subtypes. Their storytelling may include internal struggles and conflicts, typically between a dominant maladaptive part and authentic "experiencing" self. Examples include client narratives involving struggles to express adaptive anger at violation or experience emotional pain versus fear and constriction of these feelings, or a struggle between defensive anger and pushing an abusive attachment figure away versus primary sadness and longing for connection.

Full Expression of Adaptive Emotion (DRS Level 4)

Level 4 on the DRS is a turning point in EFTT and marks the beginning of the late phase of therapy and the emergence of Change narrative-emotion storytelling markers. Client narratives concerning perpetrators and traumatic events now contain clear and uninhibited expressions of adaptive anger at violation and sadness at losses and the associated meanings, including unmet needs. Arousal levels are initially high and then moderate to enable deeper level experiencing or exploration of the meaning of feelings. Adaptive anger and sadness are catalysts for change because the information associated with these emotions is now available for adaptive self-narrative coconstruction. At this stage in the resolution process, clients are able to identify unmet needs, but may not yet feel fully deserving of them. For example, the client Charlize expressed sadness and identified deep longing for connection with her mother but repeatedly collapsed into self-criticism and self-invalidation ("I sound like a spoiled brat insisting on these things that I will never get. Grow up, get over it!"). Her self-narratives were still characterized by competing emotional plotlines—this struggle between longing and doubting the legitimacy of her unmet need for connection.

Increased Entitlement to Unmet Needs (DRS Level 5)

At DRS Level 5 in the resolution process, clients begin to feel increasingly entitled to having had their attachment needs met. For example, the client Charlize asserts that her childhood need for love and current needs for close interpersonal connection, whether her mother can meet those needs, are not trivial but essential to her well-being. As clients become increasingly clear and assertive, experiencing deepens as they explore perceptions of self and others and these begin to evolve—the Same Old Story begins to shift. Client self-narratives include views of self as having legitimate wants and needs, and clients begin to hold abusive and neglectful others, rather than self, accountable for harm. Client stories have an element of discovery; these indicate the clear emergence of NEP Change markers.

More Adaptive Perceptions of Self and Others (DRS Level 6)

Levels 6 and 7 of the DRS occur during the late phase of therapy, as do the highest levels of experiencing indicating construction of new meaning, along with emotional engagement at moderate levels of arousal. At Level 6, as new therapeutic experiences are integrated, client stories about the past and current relationships clearly indicate NEP Change markers involving discoveries or new perspectives about self and others, including perpetrators. The self is seen as more autonomous and powerful, and perpetrators are seen in a more differentiated and realistic light. The client may forgive the other and/or clearly hold the other, rather than self, responsible for harm. Clients also begin to report experiencing new and sometimes unexpected outcomes, such as new feelings and reactions in their current lives—for example, they are able to assert their boundaries with others.

Full Resolution (DRS Level 7)

At DRS Level 7, clients feel more powerful in relation to the other and no longer blame themselves. They have let go of expectations, for example, that the other will apologize or respond to unmet need and instead look to their own resources to meet existential or interpersonal needs. They feel finished in terms of issues with the other who was the focus of therapy, and they focus more on personal strengths. Their storytelling reflects new outcomes, and they may express acceptance, surprise, relief, or contentment.

An Integrative Approach to Assessing NEP in EFTT

The NEP model is intended to provide clinicians with a simplified, integrative process-diagnostic map for the assessment of a combination of client processing indicators such as (a) level of client reflective engagement (e.g., EXP; Klein et al., 1986); (b) expressed emotional arousal; and (c) degree of narrative coherence, on a moment-to-moment basis, in EFTT sessions. Each NEP marker differs in the degree to which clients disclose specific autobiographical memories; symbolize bodily felt experience; express emotion; reflect on their own or others' minds and behaviors; coherently integrate actions, emotions, and personal meaning; and articulate change. As is discussed in the following chapter, it is important that individual storytelling markers also point to opportunities for the implementation of specific EFTT interventions, and marker-guided responses, to enhance autobiographical memory narrative disclosure, emotional engagement/transformation, and reflectivity for heightened self-narrative coherence. Based on empirical research outcomes presented in Chapter 4 (Angus et al., 2016), the 10 NEP markers are clustered into Problem, Transition, and Change subgroups that reflect stages of narrative and emotion process change. These are described in Table 5.1 and the following sections.

NEP Problem Markers

NEP Problem markers represent underregulated, overregulated, or unintegrated emotion and client storytelling episodes that are incoherent, rigid,

TABLE 5.1
Narrative-Emotion Process Markers

Marker	Process indicators	Examples
Problem		
Same Old Story	Expressing dominant, maladaptive, overgeneral views of self and relationships marked by lack of agency, stuckness	"She was never concerned about me, she was only concerned with herself. Behave, be good, don't cause me any trouble."
Empty Story	Describing an event with a focus on external details and behavior, and a lack of internal referents or emotional arousal	"I was crying on the floor. The lady next door, her daughter was our babysitter, she was 16. She made me some eggs with cheese on top."
Unstoried Emotion	Experiencing undifferentiated, under- or over-regulated emotional arousal, without coherent narration of the experience	*Therapist:* Sad, so sad. [*25-second pause, client stares at ceiling*] Are you holding back right now? *Client:* Yes. 'Cause I have to take a bus later. I can't be on the bus with tear-stained eyes.
Superficial Story	Talking about events, hypotheticals, self, others, or unclear referents in a vague, abstract manner with limited internal focus	"The way that she talked to me and treated me in front of friends, and family. Even like my sister and father, just things that she says and does."
Transitional		
Competing Plotlines	An alternative to a dominant view, a belief, feeling, or action emerges, creating tension, confusion, curiosity, doubt, protest	"I have three healthy children, a house, we're not wealthy but we're okay, and I sort of go . . . why am I not . . . happier? I don't know."
Inchoate Story	Focusing inward, contacting emergent experience, searching for symbolization in words or images	"Things seemed OK on the outside. But inside, there's . . . [closes eyes, frowns] a, like a [silence] black hole or a void, or . . ."
Experiential Story	Narrating an event or engaging in a task as if reexperiencing an autobiographical memory or interpersonal scheme	"I walked and walked and walked like I was in a fog. It was raining and dark, and I got wound up, and I just had to walk it off. I was soaking wet but didn't care."
Reflective Story	Explaining a general pattern or specific event in terms of own or others' internal states (thoughts, feelings, beliefs, intentions)	"There was nobody who cared, and so eventually I stopped showing them how I felt. Somewhere between there and here I stopped feeling it."

TABLE 5.1
Narrative-Emotion Process Markers *(Continued)*

Marker	Process indicators	Examples
	Change	
Unexpected Outcome	Describing a new, adaptive behavior (action, thought, feeling, response) and expressing surprise, pride, relief, contentment	"I was so anxious, but instead of wallowing in it like usual I thought 'what can I do?' So I [did] the muscle relaxation stuff . . . it felt so good. After, I felt like a different person."
Discovery Story	Reconceptualizing, or articulating a novel understanding of the self, others, key events, behavior patterns, or change processes	"I've been thinking about the theme of being uninvited in the world. I think, I never did it consciously, but I realize that I've seen myself as an intrusion for a very long time, and . . ."

undifferentiated, or repetitive. Taken together, this group of markers represents NEPs that are thought to maintain the presenting clinical issue(s)—emotional dysregulation, self-incoherence, and interpersonal distress—and do not facilitate therapeutic recovery. These are typically observed early in therapy and the resolution process described previously. The four NEP Problem markers and their descriptions presented in Table 5.1 include Same Old, Empty, and Superficial Storytelling and Unstoried Emotion.

Same Old Storytelling. The Same Old Storytelling marker is similar to a maladaptive emotion scheme (Greenberg et al., 1993), or negative core beliefs, and refers to client overgeneral descriptions of intra- or interpersonal processes, including maladaptive behavioral, thought, and emotional patterns accompanied by a sense of low personal agency (i.e., stuckness, hopelessness, or resignation). Experiencing levels are typically low. These problematic patterns are seen as unalterable and maintained by forces outside of the self. These are characteristic of classic "unfinished business" related to unresolved trauma, and helping clients to affectively reengage and begin to protest the constraints of their Same Old Story becomes an important focus of intervention during early therapy sessions.

Empty Storytelling. The Empty Storytelling marker entails the description and elaboration of personal memories or information, accompanied by a lack of reflexivity, externalizing voice (low-level experiencing), and absent or low-expressed emotion and emotional arousal. The Empty Story is an overly detailed, factual description of an event, with minimal reflexivity or analysis.

The term *empty* refers to the absent or limited emotional expression in verbal content, voice, or body, and as a consequence, the significance of the story often remains unclear to the listener. Accordingly, as will be seen in the case analysis of Mark, in later chapters, helping clients to emotionally reexperience their narration of emotionally salient personal memories becomes an essential entry point into primary adaptive emotions and new meaning making in middle-phase sessions.

Unstoried Emotion. The Unstoried Emotion Storytelling marker refers to a distressing, strong, emotional experiencing during therapy sessions that lacks a clear personal narrative context. Although the client may be either emotionally underregulated (i.e., emotional overflow as in the highest levels of arousal) or overregulated (i.e., dissociative emotion) in the moment, the client is unable or unwilling to focus on the bodily felt feeling to symbolize his or her feelings for further elaboration and reflection. As the overwhelming and often painful emotional state remains unacknowledged or unelaborated by the client, what the feelings are connected to remains unclear and as such out of control; thus there is accompanying low-level experiencing. Unstoried Emotion is often identified in long durations of client pausing and is notably evident in treatments of complex trauma (Carpenter, Angus, Paivio, & Bryntwick, 2016). Helping clients to emotionally self-regulate overwhelming emotions are important tasks for EFTT therapists.

Superficial Storytelling. The Superficial Storytelling marker refers to a generalized, vague, incoherent, or abstract narrative in which the client may discuss his or her own feelings, ideas, beliefs, or preferences in an intellectualized manner, but with little evidence of exploration or discovery. Content is also frequently depersonalized or is other focused. Consistent with low levels of experiencing described previously, this marker is identified when clients are recounting events or hypothetical situations in a vague, abstract manner with limited internal self-focus. Again, helping clients to identify and explore specific autobiographical memories for further reflective meaning making and new emotional awareness, evident in more NEP Transitional markers described next, is an important goal of EFTT therapists.

NEP Transitional Markers

The four NEP Transition markers—Reflective, Competing Plotlines, Inchoate, and Experiential Storytelling—capture clients' increasing movement toward narrative and emotion integration through the expression of more differentiated emotions within a coherent, specific, flexible narrative during therapy sessions. This NEP subgroup comprises markers that are conceptualized as an impetus for new meaning making and more adaptive and flexible self-narratives. These markers are thought to pave the road toward therapeutic change and, in recovered clients, would be increasingly observed in the middle phase of EFTT and the resolution process, described earlier.

Reflective Storytelling. The Reflective Storytelling marker is defined as a coherent analysis of or reflection on cognitive, emotional, or behavioral patterns, or on an autobiographical memory, that emphasizes the thematic connections between experiences or events. Reflective Story identifies client engagement in constructing a coherent narrative account from his or her personal perspective (i.e., referencing internal thoughts and feelings), which also corresponds with Level 5 of the EXP (Klein et al., 1986) and mid-level depth of emotional arousal and engagement. This form of client reflective engagement is self-focused, and although internal experiences may be elaborated within this marker, there is limited evidence of present-centered emotional exploration (see Inchoate Story). An important distinguishing feature between the Superficial Story and the Reflexive Story is that the latter provides explanatory information about intra- or interpersonal themes (i.e., the "why" or "how"); however, these explanations do not occur in the context of novel understanding (see Discovery Story) that would be evident at the highest levels of experience.

Competing Plotlines Storytelling. The Competing Plotlines Storytelling marker is identified when there is tension and incongruence between two parts of the self that is accompanied by emotions such as confusion and frustration. The Competing Plotlines marker refers to the expression of competing or opposing emotional responses, lines of thinking, or behavioral tendencies in response to a specific event or life domain. This is accompanied by confusion, self-doubt, protest, anger, or frustration, resulting in an overt sense of tension or self-incongruence. Often the competing emotional reactions, beliefs, or action urges stem from a breach of deeply held assumptions such as the failure of a trusted parent to provide protection from abuse, a deeply painful breach of trust. As such, Competing Plotlines Storytelling markers are identified when clients experience challenges to their Same Old Stories wherein states of emotional incoherence, confusion, and puzzlement begin to emerge in therapy sessions. Examples can be intrapersonal, as in conflict splits, self-interruption of or self-doubt about emerging experience, and self-critical or catastrophizing processes, or they can be interpersonal, as in conflicting feelings concerning an attachment figure. Levels of experiencing and emotional arousal are moderate, indicating emotional engagement with exploring the meaning of new feelings and the conflict. Therapists help to support the emergence of new adaptive emotions and needs, for further reflection and meaning making, that challenge core maladaptive beliefs and plotlines of the clients' Same Old Storytelling.

Inchoate Storytelling. Inchoate Storytelling markers are identified when a client turns his or her attention inward to sort through, piece together, articulate, and make sense of an emerging bodily felt experience that can be facilitated through the use of client experiential focusing strategies (Gendlin, 1997) described in Chapter 9 in the middle phase of EFTT. Inchoate stories include heightened client self-exploration and emergent emotional experiencing, which corresponds with Level 5 of the EXP (i.e., client is focused on exploring his or her internal experience). These story types are characterized by the client's search or struggle for the appropriate symbolization in language. This symbolization is often disjointed and involves extensive pausing, as well as the "trying on" of various words, symbols, or metaphors to accurately represent the internal experience. Helping clients to symbolize and reflectively explore the meaning of new primary adaptive emotional responses and needs, and support emotional transformation, for new story outcomes and self-narrative change is a key EFTT therapeutic task.

Experiential Storytelling. Experiential Storytelling represents the capacity to narrate an emotionally evocative, personal story in a coherent and descriptive manner. This would correspond to at least Level 4 on the EXP and moderate to high levels of emotional arousal, especially if the story refers to traumatic memories. The Experiential Story involves experiential reentry into a specific autobiographical memory, often of a traumatic nature, during which thoughts, emotions, and sensory details associated with the event are experienced in the present moment and richly described in narrative form. These trauma narratives emerge in the early phase of EFTT and the resolution process and are explored in the middle phase. This is similar to the process of reexperiencing trauma feelings and memories that is recommended in most approaches to trauma therapy (Courtois & Ford, 2013). Experiential stories can concern past traumatic events or upsetting current situations in which the core maladaptive emotion or sense of self is evoked. Helping clients to more fully integrate and construct an emotionally coherent account of their trauma narrative, for further meaning making and memory reconsolidation, is a key intervention strategy for trauma intervention treatments, including EFTT.

NEP Change Markers

Two key NEP Change markers are identified: Unexpected Outcome and Discovery Story. These demonstrate the emergence of client engagement in new adaptive actions and self-narrative reconstruction in light of positive change experiences in therapy and salient interpersonal relationships. These begin to emerge in the middle phase of EFTT and are fully evident in the late phase and later stages of the resolution process (DRS Levels 4–7, described previously and in the Appendix). The highest levels of experiencing involving constructing new meaning or understanding regarding self and others are evident in Change storytelling. The Change markers subgroup refers to client story types featuring the greatest degree of narrative-emotion integration, including more flexible, coherent, emotionally differentiated, and effective narratives. The Change marker category captures novel action tendencies, or emergent meaning making, and therefore reflects actual adaptive change—whether concrete behavioral or new conceptual understandings. As noted in Chapter 4, NEP change markers overlap with White and Epston's (1990) concept of a Unique Outcome Story, and with reconceptualization innovative moments identified in the Innovative Moments Coding System (Gonçalves, Mendes, Ribeiro, Angus, & Greenberg, 2010).

Unexpected Outcome Storytelling. The Unexpected Outcome Storytelling marker refers to descriptions of new, adaptive behavior, emotional responses, or thought patterns, which are accompanied by expressions of surprise, excitement, pride, inner peace, relief, or protest in response to new emotional responses and/or taking positive action in the context of fulfilling intrapersonal needs and goals. These new outcomes emerge in the context of salient interpersonal relationships or as an outcome of a resolved IC/EE dialogue (DRS Levels 6 and 7, described previously and in the Appendix). A sense of agency is additionally expressed in the narrative, as the client identifies his or her own active role in the change. Therapists help clients to identify and reflect on changes for further integration into their self-identity narrative.

Discovery Storytelling. Discovery Storytelling is defined as the articulation of a new understanding or view of the self that results in narrative reconstruction and consolidation of client experiences of change. Discovery Storytelling is a reflexive or interpretive reflection or analysis of a specific event, subjective experience, and/or cognitive or behavioral pattern, which is accompanied by a sense of discovery connected to new self-understanding. Whereas the Unexpected Outcome Story pertains to novel, adaptive responses to a concrete event, the Discovery Story captures innovative meaning making or the reconceptualization of old beliefs about the self in the form of a more compassionate, coherent self-narrative. Discovery Story, in particular, also appears to be reflective of Level 6 or 7 of the EXP, wherein a client's awareness and understanding of the self is leading to construction of a new self-narrative. As mentioned previously, Discovery Storytelling is a key change process wherein clients' maladaptive emotion schemes and autobiographical trauma narratives are reengaged and updated with new, more adaptive emotional outcomes resulting in positive self-narrative change (Angus, Gonçalves, Boritz, & Mendes, in press; Angus & Kagan, 2013; Angus et al., 2016).

CONCLUSION

In this chapter we have presented a typology for identifying different types of emotion, as well as several process maps for assessing the client's degree of resolution of issues with perpetrators (the primary task of EFTT) and the quality of NEPs at each stage in the resolution process over the phases of therapy. These process maps are intended to act as guides for the implementation of effective therapist interventions, which are the focus of the following chapter.

6

PRINCIPLES OF INTERVENTION WITH NARRATIVE-EMOTION PROCESSES

The following intervention principles and guidelines are presented in order of specificity, from those that are more generally applied to all sessions with all clients and all tasks to those that apply to particular therapist statements within specific tasks and procedures.

ESSENTIAL INTERVENTION PRINCIPLES IN EFT AND EFT FOR TRAUMA

Before describing intervention in specific process models, it is useful to specify fundamental intervention principles that characterize every session of emotion-focused therapy (EFT), in general, regardless of the client problem, including EFT for complex trauma (EFTT; Paivio, 2013). These processes correspond to the posited mechanisms of change in EFTT. Effective therapists

http://dx.doi.org/10.1037/0000041-007
Narrative Processes in Emotion-Focused Therapy for Trauma, by S. C. Paivio and L. E. Angus

should be implementing these principles every session regardless of the focus, the specific task being worked on, or the procedure being implemented.

Establish a Focus for the Session

The first principle is to establish a focus for the session. This focus is consistent with the goals and tasks of therapy and is collaboratively determined as part of the therapeutic alliance. Without a clear focus, sessions and therapy are unproductive. The focus for the session can be initiated by the client who comes in with a specific concern or in response to the therapist's inquiry "What is most important thing for you to talk about today?" or it can be suggested by the therapist as a part of initiating or ongoing work on a core therapeutic task. For example, in the first session the therapist explicitly describes the focus of the first few sessions as establishing a clear understanding of client problems and collaborating on therapy goals and tasks or, in Session 4, the therapist suggests a focus on in-depth exploration of trauma autobiographical memory narratives and initiates the first imaginal confrontation (IC) or empathic exploration (EE). When clients are unclear about where to start, experiential focusing strategies (Gendlin, 1997), described in Chapter 9, can help them identify their most pressing concerns.

Communicate Empathy and Compassion for Client Struggles and Pain

The second fundamental intervention principle is to listen for clients' disclosures of their most poignant personal stories (Angus & Greenberg, 2011) and empathically respond to and communicate compassion for their struggles and pain. This is what Greenberg (2011) called the "pain compass," which helps to guide intervention processes in EFT. In general, *compassion* refers to "suffer with," whereas *empathy* refers to understanding. Paivio and Laurent (2001) specified the functions and advantages of empathic responding, especially in helping clients to reprocess trauma feelings and memories. For instance, empathic attunement and responsiveness to the painful emotional undertones of clients' Same Old Stories reduces their sense of isolation and distress in the session. Experiencing a sense of emotional validation and safety in the therapeutic relationship, clients are now more able to disclose avoided or suppressed traumatic memories and emotional responses for further reflection, differentiation, and meaning making. This is a combination of Reflective and Experiential Storytelling that supports the narration of a new, more emotionally coherent and differentiated account of the full story of what happened.

Moreover, a sense of shared understanding and relational safety in the context of disclosing emotionally salient personal stories—what has been termed *reflective functioning* (Macaulay, Angus, Carpenter, Bryntwick, & Khattra, 2016) in the developmental research literature—can also be a kind of corrective interpersonal experience that helps clients to counter the profound empathic failures and breaches of trust associated with childhood abuse and neglect. It is important not only to communicate accurate understanding of client feelings and needs but also to convey compassion for how much clients have suffered, how hard they have struggled, the depth of their pain, and to empathically affirm their vulnerability in session as they access these painful feeling and memories. This strengthens the relational bond, reduces anxiety, and facilitates disclosure of painful autobiographical memories and the construction of coherent and self-compassionate self-narratives.

Promote Client Experiencing and Reflective Storytelling

The third fundamental principle is to promote client experiencing, that is, exploration of feelings and meanings, in relation to salient personal memories and stories, with a particular emphasis on increasing awareness of and entitlement to unmet needs. As articulated in the preceding chapter, client experiencing, as captured in Reflective Storytelling markers, is a primary source for the emergence of new self-understanding and views of self in EFT and EFTT and is fundamental to all tasks and procedures used in EFTT. Angus and Greenberg (2011) noted that emotions can only be meaningfully understood when contextualized within an associated personal memory or maladaptive emotion scheme that is conveyed in clients' Same Old Stories. It is essential to flesh out the emotional meaning of clients' narratives so they can understand and make sense of their own internal world of feelings, intentions, and expectations of self and others that are now connected to a more differentiated and coherent narrative account. Clients frequently have difficulty making coherent sense of and thus coming to terms with their autobiographical memories of upsetting or traumatic events, especially when these experiences happened during crucial periods of childhood development. The client Charlize, presented in later chapters, was highly distressed at treatment onset because she could not understand how she could come to terms with an awareness of her mother's abuse while at the same time feeling a strong need to protect her mother and establish a secure, emotional bond with her.

Promoting a reflective, experiential awareness of emergent primary adaptive emotions and associated needs and action tendencies that emerge from the narration of salient personal memories promotes a sense of narrative self-coherence, acceptance, and relief. Accessing client unmet needs for love, attention, and protection, for example, and promoting entitlement to these unmet needs, are particularly important parts of new narrative and meaning construction. Clients shift from a view of self as powerless victim who was somehow complicit in, or deserving of, the abuse and neglect they experienced to a more self-affirming view of self who, like all children, deserved to have important emotional and physical needs met. They now appreciate the importance of their deepest desires and longings for emotional and physical safety, rather than ignore, minimize, or invalidate them as others did, and are motivated to find ways to have these needs met in their current lives.

Paivio and Pascual-Leone (2010) specified general guidelines for promoting experiencing. Briefly, this first involves creating an environment that is quiet, slow, contemplative, and conducive to an internal focus. This is similar to the environment conducive to mindfulness. It also is essential to cultivate an attitude of exploration, curiosity, and discovery. The therapist cannot have preconceived theories about what will be discovered, but rather cultivate an attitude of mutual exploration and discovery ("Let's understand this better."); the therapist is expert on the exploration process, not on the content of client experience. Second, exploration moves from concrete aspects of experience to more ephemeral aspects, from a bodily felt sense to feelings to the meanings of feelings. If a client already can identify feelings, it is not helpful in terms of deepening experiencing to direct attention to bodily sensations. This is useful to emotion coaching and increasing awareness of emotion but not to deepening experiencing, which is about meaning exploration and construction. Third, the therapist also must cultivate an attitude of acceptance of what emerges in the process. In some instances this will be extremely emotionally painful or involve new views of self and others that may be unsettling.

In general, experiencing is deepened step-by-step (see the preceding chapter for a description of levels of experiencing). Intervention to help clients shift from externally focused low-level experiencing to moderate levels that provide a window into the clients' inner world involves focusing client attention on personal values and concerns and then feelings. Intervention to facilitate shifts to deepen experiencing further focuses on exploring and symbolizing the meaning of, and reflecting on the meaning of, feelings and events in terms of causes and the effects on self and relationships. Intervention to facilitate shifts to the deepest levels of experiencing, and Reflective Storytelling, helps clients begin to identify problems and pose questions about self and then search for answers. Interventions maintain attention on evolving internal moment-by-moment process, scaffolding the client's search for accurate labels and understanding of experience with empathic responses that are close to the client's experience. The integration of primary adaptive emotional responses (see the following section) provides an important experiential platform for further reflective meaning making and the articulation of a more coherent trauma narrative and new self-understandings.

Respond to the Emergence of Adaptive Experience and Emotional Plotlines

The fourth fundamental intervention principle that is the basis of all interventions used in EFT and EFTT is attunement and responding to the emergence of healthy resources such as adaptive emotional responses and associated needs that directly challenge the maladaptive assumptions, and expectations, of a client's Same Old Story. EFTT therapists are continually attuned to openings or opportunities to respond to, and reinforce the emergence of, a subdominant healthy aspect of self—as an alternate, competing emotional plotline—in the context of client Same Old Storytelling. Key indicators of childhood maltreatment are repetitive stories that express secondary emotional reactions such as rejecting anger, powerlessness, resignation, or depression. For clients such as Mark, who is described more fully in later chapters, the early phase of therapy was dominated by the expression of anger and resentment toward his mother. It was important for his therapist to validate his anger, but also be aware of, and respond to, subtle indicators of vulnerability, sadness, or pain for further elaboration and reflective exploration (e.g., Reflective Storytelling) in their therapy sessions. Empathic attunement for indicators of the underlying emotional landscape of client accounts of childhood abuse and neglect is fundamental to all procedures used in EFTT and to the change process itself, transforming the painful and demoralizing Same Old Story of childhood maltreatment through the emergence of healthy, adaptive emotional plotlines and the discovery of new views and experiences of self that instantiate a more compassionate and agentic self-identity narrative.

NARRATIVE-INFORMED EFTT INTERVENTION PRINCIPLES

Previous volumes on EFT (Greenberg & Paivio, 1997) and EFTT (Paivio & Pascual-Leone, 2010) have outlined specific intervention principles that apply across particular tasks and procedures. These are similar to therapist intentions that can be realized through a number of therapist operations, including empathic responding, directives, and questions. Principles that are particularly relevant to therapy with complex trauma are as follows.

Evoke Autobiographical Memory Narratives

Evoking trauma memories is the hallmark of trauma therapies and exposure-based procedures. However, memories of recent situations in which the core maladaptive emotion scheme with sense of self and others, the

Same Old Story, is evoked are equally important foci for therapy. Therapists ask clients to recall specific examples of situations, whether distal or recent, with attention to imagery; concrete, sensorial detail; and internal experience (bodily, feelings, thoughts) at the time of the event. Often the external detail can help evoke internal experience. For example, in IC/EE procedures, asking clients to imagine perpetrators in the empty chair or their "mind's eye" functions specifically as a stimulus to evoke an emotional reaction. Similarly, recalling sensory-affective details (sounds, smells, bodily experiences; e.g., frozen or holding one's breath) can fill in memory gaps and help clients make sense of distressing traumatic events, understand their own reactions, and thus construct richer and more coherent narratives.

Direct and Redirect Attention to Internal Experience: Experiential Storytelling

Because internal experience (particularly feelings and associated meanings) is the primary source of information used in the construction of meaning and new self-narratives in emotion-focused therapies, directing attention to and symbolizing or articulating the meaning of internal experience (e.g., feelings, wishes, hopes, and sensations) are the basic intervention principles used throughout therapy. Directing a client's attention and awareness to bodily felt feelings and emotions that often emerge in the context of recounting painful personal memories is accomplished through the use of empathic responses that highlight or underscore the most poignant or painful aspect of a client's autobiographical memory disclosure (e.g., "I hear a lot of sadness, so much you missed out on, with your mother.") and a shift to Reflective Storytelling. Directing attention to presently felt experience is an important variant of this intention (e.g., "I see how distressing it is for you recall that memory. Can you put some words to what you are feelings now?" or "Put some words to those tears.") is a key intervention strategy that can shift clients' problematic Empty Storytelling to an emotionally enriched narrative account and deepen a moment-by-moment experiencing process.

Some clients who are particularly fearful, avoidant of feelings, and externally oriented (e.g., Empty Storytelling and low-level experiencing) may not respond to therapist empathic responses. These clients require more directive responses and explicit guidance (e.g., "How did you feel when he said that? Go inside.") and empathic conjectures about what they might be feeling (e.g., "I would be so hurt if my own father said that to me.") to deepen experiencing. EFTT therapists need to be patient and persistent in redirecting their client's attention during externally focused storytelling ("A lot going on. Let's go back to that incident with your father. That seems important to explore in more detail."). This is because emotionally avoidant clients will easily deflect away from a focus on emergent emotions and feelings. To engage in process-directive refocusing and avoid an alliance rupture, therapist and client need to establish a shared understanding that emotional awareness and meaning making is an important therapeutic goal. One caveat is that questions about internal experience can increase anxiety and blocking for clients who are socially anxious or alexithymic and do not know what they are feeling. In these instances asking the client to recall and describe a specific event (autobiographical memory) for heightened emotional awareness, empathic conjecture, offering prompts (e.g., "Sometimes people feel afraid they will make a mistake and be judged, sometimes people fear they will lose control. Do these resonate with you?"), or explicit emotion awareness training may be more effective.

Symbolize Meaning: Reflective and Experiential Storytelling

Symbolizing meaning refers to exploring all the facets of sensorial, perceptual, and emotional experience embedded in memory-based emotion schemes and autobiographical trauma memories to construct a rich and coherent narrative account. The disclosure of specific, autobiographical memory narratives in therapy sessions offers EFTT therapists a rich opportunity to help clients reflectively explore emerging feelings, sensory experience, beliefs about self and others, unmet needs, wishes, desires, longings, other memories, connections between situations, causes and effects—all of which are aspects of meaning. The basic intention is to help clients engage in Experiential Storytelling that supports the articulation of an integrative, coherent account of what happened, how did it feel, and what did it mean (Angus, 2012; e.g., "That sounds important. Say more about what was happening inside you, as you heard your father come inside the room. Almost frozen or paralyzed . . . ? Imagining what . . . ?"). However, it is better if this is a dyadic, coconstructive process whereby therapist responses (empathy, directives, and questions) provide scaffolding for narrative coconstruction that helps to support and move the process forward.

Regulate Emotion: Empty Story and Unstoried Emotion

When emotions are underregulated or overcontrolled, client storytelling often has an unclear quality in which the personal significance of an event and its meaning for the client are not expressed. Without the expression of the emotions felt, and their meanings, in relation to actions taken, personal stories are confusing, do not make sense, and create a sense of narrative incoherence that is further dysregulating. EFTT therapist responses need to intensify and evoke constricted experience through the facilitation of detailed autobiographical memory disclosures and/or evocative empathic responses (e.g., "a big hole in your heart, wanting to crawl in a hole and die, cuts to the quick" or directives to "say it again . . . louder"). Interventions that direct attention to clients' experience of themselves as a child can be particularly evocative (e.g., "sad little thing, dying for someone to just love her"). Words and phrases such as *furious, outrage, how dare you* can intensify anger. These must be stated in a firm but controlled vocal quality. On the other hand, soothing empathic responses can decrease clients' feelings of isolation and distress (e.g., "Yes, this is where it hurts.") in response to tears welling up in a client's eyes or their voice quivering. Standard emotion-regulation strategies such as attention to breathing, grounding, and present-centered awareness (e.g., Linehan, 1993; Najavits, 2002) can be used when clients are having severe emotion-dysregulation problems. It is important to note that clients who are highly distressed when telling a particularly painful or disturbing trauma memory are not dysregulated as long as they can continue with their experientially alive storytelling. Dysregulation occurs when clients' intense feelings are not connected to a specific narrative context—a key indicator of Unstoried Emotion markers—either because there is too much distress or because of dissociation where the client completely withdraws out of fear.

Affirm Vulnerability

When clients are sharing painful, autobiographical memories and disclosing their inner feelings, intentions, and fears about those traumatizing and humiliating experiences, they often feel exposed and afraid of losing control, overwhelmed, misunderstood, or judged as weird or defective and, as such, are at risk for retraumatization. This is especially true when clients are disclosing specific, autobiographical memory accounts of shameful experiences involving sexual abuse. An experience of profound victimization is always humiliating, and clients will understandably cringe and feel highly vulnerable when disclosing those personal memories. Therefore, to reduce client anxiety, it is important for EFTT therapists to acknowledge and actively affirm client feelings of vulnerability so that they can continue to tell their story (e.g., "I know how hard it is to talk about these things, so painful, and so important."), followed by an explicit encouragement to disclose (e.g., "It's OK, you're doing fine, take your time. It's important that you get it out, that you not be alone with this stuff anymore."). The general intervention guideline is to affirm vulnerability and thus reduce anxiety before exploring meaning.

Validate Experience

Although there is overlap between *validation* and *empathy* and some experts (e.g., Linehan, 1997) use the terms interchangeably, in EFTT empathic responses communicate understanding, whereas validation communicates normality when clients explicitly or implicitly are worried whether their personal stories, perceptions, or reactions are normal or weird. Abuse survivors typically have grown up in invalidating environments where their personal accounts and stories of traumatic events were minimized or denied, they were told they were exaggerating or crazy, or they were ignored. These responses from significant others (and society) have been internalized, and self-doubt and second-guessing are common. Therapist validation helps to create a therapeutic relationship that is both secure and trustworthy, so a client feels safe to disclose painful personal memories to the therapist. Additionally, validation responses promote client self-development and trust in their own internal experience—often for the first time, they experience a new sense of certainty, and clarity, regarding what happened, how it felt, and the impact that it has had on their life.

Promote Agency

An important goal in EFTT is to increase client sense of agency or control in the narration of their most important personal stories and the primary adaptive emotions, meanings, intentions, needs, values, goals, and beliefs that truly define them. This is a key goal of two-chair dialogues, described in Chapter 9, that aim to increase client awareness of how they contribute to their own bad feelings evidenced in Same Old Storytelling. Interventions intensify the emotional impact of client maladaptive nonassertiveness (e.g., "So you must sacrifice yourself to your mother, be her doormat. That is your role. How does it feel to hear that?"). Once clients are aware of how they contribute to their own suffering, they can begin to understand how they can change. Thus awareness of agency facilitates the emergence of a new, adaptive, and agentic emotional plotline (Competing Plotline Storytelling) that facilitates the discovery of adaptive action tendencies, unmet needs, and a new view of self and self-narrative change. As well, when clients discover new aspects of self and relationships or describe positive unexpected outcomes in personal relationships (Unexpected Outcome marker) during the midtreatment review or in the late phase of therapy, it is important for their EFTT therapist to highlight and validate the significance of these new developments and encourage them to go beyond a simple report of their new understandings, events, reactions and/or behaviors, to further elaborate their contribution to making that change happen. This is accomplished by directing their attention to changes in their thoughts, feelings, interpretations, expectations, and intentions and by including them in a more coherent, differentiated change narrative.

Specify Intentions (Needs, Desires)

In responding to the emotional meanings embedded in client personal stories, it is critical to also identify implicit associated existential and relational needs—sadness and the need for contact, comfort, and connection; fear and the need for safety, protection, or soothing; anger and the need to self-protect, to assert boundaries, or for interpersonal distance. Identifying needs enhances clients' motivation to have needs met and moves the process of change forward. Evocative expressions of need, such as *longing*, *heart's desire*, *craving*, and *hungry*, help to increase emotional arousal and evoke a corresponding emotional response. In the general model of change in EFT (Greenberg & Paivio, 1997), identifying unmet intrapersonal and interpersonal needs, associated with maladaptive emotion schemes and repetitive Same Old Stories, is the first step toward accessing primary emotional responses and new, adaptive action tendencies. This represents the emergence of a new emotional plotline that directly challenges the negative expectations and criticisms and is a key indicator of more adaptive storytelling.

This important change process occurs by first helping clients to identify and feel entitled to fulfilling unmet needs, and then supporting the emergence of a new emotional plotline. Especially in the context of two-chair dialogues and/or to the imagined other in IC/EE, a new resolution and integration process unfolds when clients assertively state their entitlement to intra- and interpersonal wants and needs, directly challenging the suppressing and catastrophizing criticisms and fears expressed in clients' Same Old Stories. Expression of need can become increasingly assertive, moving from "I want" to "I deserve" to "I insist" or "I refuse." Such expressions in IC or EE are markers for shifting the client to enact or imagine the response of the other to the stated need. This now occurs in the context of a brand new kind of conversation with the emergence of new, more assertive, compassionate emotional outcomes (Unexpected Outcome Story) and an agentic view of self.

INTERVENTION WITH SPECIFIC EMOTIONS

The previous chapter described specific emotions—anger, sadness, fear, and shame—for appropriate assessment. In this chapter we focus on intervention aimed at helping clients access and explore these particular emotions and integrate them into a coherent personal narrative. Effective intervention needs to be consistent with the nature of these specific emotions, in terms of bodily posture, vocal quality, and content that was described in the preceding chapter. In therapy sessions, clients are most successfully helped to differentiate emotional reactions and responses in the context of reflectively exploring specific autobiographical memory narratives and/or two-chair dialogues and IC/EE EFTT interventions.

Intervention With Anger

Anger is accessed to help increase client assertiveness, assert interpersonal boundaries, and set limits. Therapists speak in a firm and controlled voice and may use intensification strategies (e.g., "Say it louder."). Clients should be encouraged to sit up straight with their feet on the floor, to speak in a firm voice, and to look directly at the therapist or imagined other. Successive approximations can be used for clients who are afraid and reluctant to explicitly use the term anger. Moving from "I don't like" to "I resent" to "I hate" or "I am furious," as appropriate to the situation, is a form of gradual exposure to anger experience and expression. As noted earlier, assertiveness can be increased by gradually shifting expressed wants and needs to insistence and refusals ("I will." or "I will not."). According to criteria for healthy anger expression presented in the preceding chapter, therapists encourage clients to direct anger at specific others and to specify the harms done, use I–you language instead of blaming and hurling insults, and articulate the meaning of their anger in terms of the consequences and preferred behavior, thus helping clients to stay focused on anger that is clearly differentiated from other emotions. They can validate that many emotions are present but collaborate on experiencing and expressing one at a time. Paivio and Carriere (2007) reported that anger expression during IC using these criteria was related to interpersonal dimensions of change.

Intervention With Sadness

Sadness is accessed to help clients acknowledge and grieve losses and elicit compassion (as opposed to self-criticism) toward self and sometimes others. In helping clients to access sadness, the therapist is minimally active, to allow the client to turn inward. Affirmation of vulnerability can be used to reduce anxiety about approaching the pain of profound loss. Evocative empathic responses can be used to increase arousal, access the emotion scheme, and activate sadness that is suppressed or interrupted. Therapists can use certain words and phrases (e.g., *a broken heart, a hole in the heart, emptiness or ache inside, what a shame, it kills you to think . . .*) in empathically responding to client personal stories about particular intra- and interpersonal losses. It is important that interventions direct attention to what was missed or missed out on, and is longed for, and explore the meaning of the loss to the client, for example, the effects on self and relationships. Clients should not be expected to fully express their sadness and grief to an imagined cruel or rejecting other in IC. Rather, sadness is more appropriately accessed and expressed in the context of the therapeutic relationship or to an imagined responsive other, for example, an attachment figure who is seen as genuinely sorry for the harm they have caused.

Intervention With Fear and Shame

Intervention with primary maladaptive fear and shame involves accessing the core maladaptive emotion scheme, which includes negative self-appraisals and unmet needs that emerge in the context of client storytelling—the Same Old Story they want to change. As described previously, identifying and increasing entitlement to unmet needs for safety and self-respect, for example, is an important part of the change process that activates the emergence of alternate adaptive experience such as anger at maltreatment and sadness at loss. Because fear and shame are associated with anxiety, withdrawal, and hiding, interventions involve affirmation of vulnerability about the difficulty of talking about terrifying and shameful experience, as well as soothing empathic responses to reduce distress. In instances of secondary fear and shame that emerge as internal conflicts in Competing Plotline Storytelling, intervention involves identifying both sides of the struggle, for example, the self-critical cognitions along with associated feelings toward self (e.g., anger, contempt, disgust, disappointment) as one side of the emotional plotline and the impact of this on the experiencing self (e.g., feelings of shame and then healthy protest or rejection of the criticism) as the other side of the plotline.

Again, promoting awareness of agency in contributing to secondary maladaptive fear and shame is important to the change process. Once clients are experientially aware of how they contribute to their own bad feelings, they have increased self-control and are in a better position to change maladaptive processes. Competing Plotline Storytelling that indicates access to healthy internal resources (i.e., adaptive feelings, needs, action tendencies, perspectives) and readiness to change have client awareness of agency as one criterion. Shame is a particularly painful experience that is difficult to approach and allow in therapy. Affirmation of vulnerability is important in initially reducing anxiety before these experiences can be explored for meaning. Process maps for helping clients approach and allow emotional pain are presented in Chapter 9 on the middle phase of therapy.

EFTT THERAPIST OPERATIONS IN CORE TASKS

The following sections describe therapist operations in the core tasks of promoting resolution of issues with perpetrators and facilitating a more productive narrative-emotion process (NEP). These specific operations incorporate the intervention principles described previously.

Promoting Resolution of Issues With Perpetrators

The primary task in EFTT is resolution of issues with particular abusive and neglectful others who are the focus of EFTT. Therapist operations to facilitate this task are designed to promote client movement through each of the steps in the Degree of Resolution Scale (DRS; Singh, 1994) presented in the preceding chapter on assessment and in the Appendix. Because the model of EFTT is based on this model of resolution, these therapist operations apply over the phases of EFTT as well as during implementation of the IC/EE procedure in individual sessions. The following sections outline therapist operations at each stage in the resolution processes and phase of therapy. As noted earlier, client movement through stages in the resolution process is a reiterative process in which they cycle through the stages, gradually moving closer to resolution.

Early Phase of Therapy

The early phase of EFTT and the resolution process consists of helping clients to identify the thoughts and feelings that have kept them stuck (the Same Old Story) and gradually confront trauma feelings and memories and imagined abusive and neglectful others.

Identify Elements of the Same Old Story (DRS Level 1). At this earliest stage in the resolution process, therapists empathically respond to clients' bad feelings concerning trauma and abusive, and neglectful others, including their sense of hopelessness at not being able to change the Same Old Story. It is important that interventions also need to highlight the client's desire to change. The therapist provides a rationale for reexperiencing trauma feelings and memories (e.g., "Things are stuck at an emotional level. We need to help you reprocess all those bad feelings."); direct and redirect client attention to their internal experience; and help them to articulate the feelings, beliefs, and behaviors associated with the repetitive narrative (symbolize meaning). Therapists are listening for and responding to the emergence of client healthy internal resources (adaptive feelings and needs, views of self and others) that can be used to help shift the maladaptive pattern and move the resolution process forward.

Evoke Trauma Feelings and Memories (DRS Level 2). Intervention to shift the client to this level of resolution involves introducing the IC or EE procedures to evoke trauma feelings and memories. Therapists elicit specific, sensorial, autobiographical trauma memories and ask clients to imagine the abusive/neglectful others involved. Interventions direct client attention to and help them express the thoughts and feelings evoked directly to the imagined other or to the therapist in the case of EE. Therapists affirm client vulnerability and acknowledge their hurt, fear, and collapse into resignation or powerlessness; validate these as part of the pattern of shutting down, blocking, and suppression that has kept them stuck; and encourage them to continue with their disclosures. Again, it is important to highlight client adaptive resources that emerge. For example, the client Mark presented in later chapters describes his mother as a "monster" and himself as "an asshole just like my mother," hurting his wife and children and pushing them away. The therapist asked him to give a specific example of hurting loved ones and highlighted his feelings of regret and his desire for connection.

This stage in the resolution process also involves differentiating global distress and bad feelings into specific emotions, typically fear, shame, rejecting/blaming anger, and sometimes sadness that are activated as part of the core maladaptive emotion scheme. The therapist acknowledges and reduces distress with soothing empathic responses, acknowledges or elicits the source of distress (e.g., "that look on his face, so upsetting to remember that incident"), elicits specific autobiographical memories and examples—stories of abuse and neglect—followed by empathic responses, conjecture, or questions to differentiate the experience and access implied feelings and associated meanings.

Middle Phase of Therapy

During the middle or working phase of EFTT and resolution process, interventions help clients work through self-related difficulties that interfere with resolution of issues with perpetrators.

Work Through Self-Related Difficulties (DRS Level 3). Intervention to move clients to this stage in the resolution process involves helping them to work through intrapersonal difficulties typically related to fear and avoidance of emotional pain, guilt, shame, and self-blame for the abuse that act as blocks to resolution that keep them stuck. These blocks are evident in Problem Storytelling that is superficial or devoid of emotion or narrative content. Interventions increase or decrease arousal to optimal levels, so that coherent narratives can be constructed and deepen experiencing step-by-step so that narratives are more emotionally alive and reflective (Experiential and Reflective Storytelling). Therapist responses highlight and reinforce the emergence of healthy resources (more adaptive views of self and others, adaptive anger and sadness, and unmet needs) evident in Competing Plotline Storytelling that can be used to challenge the repetitive maladaptive pattern. Specific procedures for reducing these blocks to resolution are presented in Chapter 9.

Late Phase of Therapy

During the late phase of EFTT and the resolution process, intervention focuses on helping clients to fully experience and express adaptive anger and sadness, explore associated meanings, construct more adaptive narratives regarding self and others, and bring closure to issues with perpetrators.

Promote Full Expression of Adaptive Emotion (DRS Level 4). Interventions that help clients move to this stage in the resolution process may intensify arousal to evoke clear, assertive expressions of adaptive anger and sadness to strengthen interpersonal boundaries, grieve losses, and help them articulate the associated meanings in deeply Experiential and Reflective Storytelling. The therapist helps clients construct narratives about past experiences with perpetrators that are specific (e.g., "Give an example, bring the scene alive.") and imbued with emotion (e.g., "How did you feel, what was going on for you on the inside?") and emotional meaning (e.g., "That is so painful and so important, say more. Speak your truth, speak from your heart.").

Interventions help clients coconstruct a coherent narrative specifying what made and still makes them angry and why, what they missed or missed out on, the effects of abuse and neglect and unmet attachment needs on self, the damage caused, and how life would have been better if these needs had been met (e.g., "make him/her understand"). Interventions also elicit client perceptions of how the other would respond to their expressed feelings and needs. This is part of tracking shifting perceptions of self and other who is the focus of therapy and coconstructing a new narrative.

Promote Increased Entitlement to Unmet Needs (DRS Level 5). Interventions that help clients move to Level 5 in the resolution process promote an increased sense of entitlement to unmet needs. At first therapist directives might be tentative (e.g., Try saying, "I deserved to be treated like a human being." or "I deserved to have a carefree childhood, innocence.") and always include directing client attention to their internal experience in response to these assertions (e.g., "How does it feel to say that?"). This is repeated until the client feels comfortable with these assertions. Gradually the client's sense of self (Same Old Story) shifts, and their narratives contain views of self with legitimate wants and needs that are clearly and assertively expressed. Again, interventions elicit client perceptions of the imagined other and their reactions to client expressed feelings and needs (e.g., "How do you imagine she would react to knowing how you feel?").

Coconstruct New View of Self and Others (DRS Level 6). As client self-narratives include deeply felt and assertive expressions of adaptive feelings and needs, interventions help them coconstruct more adaptive self-narratives that contain perceptions of self as more separate, autonomous, and empowered (Discovery Storytelling). Interventions help clients to assert interpersonal boundaries with imagined others by imagining specific situations. As clients feel stronger and are better able to clearly and assertively express feelings and needs to the imagined other, their perceptions of the other shifts. Interventions help clients to construct narratives with more differentiated and realistic perspectives of these significant others. This involves the activation of client empathic capacities and might be accomplished by asking clients to imagine what the other is thinking or feeling underneath their behavior (e.g., "He would never admit he was wrong, but I do think he feels bad about what he did." or "I just don't think she knows any better, has the capacity to understand or change.").

Support Full Resolution (DRS Level 7). Interventions to help clients move to this final phase in the resolution process encourage and support their acceptance and letting go of the past and expectations that the other will change, apologize, or respond to unmet needs. Interventions support them in their new focus on personal strengths and in clearly holding abusive/neglectful others accountable for harm and possibly in forgiving them. Therapists acknowledge; reflectively explore; and celebrate clients' new feelings of acceptance, relief, and confidence and new reactions and behaviors in their current lives told in Discovery and New Outcome stories.

Guidelines for Intervention Using Narrative-Emotion Storytelling Markers

Working with NEP Problem, Transition, and Change markers is the other key process map that supports the implementation of EFTT interventions on a moment-by-moment basis. The NEP model described in the preceding chapter was developed to provide therapists with a simplified, integrative process-diagnostic map to quickly assess client process indicators—level of experiential engagement, emotion regulation, and narrative coherence/specificity—and guide interventions to facilitate emotional transformation and self-narrative change over the course of therapy. As such, strategies to enhance both client depth of experiencing and level of emotional arousal are discussed in the context of facilitating productive shifts from NEP Problem markers to key Transition and Changer markers, in EFTT therapy sessions. These strategies are described next.

Facilitating Emotion Regulation, Specificity, and Self-Reflection

The following sections present strategies for helping clients shift to storytelling with increased access to alternate healthy resources (responses, views of self and others), emotional experience, and reflection on experience.

NEP Problem Markers

Table 6.1 presents examples of effective intervention with each of the Problem Storytelling marker subtypes that were described in the preceding chapter. The following sections further elaborate on marker-guided interventions to address each of these Problem markers that are evident in the early phase of EFTT and the resolution process.

Same Old Storytelling. The first step in intervention to change the Same Old Story that clients present with early in therapy involves accessing the core maladaptive emotion scheme, for example, through evocative empathy, memory evocation, or the IC/EE procedures. This involves identifying and exploring (promoting experiencing) the maladaptive pattern of feelings, beliefs, and behaviors embedded in the Same Old Story with specific examples. The therapist heightens and empathizes with client bad feelings, such as hopelessness, and listens for and tentatively reflects the emergence of implied alternative protest or frustration with the old story or pattern. The goal is to access adaptive emotion and unmet needs to help modify the maladaptive emotion scheme, shift the Same Old Story so that it becomes only one side of a competing plotline.

Empty Storytelling. The goal with Empty Storytelling is to help the client construct a narrative that is more affectively alive, to help the listener connect with what it is like to be this person, to transform a monologue into a dialogue for heightened coconstruction, and to reflect on emotional meanings. Fifteen-minute externally oriented monologues should not be allowed; the therapist must engage. Intervention is different depending on the underlying determinants of limited emotional presence. Limited awareness of emotional experience, as in alexithymia, for example, will involve implicit or explicit emotion awareness training, starting with awareness of bodily experience and associated feelings, as well as explicit guidance and directives in exploring affect. Fearful avoidance and overcontrol of emotional experience will involve reducing anxiety and collaboration on the tasks of reducing avoidance and allowing emotional pain. Access to emotion words but low arousal indicates overcontrol and anxiety about emotional expression. Strategies to help clients relinquish overcontrol are presented in Chapter 9 on the middle phase of EFTT.

TABLE 6.1

Intervention With Narrative-Emotion Problem Markers

Problem	to	Transition	
Unstoried Emotion	Symbolizing painful emotion in context, by reexperiencing and narrating troubling ABM events	Experiential	Facilitate narrative retelling of sensory-rich event memory. Ask client to reflect on experience of the ABM, using all five senses.
	Symbolizing painful emotion by attending to internal felt sense to locate an image, word, or action representing felt experience	Inchoate	• Direct attention inward. • Employ focusing strategies (Gendlin, 1997). • Offer empathic guesses. • Offer feedback about observed facial and body expressions indicating emotional arousal (e.g., "you are clenching your hands").
Same Old Story	Opening up to alternative aspects of experience that challenge or destabilize the dominant, maladaptive view of self	Competing Plotline	• Request specificity regarding events, actions, behaviors, and responses that are repeatedly referenced without explanation or elaboration (i.e., define the Same Old key terms). • Listen for and tentatively reflect any alternative views, protest, and frustration emerging "at the edges." • Reflect absolute views using "as if" and "parts of self" language to make space for eventual alternatives. • Heighten and empathize with the hopelessness until an alternative voice emerges. • EFTT IC/EE task interventions

	Moving out of stuckness by talking about the repetitive pattern or maladaptive view of self, rather than talking from inside it	Reflective	Invite the client's reflection on: origins of beliefs about problematic interpersonal patterns; intentions and mental states of key figures; the meaning and implications of repetitive patterns and experiences.
	Moving out of stuckness and overgenerality by opening up experience to alternative, possibly competing information	Experiential Story	Identify a specific ABM associated with the Same Old Story and facilitate vivid, sensory-rich narrative retelling of the ABM for emotional differentiation of global negative emotions and new meaning.
Empty Story	Attending to and inclusion of internal experiences	Experiential	• Direct attention to/query internal experience. • Evocative reflection
	Exploring, articulating the felt impact or meaning of the (so far) empty story	Reflective	• Ask about significance, meaning, impact, or client's interpretation of event.
Superficial	Increasing self-focus, attention to or reflection on internal experience, making connections between events, making meaning	Reflective	• Direct attention to internal experience. • Redirect attention to internal experience. • Redirect focus to self (to client). • Inquire about impact, or understanding of the content being discussed. • Request specificity.

Note. ABM = autobiographical memory; EFTT = emotion-focused therapy for trauma; IC = imaginal confrontations; EE = empathic exploration.

Unstoried Emotion. Overwhelming emotion without narrative content may emerge at the introduction of the IC procedure or other interventions that evoke trauma memories. The goal of intervention is to reduce arousal so that the client can begin to construct a coherent narrative around his or her emotional experience. This is accomplished through the use of emotion-regulation strategies introduced earlier in the chapter to first reduce client arousal, bring the client into the present and into experiential contact with the therapist so that experience can be empathically supported and validated, and then help the client construct a coherent narrative around his or her feelings and where they come from. Labeling emotional experience increases understanding and a sense of control and thus reduces arousal— the experience of having an emotion as opposed to being an emotion. In instances of dissociation, grounding strategies that bring clients into the present and keep them connected to the therapist are helpful. Similarly, for high levels of distress, therapists first empathically acknowledge the distress, then invite the client to put words to their distress/tears, offer process observations and empathic conjectures, and state the importance of not being alone and staying connected.

Superficial Storytelling. The goal in shifting stories focused on external events and behaviors (low-level experiencing) is to help shift the client to engage in more reflective or experiential self-focused storytelling or to deepen experiencing in a step-by-step process. General guidelines were presented in the previous section. To review and elaborate, first focus on more personal values and concerns, then conjecture about feelings, ask about what was the most important or worst part of the experience, provide tentative prompts for exploring meaning (e.g., "Some people are afraid of looking foolish or losing control."), and elicit autobiographical memories with specific details for heightened self-reflective engagement rather than focus on others.

Enhancing Client Experiencing, Reflection, and Self-Narrative Change

The following sections present strategies for helping clients shift to storytelling with greater integration and reflection on emerging bodily felt experience, episodic memories, alternative or conflicting action tendencies, and views of self.

NEP Transition Markers

Table 6.2 presents examples of intervention with NEP Transition markers. Therapist responses to help clients shift to Transitional Storytelling focus on helping clients to access and articulate adaptive feelings and emotional meanings; coconstruct coherent trauma narratives; and integrate

TABLE 6.2
Intervention With Narrative-Emotion Transition Markers

Transition	to		Interventions
Inchoate	Reflective	Further elaboration and differentiation of the symbol, differentiate meaning of the experience	• Ask about significance, meaning, impact, or client's interpretation of articulated internal experience. • Inquire about impact or understanding of the content being discussed. • Request specificity.
	Experiential	Connecting the experience to a specific ABM	• Query about specific times "that feeling" has come up in the past, and encourage clients to provide a sensory-rich narrative account of the ABM.
Competing Plotline	Reflective		• Elaborate the emergent voice challenging the SOS. • Make sense of the protest or the tension; making meaning of the SOS, competing values, discrepancies. • Ask client to reflect and elaborate on the confusion, surprise, frustration, etc., they are experiencing as a result of the competing plotline story. • EFTT IC/EE task interventions
Experiential Trauma Memory	Reflective	Allowing to fully process, experience, tell the story, in a coherent manner. Enable coherence and integration	• Continue to provide relational conditions to maximize client's sense of safety. • Empathic validation • Encourage clients to express the thoughts and feelings they experienced in the ABM. • Ask clients to connect how this specific trauma ABM may have impacted the client then and now.

Transition	to	Change	Interventions
Reflective		Discovery	• Invite new understanding of self ("What does this mean about you/for you . . . ?")
Competing Plotline		Unexpected Outcome	• Ask for experiences that cohere with the challenging, competing voice. • Make it concrete and specific. • Introduce behavioral experiments. • Explore evidence that supports, does not support.

Note. ABM = autobiographical memory; EFTT = emotion-focused therapy for trauma; IC = imaginal confrontation; EE = empathic exploration; SOS = Same Old Story.

emerging, adaptive emotional plotlines as part of a more differentiated and empowered self-narrative.

The following Transitional markers represent a shift from conflicted or Superficial Storytelling, to Inchoate search for understanding, to more experientially alive and Reflective Storytelling, and eventually to new understandings evident in Discovery Stories.

Competing Plotline Storytelling. These narratives can be attachment or identity related and can be decisional conflicts or include a struggle between maladaptive and adaptive resources. Intervention first involves identifying both sides of the internal conflict or struggle. The therapist specifies the dominant maladaptive part of self-narrative (e.g., specific criticisms or fears), and in doing so, it is helpful to refer to "parts" of the self to help the client open to other more adaptive possibilities. Next, direct attention to and support the subdominant aspect of the narrative, healthy resources (adaptive thoughts, feelings, and needs), authentic self; explore this part of the self and use empathic responses to coconstruct a new narrative integrating this new information. Two-chair dialogues described in Chapter 9 can be used to explore intrapersonal Competing Plotline Stories. IC or EE can be used to explore the push/pull with attachment figures, for example.

Inchoate Storytelling. The goal here is to shift the client to more reflective, experiential, and coherent storytelling. Intervention involves helping the client search for words or images to symbolize unclear or confusing experience. Guidelines for deepening experiencing and Reflective storytelling were presented earlier in the chapter. The therapist must foster an attitude of curiosity and exploration, attention to bodily experience, and acceptance of what emerges. Therapist responses closely reflect the emerging client emotional responses for further symbolization and later shift to Experiential Storytelling, described next.

Experiential Storytelling. Promoting Experiential Storytelling is important in the recall of traumatic events or current events in which the core maladaptive sense of self was evoked. The goal of intervention is to shift trauma narratives or stories of these distressing events that communicate facts alone to storytelling that is more affectively engaged. Therapists need to provide a lot of process guidance and support. This begins with detailed retelling of what happened from beginning, middle, to end; providing support to stay with the memory; and then directing attention to internal experience (sensorial, thoughts, feelings). Therapists provide empathic support; affirmation of vulnerability when approaching painful, shameful, or frightening experience; and evocative empathy to activate emotion memories. Therapists' empathic responses help scaffold narrative retelling with attention to internal experience (bodily experience, feelings, thoughts, and perceptions) to deepen experiencing to moderate levels. For many clients the trauma story will be told repeatedly over the course of therapy and become increasingly experiential in quality. This is beautifully illustrated in the case of the client Mark who is presented in later chapters. In cases where clients blame themselves or feel complicit in the abuse, it is important to direct attention to and heighten experiences of disgust, powerlessness, and lack of complicity. Once the client has experienced himself or herself as a powerless frightened child, it can be transformative to access healthy adult resources in the form of anger expressed toward imagined perpetrators or sadness expressed to the therapist.

Reflective Storytelling. Once stories are told in an experientially alive manner, clients are encouraged to reflect on the causes, implications, effects on self and relationships, meanings, and understandings of these experiences, and to explore patterns and connect to the present and themes across relationships. Reflective Storytelling functions as a check-in to the client's understanding of an experience as it currently stands, including internal referents, interpretations, connections between events, and meaning. This reflective processing moves the process along by revealing points of conflict or confusion, missing information, evoking the disclosure of a specific autobiographical memory, and/or inviting further self-reflectivity and meaning making. By inviting the client to put pieces together but with some reflective distance, Reflective Storytelling reveals "what else is missing or incoherent," which acts to string together and catalyze shifts between other Transition and Change markers. This is the process of deepening experiencing from moderate to higher levels and will result in new understandings of self, others, and traumatic events evident in Discovery Storytelling described in the next section.

NEP Change Markers

Change markers typically occur during the late phase of EFTT and the interpersonal resolution process. The goal of intervention with the following Change marker subtypes is to help clients to coconstruct new, coherent, adaptive narratives concerning self and abusive/neglectful others who were the focus of therapy. Table 6.3 presents examples of intervention with NEP Change markers. These are elaborated in the following sections.

Unexpected Outcome Storytelling. Here, clients are encouraged to elaborate on their reports of changes in view of self; their feelings, including feelings of surprise and relief; and their behavior, reactions, and reactions of others that are discrepant with the way things were, the old story. This involves directing attention to and exploring internal experience during the new experience or in the present as they are telling the story (i.e., deepen experiencing). This process is identical to the process of exploring the meaning of maladaptive or negative experiences in earlier phase of therapy. Therapists validate the

TABLE 6.3
Intervention With Narrative-Emotion Change Markers

Change	to	Change	
Unexpected Outcome	Making sense of new experience at the level of self-understanding, agency	Discovery Story	• Further elaboration of the unexpected outcome experience • Invite reflection on meaning of the unexpected outcome for the future. • Explore impact of change events on view of self, challenge to Same Old Story. • Support self-narrative coconstruction.
Discovery Story	Make it real, heighten it Elaborate impact of change Experiences and new views of self	Unexpected Outcome	• Ask for specificity: How has this new view manifested in the client's daily life (e.g., work, relationships, self)? • Explore client agency, e.g., "How were you able to do that?" (White, 2007)

importance of and share the client's excitement about these changes, promote client agency in contributing to the new outcome (what did they do or think differently), and connect to possible or desired future events.

Discovery Storytelling. Stories about new discoveries or understandings emerge from unexpected outcome, which causes reconceptualization of the self, others, and traumatic events (before–after, *I understand now*). Intervention involves exploration of these new discoveries and the process of deepening experiencing to the highest levels in which clients construct new meaning. This helps to consolidate change. As in Unexpected Outcome stories, interventions support and validate these new understandings, may provide clients with feedback in the form of therapist observations, and help clients connect to the future. These interventions with Change Stories are particularly important during the midtreatment review when clients report early changes and discoveries and again at therapy termination when reviewing the entire course of therapy and outcome.

CONCLUSION

One of the distinguishing features of EFT, including EFTT, is the use of empirically derived standardized measures used in clinical research to analyze therapy processes. Because higher level processes on these measures are associated with better client outcome, these measures act as "process maps" to help guide effective intervention, that is, to move clients forward in the process of resolving issues with perpetrators and enhance self-narrative change. In the following chapters we describe how these process maps and intervention strategies are applied to the early, middle, and late phases of therapy.

7

CULTIVATING THE ALLIANCE: EARLY-PHASE EFTT

In this chapter we introduce key narrative and emotion-based intervention strategies that effective therapists can implement to enhance productive processes and storytelling in early-phase emotion-focused therapy for trauma (EFTT) sessions. Because complex trauma results from the repeated occurrence of abuse and/or neglect in childhood, the narration of the lived experience of those events—vivid, painful images and autobiographical memories—as an emotionally coherent told story is a key goal of early-phase EFTT sessions. Therapist empathic responding is the primary mode of intervention in early EFTT therapy sessions. Session 1 is particularly important because it sets the stage for the development of a strong, collaborative therapeutic bond and the remainder of therapy. Therapist relationship qualities such as empathic attunement, prizing, genuineness, acceptance, and validation of the client's experience contribute to the creation of a secure, relational bond and an overall productive working alliance (Angus & Greenberg, 2011; Angus & Kagan, 2007; Greenberg, Rice, & Elliott, 1993). It is when clients feel safe

http://dx.doi.org/10.1037/0000041-008
Narrative Processes in Emotion-Focused Therapy for Trauma, by S. C. Paivio and L. E. Angus

and truly heard by their therapist that they can fully access and disclose their most vulnerable and painful lived stories to therapists for further emotional differentiation, transformation, restorying, and new meaning making. Rather than the client independently discovering new personal meanings, therapist and client both contribute to the coconstruction of new personal meanings and narrative reconstruction in productive EFTT sessions.

During the first session clients are encouraged to disclose their personal story of what happened to them during their childhood, particularly auto-biographical memories of childhood maltreatment, and describe what it was like for them growing up, more generally. Clients are also encouraged to share personal stories about their current areas of struggle, what they would like to change, and how they imagine therapy might help them move forward in their lives. In the context of empathically responding to clients' disclosure of painful childhood memories and current concerns, EFTT therapists can also listen for narrative and emotion Problem markers indicating emotion-regulation and experiencing difficulties with the aim of helping clients shift to more productive Transitional storytelling that is experientially alive and reflective. In turn, both the assessment of narrative-emotion process (NEP) storytelling markers and the empathic exploration of clients' trauma stories set the stage for the collaborative development of a process-informed EFTT case conceptualization, including therapy goals and a treatment rationale.

In Sessions 2 and 3, case conceptualization and therapy goals can be further refined in the context of clients' further emotional and reflective elaboration of their most important memories and personal stories. The initial EFTT imaginal confrontation (IC) and empathic exploration (EE) trauma-focused reexperiencing procedure, which is usually introduced during Session 4, will typically activate core maladaptive emotion scheme and narrative-emotional process difficulties (fear/avoidance, shame, views of self and others) that emerged in earlier sessions. These are the focus of intervention in Phase 2 therapy sessions.

Key EFTT therapeutic tasks during the first phase address (a) cultivating the therapeutic alliance, (b) promoting client narrative disclosure of memories of childhood maltreatment, (c) assessment of narrative-emotion processing difficulties, (d) case conceptualization, and (e) introduction of IC/EE trauma memory reexperiencing procedures.

ELEMENTS OF THE THERAPEUTIC ALLIANCE

As previously outlined, the alliance in EFTT consists of three basic elements. The first element is a secure attachment bond, in which the therapist is empathically responsive to client suffering and pain, that often emerges in the context of disclosing autobiographical memories of childhood neglect and/or physical and sexual abuse. Therapist empathic responsiveness creates an atmosphere of safety and trust that supports clients' disclosures of important trauma memories while at the same time helping to coregulate the emergence of strong emotional reactions in the therapy sessions. Mlotek (2015) found that therapist-expressed empathy during Session 1 predicted engagement with trauma memories and emotions during IC/EE intervention in later EFTT sessions and was also associated with reduced trauma symptoms and resolution of issues with perpetrators at treatment termination.

Additionally, it is important to provide clients with a clear understanding of how their early-phase EFTT sessions will unfold. For example, "We will spend the first few sessions getting to know each other, getting a clearer understanding of your story and what is contributing to your difficulties so that we can identify how best to work on the changes you want to make." The therapist also explains to the client how the disclosure and emotional exploration of painful trauma memories contribute to therapeutic change. This discussion provides EFTT therapists with an opportunity to normalize and validate client fears about the emotional impact of engaging past trauma memories and to provide explicit reassurance that therapy will go at the client's pace.

The second key element is collaboration on the goals and tasks of EFTT. Unlike during more structured cognitive–behavioral therapy (CBT) approaches, in EFTT this happens in the context of therapist process-diagnostic responses to client pain, distress, and unmet needs, wants, wishes, and desires that emerge from the disclosure of their most poignant and troubling personal memory narratives. Client storytelling in the first session is marked by a profound sense of feeling stuck in the Same Old Stories of guilt, shame, or self-blame for the abuse, confusion and self-doubt about conflicting internal feelings and self-criticisms (e.g., "I feel angry and then end up second-guessing myself."), hatred toward the perpetrator, and/or recurring posttraumatic stress disorder (PTSD) symptoms. It is important for therapists to identify the emotional themes expressed in clients' Same Old Storytelling as a consequence of the unfair negative impacts of abuse and to assure clients that a key goal of EFTT therapy will be to better understand and change this legacy of negative and confusing feelings of self-blame, rage, guilt, and shame in the context of a more coherent, and differentiated, trauma narrative.

A key element of task collaboration in trauma-focused therapy is a shared understanding that the route to change is the narrative disclosure of distressing trauma memories for the exploration and transformation of painful emotions and new story outcomes. For example, "I see there is still a lot of pain when you talk about your dad's explosive anger and how he made you feel so small, and so frightened as a little girl . . . we need to help you heal these emotional wounds, not just Band-Aids, but at a deep level, from the inside out." As needed, the therapist can also explicitly provide information on the role of emotional avoidance and narrative incoherence for complex trauma symptoms and highlight the importance of facilitating enhanced narrative-emotion integration, emotional transformation, and new self-narrative outcomes for recovery.

The third element of the alliance is developing a collaborative understanding of factors that contribute to current intra- and interpersonal difficulties and problems in living—including autobiographical trauma memory/emotional avoidance, emotional dysregulation, and narrative incoherence—and how to address them. This is all part of formulating a process-informed case conceptualization that highlights the importance of emotion, narrative, and meaning-making processes for successful treatment outcomes. To arrive at a shared, mutual understanding of therapy tasks and goals, it is also important to ask clients about their own theories of why they are psychologically distressed and the factors that may have interfered with healing. The therapist's initial case conceptualization should be discussed with the client at the beginning of Session 2, and a clear working understanding should be established by the end of Session 4 as part of establishing goals and tasks for the second working phase of therapy. The elements of case conceptualization are presented later in this chapter.

PROMOTING DISCLOSURE OF CHILDHOOD ABUSE MEMORY NARRATIVES

The early phase of EFTT involves promoting disclosure of traumatic autobiographical memory narratives, first through written trauma narratives before the first session and then through therapist attunement and responding to client narrative and emotion-processing difficulties and explicit encouragement to disclose in the early-phase session. The following four steps provide helpful guidelines for therapists to promote their client's emotional reexperiencing of trauma memories.

1. The first guideline is gradual exposure. For example, Session 1 involves telling the trauma story, but explicit deepening of experience usually does not begin until Session 4 when the alliance is established and the client feels safe.
2. Second, affirmation of clients' feeling of vulnerability as they approach painful, shameful, and frightening trauma experience can be used to help reduce anxiety and distress before moving to exploration of meaning. For example, therapists can validate how difficult it is to disclose and stay in touch with memories of abuse or validate that feelings of humiliation often emerge

when clients begin to admit the degree to which they were so unfairly and profoundly victimized.

3. The third guideline for promoting reexperiencing is to encourage autobiographical memory specificity by encouraging clients to disclose personal memories of abuse experiences that activate emotion memories and enhance emotional engagement in storytelling.

4. The fourth guideline is to focus on aspects of clients' narratives that are personal, affective, and sensorial to deepen client experiential storytelling. For example, "So, as he approaches in your bedroom, you are feeling queasy in your gut, sensing something bad is going to happen, but you are paralyzed in your bed, unable to move or cry out for help."

5. Finally, therapists need to differentiate global distress into specific emotions, such as fear, shame, anger, or sadness, in the context of the trauma narrative to access the associated affective meaning and enhance narrative coherence.

PROVIDING INFORMATION AND EMOTION COACHING

In the first session, the therapist provides information about the relational impact of childhood experiences of physical/sexual abuse and neglect, the role of trauma memory in activating and heightening emotional distress and self-incoherence, and key therapeutic strategies to achieve trauma recovery. For example, "These fears are engrained at an emotional level and embedded in your traumatic childhood memories. Healing will involve getting in touch with, disclosing, and reprocessing the emotional meanings and impact of your actual experiences of childhood abuse, in therapy, where it's safe." Therapists also provide information about types of emotions and emotional processes. For example, "You have every right to be angry at the way you were treated, but I also think that a lot of your anger is defensive, covering more vulnerable feelings of fear, shame, or sadness that you experienced when you were a little boy. We need to help you also get in touch with those feelings, in those childhood memories, this is where the pain lies." Finally, EFTT therapists provide guidance and clear expectations in terms of participating in therapy to reduce client anxiety. For example, "Your job is to disclose, and tell your story of abuse, as much as you feel comfortable, particularly what's going on for you on the inside. My job is to help you feel safe doing that, put words to your emotions, and help you gradually express the feelings you have kept locked inside for so long. I know it won't be easy, but I will make sure there is time to process things at the end of sessions so you leave feeling put together. We will keep monitoring how you are doing and adjust things accordingly." This information is provided as needed at appropriate markers and in the context of narrative exploration. Provision of information and clarification of expectations help to reduce client anxiety and strengthen the therapeutic alliance.

Finally, clients who are alexithymic require explicit process-diagnostic guidance and emotion coaching to help them identify, label, and explore the meaning of emotional experience. Empathic responses and directives are not effective in eliciting feelings, and questions about feelings elicit conceptual descriptions or anxiety because these individuals do not know what they are feeling. Tentative empathic conjectures that name emotion words (e.g., "I would be so hurt if someone said that to me.") would be more helpful, along with explicit education about specific emotions, starting with bodily sensations, associated appraisals, and needs. Structured experiential focusing presented in the following chapter also can be helpful in working with alexithymic clients.

NARRATIVE-EMOTION ASSESSMENT AND INTERVENTIONS

During the early phase of EFTT, therapists identify and begin to address emotional processing difficulties evident in NEP Problem storytelling markers indicating emotion-regulation and experiencing difficulties as well as maladaptive patterns of feelings, beliefs, and reactions. The following sections describe case examples of effective and ineffective intervention with these processing difficulties during the early phase of EFTT.

Same Old Storytelling and Accessing Adaptive Emotional Plotlines

Clients who have not been able to resolve or come to terms with past issues concerning childhood abuse and neglect are by definition stuck in the Same Old Story. Old thoughts, feelings, and maladaptive behavioral patterns developed in past relationships are activated as part of the core maladaptive emotion scheme in current situations. This is accompanied by a sense of low personal agency and hopelessness. This can be observed in symptoms of PTSD, depression, social anxiety, or personality pathology, for example. Intervention involves activating or listening for and reinforcing the emergence of healthy resources, especially needs and desires, and new alternatives, such as assertiveness, approaching emotional pain, and accessing vulnerable experience, that challenge the Same Old Story.

For example, during Session 1, Richard, who had been sexually molested by a priest, described his rage ("Is it so wrong to wish he was dead?") and intrusive and reexperiencing symptoms (nightmares) that emerge whenever he hears about children being molested. He also repeatedly stated that he blames himself for not doing something about it, that he didn't understand why he never disclosed to anyone and kept going back to church. These recurring symptoms and his repeated collapse into self-blame are parts of the old maladaptive pattern or story. This became the focus of exploration and more narrative context about the circumstances of his life as a child. It became clear that Richard intellectually understood that he was not to blame, but the conflict remained at an emotional level. Resolving the conflict became a goal for therapy.

Another example is Sarah, who had a history of repeated victimization from multiple perpetrators her entire life. At the beginning of Session 1, she described incidents of physical abusive by her mother, sexual abuse by a neighbor, and sexual and physical abuse by her husband and other male partners. She described herself as being "so damaged" and perhaps not capable of change—there was little hope for change in the Same Old Story. Her goals for therapy were to be a better parent so that her children would have a better life; she would experience happiness through them. Intervention in this case involved conveying compassion for her lifelong struggles and pain, responding to her healthy desire to create a better life for her children, and expressing a genuine wish that she herself could experience some joy. This left the door open to the possibility of change.

In contrast, an example of poor process working with limited access to adaptive feelings and needs took place during an early session with a client who was dealing with childhood emotional abuse. The therapist observed the client's analytical stance and provided information on the process of attending to emotional experience. Thus he identified her emotional processing difficulty and attempted to collaborate on the task of deepening experiencing. The client responded, "I don't see how I will ever be able to stop, it's so engrained." This was her core maladaptive belief that is part of the Same Old Story that keeps her stuck. The therapist empathically responded in an attempt to access emotional experience, "You fear you won't be able to change." The client rejected the idea of fear and said, "I just don't think it's possible," indicating limited access to healthy internal resources and readiness for change. The therapist simply reflected this, and the dialogue went nowhere and remained intellectual and superficial. The client's belief that she could not change obviously has important implications for alliance quality and for agreement on the goals and tasks of therapy. A more effective intervention would have been to validate and explore the client's core maladaptive belief. For example, "So for some reason there's a big part of you [leaving the door open for another part of her] that does not believe it's possible to change. This is such an engrained habitual way of operating. Say more." This could lead to further discussions about the process of therapy, the client's struggle with this therapy process, the origins of that maladaptive belief, the negative effects on her, and possible emergence of a part of self that would like to grow and learn about her experiencing self (Competing Plotlines Story).

Unstoried Emotion and Enhancing Emotional Regulation

Other emotional processing difficulties that are typically observed in abuse survivors concern emotion dysregulation rather than avoidance or overcontrol. The client expresses undifferentiated global upset or distress in the form of dysregulated or unintegrated emotion (e.g., difficulty breathing, pausing, sobbing, dissociation) that is disconnected from narrative content. These are not meaningful or coherent narratives devoid of emotion but expressions of emotionality devoid of a coherent narrative context or meaning. This is emotion that is "unstoried."

Intervention for Unstoried Emotion in the early phase of EFTT involves reducing arousal and distress through empathic affirmation of vulnerability, validation of distress, and soothing empathic responses. Interventions also include establishing goals for gradual exposure to trauma material at the client's pace and standard emotion-regulation strategies, such as breathing and grounding as needed, but no deepening of experience.

For example, Richard is hesitant and withdrawn, and he spoke under his breath when asked to describe his experience of sexual molestation at the beginning of Session 1. The therapist validated how hard it is to talk about this and said they did not have to talk about it right then, but he encouraged disclosure—eventually they would talk about it a lot, Richard would get used to talking about it, and it was not good to keep it inside. Richard then disclosed a memory of profound humiliation with obvious distress. At the end of the session he said he was relieved to have disclosed: "It was hard, but I'm glad I told you. Now you know."

An example of poor process with emotion dysregulation was seen with a client who had a history of aggressive behavior, including biting a coworker in anger. During an early session, while she was talking about her abusive mother and needing to "get her feelings out," she was slouching in the chair and looking at the ceiling, in a kind of spaced out, dissociative state. The therapist empathically responded to how she must have a lot of sadness and anger about never getting her needs met. However, the client continued to look at the ceiling, "I need to get this out. Maybe I should go to church." The therapist responded somewhat confrontationally with "What, ask God to help you get it out?" and the client remained distant, leaning back. The therapist missed the core issue, which was her difficulty approaching and expressing emotional pain. She needed a lot more help to articulate her experience. First the therapist needed to sit forward, validate the client's struggle, the discomfort of it, encourage her to sit up and make eye contact with the therapist, and collaborate with her. For example, "This is important. We don't want you sitting there all blocked up inside, feeling like you want to explode, desperate, and powerless. We need to find ways to help you express your feelings in here. Can you look at me? What are you feeling in your body?"

Empty Storytelling and Enhancing Emotional Engagement

The early phase of therapy with abuse survivors is frequently characterized by narratives that are devoid of or have limited expressed emotion, or wherein emotions are acknowledged but there is little arousal in voice or body. These stories feel "empty" because they lack the color or life that emotion brings to a narrative and the personal significance of the event for the client that emotion conveys. In the first session especially, clients may describe painful traumatic events in a detailed but matter-of-fact, external manner characteristic of Empty Storytelling. When trauma memory disclosures are stripped of the lived emotional experience of what happened, it is often the case that clients are trying to avoid awareness of deeply distressing feelings, fears, and maladaptive action tendencies. Emotional avoidance occurs on a continuum ranging from conscious overcontrol, where the feelings being controlled are in awareness, to absent or limited access to emotional experience without deliberate overcontrol. Interventions differ depending on degree of availability of emotional experience.

For example, at the beginning of therapy Sarah expressed minimal affect as she told the story of her childhood; rather, she focused on behavior and events. When the therapist empathically responded to the "horror" of her mother and brother's death in a fire, for example, she reported feeling nothing, only being glad the beatings and sexual abuse stopped. When asked about her feelings and needs as a little girl, she could not respond but described herself as "not a very emotional or nurturing person, more a matter-of-fact type of person." Her narrative is empty of lived emotional experience, and she has limited access to her feelings and thus limited capacity for reflection on them. Effective intervention will require considerable emotion coaching and guidance. It is important to note that early in the session, the therapist validated her difficulties with feelings as one of the effects of her childhood ("life robbed of color") and was attuned to the infrequent emergence of healthy resources. This is like attention and responding to emergence of peak levels of experiencing and reinforcing this emotional processing style. For example, tears welled in Sarah's eyes as she remembered herself as a little girl: "I remember wishing I had a different mother." The therapist empathically responded to her sadness. The goal is to support and increase the frequency/dominance of these processes.

Superficial Storytelling and Heightened Reflective Self-Awareness

Client narratives and emotional states in the first phase of therapy may also convey a kind of superficial, rehearsed quality. Traumatic events are described in a vague or generalized manner. The client may talk about intellectual or hypothetical ideas but with low-level experiencing, an external focus on events and behavior, especially the actions and intentions of others. There is limited reflective self-focus, and little or no evidence of emotional engagement, exploration, or discovery. Effective interventions increase a focus on the personal meanings of the stories told though the use of I-language to promote ownership of experience, as well as narrative specificity, by eliciting specific examples and episodic memories. An evocative use of emotion words and metaphoric responses can also bring client storytelling more experientially alive. Interestingly, Mundorf and Paivio (2011) found no relationship between depth of experiencing in pretreatment written trauma narratives and outcome in EFTT. However, depth of self-focused experiential engagement improved from early to late session narratives, and greater depth of reflective, self-focused engagement and meaning making (experiencing) in late narratives predicted better treatment outcome. These research findings support the important benefits of implementing process-guided responses and interventions to deepen client self-reflective, emotion-focused experiencing for the articulation of new emotional meanings, story outcomes, and self-narrative change over the course of therapy.

A client who was talking about how her mother always embarrassed her (part of the Same Old Story) can serve as an example of poor process in working with Superficial Storytelling. The therapist reflected her embarrassment, obviously observed her abstractness and generalities, and asked her to describe a specific example of how her mother had embarrassed her in the past. This attempt to help the client be more specific was technically correct but ineffective, as the client continued to focus on general themes and complaints. In helping clients approach and articulate shame-related experience, therapists first need to empathically affirm how difficult it is to be in touch with that "embarrassment" to reduce anxiety and to validate and reflect on the importance of these difficult emotions in terms of a client's sense of self. Both therapist and client can then explicitly collaborate on the goal of accessing and disclosing these painful episodic memories to not only fully understand what happened to her, but more important, to also fully experience and understand how her mother's actions may have emotionally impacted her and her negative view of self. Again, guidelines for the effective implementation of interventions to help clients access, disclose, and emotionally engage specific, shame-based autobiographical memory disclosures are presented in the next chapter.

Another example of emotionally avoidant storytelling was identified in an early EFTT session in which the client's narrative expression was externally focused and conveyed limited depth of reflective awareness or self-focused experiencing. The client began by complaining about her mother's boyfriend, whom she disliked, and then added that her mother had him in the house despite her feelings toward him. She then shifted to a detailed list of her father's behaviors, whom she described as deliberately doing things to upset her. In the session, her therapist was leaning forward, attentive, but too focused on following the specific event-based details of her storytelling. In the context of Superficial Storytelling markers, it is more helpful to the client when a therapist is able to adopt a process-diagnostic, observational stance and listen carefully for openings to shift the clients monologue to a dialogue and explicitly ask the client to slow down, go back, and attend to personal stories in which indicators of emerging emotional responses are present. For example, "Can we go back to that story of your mother ignoring your feelings? That sounded so important to you." An emphasis on emotion-focused story exploration could have helped this client to access a deepened awareness of her own feelings of resentment toward her mother for choosing the boyfriend over her or how hurtful it must be when her own father deliberately tries to upset her. These interventions that direct attention to clients' emotional experiencing of their personal stories must be followed by explicit encouragement to elaborate and symbolize the meaning of those emotions, in light of an expanded awareness of the intentions, actions, and expectations of others. This takes the form of implementing interventions to elicit self-appraisals (e.g., of not being loved, important, negligible) and asking questions about what the client wants alternatively (unmet needs) and how getting those needs met would be better for them. The point is, clients for whom Superficial Storytelling is their typical narrative style need empathically attuned, process direction to help them access personal and affective personal memories, to focus on an awareness of their own emerging emotions in the context of storytelling, and to deepen experiencing and capacities for reflective self-awareness. This is for the coconstruction of new meaning making and the emergence of a more coherent, compassionate view of self and self-narrative change.

FACILITATING NARRATIVE-EMOTION PROCESS SHIFTS IN EARLY-PHASE SESSIONS

To reiterate, Transitional narratives include some access to healthy resources in the form of adaptive emotion, needs, and perspectives. Client storytelling indicates struggle or conflict between maladaptive experience evident in the Same Old Story and healthy resources (Competing Plotlines). These stories are more experientially alive than the Problem narrative subtypes described previously, contain vivid metaphors and use of emotion words, and are reflective. Narratives also can be inchoate, indicating a search for the right words to describe experience. The frequent appearance of Transitional narrative quality early in therapy indicates a readiness for change and a good prognosis in terms of treatment outcome (Carpenter, Angus, Paivio, & Bryntwick, 2016).

An example of accessing new healthy resources was observed in therapy with a client who was struggling to accept her current reactions to being criticized by a friend. In the exploration, reducing self-doubt is collaboratively established as a goal for therapy. Issues of self-doubt are frequently observed in abuse survivors who have been raised in invalidating environments. The following is an excerpt from Session 3.

> *Client:* Oh, I just wanted to sit there and bawl my eyes out. It just feels like here we go again [Same Old Story].
>
> *Therapist:* Bringing up all those feelings . . . like "I'm no good" and . . . just feeling crushed.
>
> *Client:* That's the word. Like someone who should care about you doesn't give a hoot. But then I wonder if I am reacting too strongly.
>
> *Therapist:* So part of you says "should I maybe not make a big deal out of it" [identifies the Competing Plotline]. But something in your gut is telling you its important [focus on healthy resources].
>
> *Client:* Yes. Yes.
>
> *Therapist:* Is that something you would like to work on in therapy, so when that doubting part kicks in you feel more certain?

The following excerpt from an early session with another client illustrates the productive process of first identifying a conflict between maladaptive and adaptive parts of self (Competing Plotline), then searching for words to describe her healthy experience (Inchoate Storytelling), then shifting to deeper exploration and reflection to coconstruct an experientially alive and coherent narrative (Experiential and Reflective Storytelling).

> *Client:* I think of the word *fun*, I realized I accomplish lots of things like in my work [pause, inwardly focused], or when I'm walking my dog, it's like this is good for me. Whereas I know in the past, I heard the crunch of the snow, but not now. I'm working now. But I know I'm not having any fun [identifies the conflict, the Competing Plotline].

Therapist:	What does fun mean to you? [promote exploration, deepen experiencing].
Client:	[pause, searching for the right words, focusing inward, hands on stomach] It's freedom, you're not trying to lose weight, you're working out because you want to.
Therapist:	Because it makes you feel good, happy.
Client:	Happy, yes, fun is a feeling thing, it's a freedom feeling, and . . . [pause, internal focus, searching] . . . it's like I have to accidentally fall into it [Reflective Storytelling]. I think "where can I get some of that?"
Therapist:	Right, so this is a want, like noticing things in your life such that you do have more of that fun?
Client:	Absolutely need that, because without that I'll be dry.
Therapist:	Yes, life becomes . . .
Client:	Gray.
Therapist:	Yes, gray and dull and boring, like what's the point of getting up [empathic responding, collaborative coconstruction of more coherent narrative].
Client:	Yes, like all that other stuff is really good, but if I don't get some fun, then life loses its color.

In these excerpts, we observed therapist interventions that lead to increasingly productive storytelling in Transitional narrative-emotion markers that indicate a readiness for change. The early phase of therapy also may include early narrative Change markers, such as surprise relief about disclosure, trying out new behaviors in current life, and new experiences and insights during the first IC/EE. Again, the emergence of these Change stories early in therapy is a predictor of good outcome. We see this in the cases of the clients Charlize and Mark in later chapters.

PROCESS-INFORMED CASE CONCEPTUALIZATION

Starting in Session 1, the therapist and client are beginning to collaboratively develop an understanding of the factors contributing to disturbance and the therapeutic processes that will address those factors. The initial case conceptualization should be discussed with the client at the end of Session 2 and be fairly clear by the end of Session 4. This understanding provides direction for the working phase of therapy, but it is a working hypothesis that can be revised as therapy progresses. There are three basic process steps that contribute to the development of an EFTT case formulation:

1. Make a process-diagnostic assessment of the content and quality of client storytelling and emotional processing style, using NEP markers as a guideline.

2. Identify the core painful emotion or maladaptive emotion scheme evident in clients' Same Old Story. The core maladaptive relational patterns and emotions emerging in the context of clients' most poignant storytelling will become the key focus of therapist responses and IC/EE interventions.

3. Identify NEP markers to guide the effective implementation of task interventions in later therapy sessions. The following interrelated dimensions of case conceptualization are modified from Goldman and Greenberg (1997) and tailored specifically to clients dealing with child abuse trauma.

First, the *Diagnostic and Statistical Manual of Mental Disorders* (DSM) diagnoses such as PTSD, depression, social anxiety, substance abuse, eating disorders, and personality pathology are informative in terms of symptoms and processing difficulties that have implications for engagement in therapy and therapy processes. For example, abundant research and clinical observation indicates that particular disorders are associated with particular problems concerning emotion regulation, self-critical processes, performance anxiety, and difficulties cultivating a therapeutic relationship. The client may have been assigned a diagnosis or the therapist may conduct a diagnostic interview to get a better understanding of client difficulties, as needed.

Beginning in the first session, the therapist is listening for the content and quality of client narratives to identify the *core maladaptive emotion scheme*. This comprises recurrent maladaptive feelings (e.g., defensive anger, fear, shame) and associated thoughts, expectations, unmet needs, and behavioral patterns that contribute to a client's negative views of self and others and a confusing, often incoherent self-narrative. The latter includes the often contradictory views of past perpetrators and current significant others. This is the Same Old Story of a damaged, powerless, needy self that was developed in childhood and is activated again and again across interpersonal relationships and events. Clients with unresolved histories of childhood abuse and neglect typically experience themselves as powerless victims and have problems with low self-worth and confidence, lack of clarity about self-identity, and self-doubt concerning their own experience and perceptions. Clients also report difficulties with intimacy and trust, perceiving intimate others as powerful, controlling, hurtful, or neglectful.

An EFTT therapist is also listening for client access to healthy internal resources that emerge in the form of adaptive emotion, needs, hopes, and action tendencies that can be used to modify the maladaptive emotion scheme and challenge the dominant negative emotional plotlines of a client's stories. Competing Plotline transition markers in which clients simultaneously experience the negative emotional plotlines of the Same Old Story, as well as a new healthy part of self that recognizes that the problem lives within them, provides strong evidence of client readiness for change and engagement in EFTT task interventions. For example, the client may describe a maladaptive pattern of defensive anger as well as distress about isolation and sadness at pushing others away, or the client may describe a pattern of situations in which he or she feels angry at a perceived injustice but collapses into self-doubt, powerlessness, or resignation. Effective intervention involves identifying and validating the maladaptive relational pattern and conflict or struggle and fleshing out the adaptive emotion and implicit healthy needs and desires that are missing from their narratives—for example, a longing for connection or the need to take risks and to feel more agentic and self-confident in life.

It is important to note that in addition to attending to the content of client narratives, the therapist is also attending to their affective quality and degree of specificity and coherence to help identify emotional processing difficulties in terms of awareness and regulation. As noted earlier, EFTT therapists should also assess whether the client is able to identify feelings or if there is evidence of alexithymia in which the client can only identify experience as negative and positive or feel global upset and distress.

Throughout the process of narrative exploration, therapists also are assessing clients' responsiveness to empathic responses and/or directives to attend to and articulate their emotional experiencing of their told stories. Because it is well recognized that recovery from trauma requires emotional processing (Foa, Keane, Friedman, & Cohen, 2009), identifying specific emotional processing difficulties and helping clients to develop specific emotional competencies are also critical for recovery and self-narrative change. In instances where clients have difficulty attending to, identifying, accurately labeling, and exploring the meaning of emotional experience, interventions need to be more directive and provide more guidance and explicit emotion coaching or awareness training. Again, for clients who are alexithymic, for example, asking them how they feel is ineffective and likely will increase anxiety. Empathic conjecture, along with directing attention to bodily experience and teaching associated feelings, is more effective.

The final dimension of case conceptualization stems from the emergence of *task markers* in client narratives. These are specific statements that are indicators of particular processing difficulties and readiness to engage in a particular intervention designed to address the difficulty. Typical therapeutic tasks involve attending to the therapeutic relationship, promoting depth of experiencing and increasing clarity about internal experience, resolving intrapersonal conflicts (e.g., self-criticism, interruption, catastrophic expectations), and resolving trauma or relational issues from the past. To re-iterate, in all procedures that address these tasks, the therapist listens for and responds to the emergence of healthy processes (adaptive emotion, needs, strengths, shifting views of self and others) evident in client narratives. In the early stages of therapy these may be subtle and infrequent. The goal of therapist responding and intervention is to increase the frequency and dominance of healthy processes. Because Transitional narratives described earlier show some evidence of access to new information and healthy processes, the more frequently these occur in the early stages, the better prognosis for change.

By the end of Phase 1, tentative collaborative agreement has been reached about primary processing difficulties and associated tasks to address these difficulties. These tasks become the foci of therapeutic work during the middle phase of therapy.

INTRODUCTION OF REEXPERIENCING PROCEDURES

Traumatic experiences are disclosed and discussed in the first three sessions of EFTT, but these are not a focus of in-depth exploration and processing until Session 4, when the IC or EE experiencing procedures are first introduced. Although he or she may wait for markers of unresolved attachment injuries to spontaneously emerge, typically the therapist will explicitly suggest focusing on in-depth exploration of specific abuse issues at the beginning of Session 4. The therapist validates the client's nervousness or hesitation at this suggestion and reassures the client that he or she is "in the driver's seat." Once the client agrees to engage in the task, the therapist will elicit a specific memory or experience, then direct the client to attend to and articulate his or her internal experience in response to imagining the abusive or neglectful other. These procedures quickly evoke the core maladaptive emotion scheme for subsequent exploration. In one study (Holowaty & Paivio, 2012), clients identified the first IC as one of the most helpful events in EFTT and reported that acknowledging, for the first time, the extent of their pain was the important aspect of the procedure. Before presenting clinical material, we review early steps in the model of resolution and narrative processes most relevant to the first IC/EE.

Model of Resolution

Empirically verified steps in the process of resolving "unfinished business" with significant others (Greenberg & Foerster, 1996) were presented in

Chapter 3, describing the EFTT treatment model. Narrative processes that typically emerge during the first IC or EE procedure are the same as those that emerged in the first three sessions, only now they are being deliberately evoked and heightened as clients imaginally confront trauma memory narratives and abusive and neglectful others. These processes are now obvious and available for exploration and change in the middle phase of therapy. The following section describes the quality of productive emotional engagement with the first IC that is related to client resolution and change. Productive intervention during the first IC therefore involves promoting these qualitative dimensions.

Dimensions of Engagement

Clinical observation of EFTT clients indicated wide variability in the quality of client emotional engagement during IC, ranging from refusal to participate, to reluctance, to full emotional engagement. Early research on EFTT with IC (Paivio, Hall, Holowaty, Jellis, & Tran, 2001) examined whether high-quality engagement contributed to better outcome. To address this question, quality of engagement was operationalized in terms of the following three readily observable dimensions.

- The client is in psychological contact with the imagined other as evidenced by looking at the imagined other in the empty chair as opposed to the therapist, vivid descriptions of the imagined other, and use of "I–you" rather than third-person language in interaction with the other.
- The client is involved in the process as evidenced by initiation of dialogue with the imagined other and spontaneous elaboration, rather strictly responding to therapist directives to "tell him" or "say more."
- There are verbal and nonverbal indicators of emotional arousal.

Overall, full engagement involves an increasingly coherent narrative about the client's experience and perspective of the relationship with the significant other, with affect and reflective meaning exploration, that is communicated directly to the imagined other. Results of the Paivio et al. (2001) study indicate that high-quality engagement in the IC procedure, indeed, predicted better treatment outcome in EFTT. Later research (Chagigiorgis, 2009) found similar results for EFTT with the EE procedure. Thus, effective interventions promote high-quality engagement along the previously described dimensions and are particularly important in early sessions because they set the course for the rest of therapy.

Comparison of IC and EE

Clinicians will have a choice about which procedure, IC or EE, to implement during Session 4. Results of the randomized controlled trial comparing EFTT with IC to EFTT with EE (Paivio, Jarry, Chagigiorgis, Hall, & Ralston, 2010) indicate comparable efficacy in terms of statistically significant change, with lower dropout rates in EE but greater clinically significant change for clients who completed IC. Results of studies comparing processes during IC and EE (Ralston, 2006) reveal equal observed depth of experiencing and client-reported distress but lower levels of observed emotional arousal and higher client-reported engagement during EE. These findings suggest clients in both interventions were involved in exploring trauma material and support the intended development of EE as a less evocative and stressful procedure.

That said, there are advantages to the IC procedure. First, there is more research supporting EFT with IC for resolving attachment injuries (e.g., Greenberg & Malcolm, 2002; Paivio & Greenberg, 1995; Paivio et al., 2010). Second, IC quickly evokes core material, including maladaptive processes, making them available for subsequent exploration and change. Ralston (2006), for example, found higher levels of both client experiencing and emotional arousal in the midphase of EFTT with IC compared with EFTT with EE. Early access to core material is important in time-limited therapy. Third, although stressful, it is very powerful to stand up to imagined perpetrators in the room. This is an additional behavioral dimension of learning. Finally, the structure of IC makes it relatively easy to track changing perceptions of self and other, an essential component of the resolution process. The structure of IC also makes it easier for novice therapists or those new to EFTT to learn steps in the resolution process.

Range of Responses to Initial IC/EE

As noted previously, the dominant narrative quality observed in the first three sessions likely characterizes narrative quality and the quality of engagement in the first IC/EE in response to the imagined other. The therapist can anticipate narrative-emotion processing difficulties and strategies for intervention before introducing IC/EE. For example, for clients with severe emotion-dysregulation problems, use EE rather than IC or focus on a less threatening other in the first IC. For clients with little access to emotion words, more explicit directives and emotion coaching rather than reliance on empathic responding will likely be more helpful. For clients with low levels of experiencing, interventions focus on values and concerns, rather than on feelings, to deepen experiencing step-by-step. For vague and abstract narratives, interventions elicit specific autobiographical memories and examples.

An example of addressing client difficulties with IC was observed in Session 3 with Monica, described in an earlier volume on EFTT (Paivio & Pascual-Leone, 2010). Monica's mother committed suicide. Asking her to imagine her mother in the empty chair activated memories of her mother's suicide and severe distress as shown by difficulties breathing and pulling at her collar (Unstoried Emotion). The therapist abandoned IC, directed her and modeled deep breathing to help regulate emotion, validated and affirmed Monica's vulnerability ("I can only imagine how difficult this must be for you."), and asked her to share the specific memories that had been activated. Monica told a detailed story of coming home on Christmas Eve and finding her mother dead on the floor after having shot herself, and another story of seeing her mother in her coffin. The therapist empathically responded throughout the storytelling to reduce distress and help her articulate her experience. Once Monica was calmer, she revealed that she talked to her mother in imagination, without imagining her visually, and usually when she was angry with her. The therapist used this information to collaborate on reintroducing a dialogue with her imagined mother but removed the empty chair to make the intervention less evocative ("That's great that you do that already. It's important to tell her how you feel and say it directly to her to make it more powerful. So you should be here . . ."). Monica was able to reengage with her imagined mother and express anger and sadness at abandonment (Experiential Storytelling).

An example of introducing EE at the beginning of Session 4 is the client Richard, who had been sexually molested by priest. "Unless you have something in particular you would like to discuss, I suggest we spend this session focusing in depth on those experiences of sexual abuse. What happens to you on the inside as I suggest that?" Initially, the client was hesitant, a little incoherent, and reported feeling nervous. The therapist validated his anxiety, reassured him that they would go at his pace, got his agreement, and asked what specific memory came to mind. When Richard couldn't think of anything (Unstoried Emotion), she suggested focusing on the incident of humiliation he talked about in Session 1 and asked him how he felt when he recalled that experience: "What would you say to him if you could?" This quickly evoked anger. The client was fully engaged, able to uninhibitedly express his hatred: "Why the f—k did you do that . . . you pervert, I hope you burn in hell . . ." The therapist's empathic responses helped him hold the priest accountable for harm. At the end of the procedure, he again wondered why he didn't tell anyone at the time. This internal conflict (Competing Plotline Storytelling) became the focus of later sessions.

Common Therapist Errors

The following are commonly observed therapist errors in introducing the first IC procedure. Addressing these difficulties will help deepen the client's emotional engagement.

Too Much or Too Little Attention to Client Difficulties

Research on EFTT examined the effects of therapist skill on treatment outcome (Hall, 2012; Paivio, Holowaty, & Hall, 2004), in particular on therapist competence with the IC procedure. Competence was operationalized according to facilitating the three dimensions of emotional engagement described in an earlier section of this chapter. An additional dimension of competence was addressing client difficulties. Results of the Hall (2012) study indicated an effect for therapist experience, with novice therapists demonstrating competence but their competence not contributing to better outcome. An interpretation of this finding is that novice therapists tended to spend much more time explicitly addressing client difficulties than do experienced therapists, who were more readily able to bypass client difficulties and help clients quickly engage (e.g., "Yes, I know it seems a little strange, but therapy is a place where we can try new things. You'll get used to it. Can we try? If it doesn't work we can do other things."). Too much time spent on addressing difficulties detracts from the process. The other side of the coin, of course, is inadequate addressing of client difficulties, particularly emotion dysregulation, which can result in retraumatization or misunderstanding of client difficulties.

An example of poor process in working with Unstoried Emotion during the first IC occurred with a client who fell silent and withdrew when the novice therapist asked her to imagine her sexually abusive stepfather in the empty chair. The therapist assumed the IC was too evocative and focused on rearranging the chair, moving it farther away, providing a rationale that the father could not hurt her. This was ineffective and detracted from helping the client open up and become more engaged in the procedure. Instead, when clients withdraw, it is better to understand what is going on for them, to direct their attention to their internal experience, and to give them space to attend to that experience. For example, "Something happens on the inside as I ask you to do this? Can you tell me?" In cases of dissociation in response to activation of trauma memories, several experts (e.g., Najavits, 2002) have written guidelines for helping clients become more grounded in the present.

Too Much Attention to Expression Rather Than Internal Experience

One of the distinguishing and attractive features of EFTT and similar experiential therapies is the use of gestalt-derived enactment procedures that quickly evoke emotional experience. Therapists learning EFTT, therefore, can focus attention on the expressive aspects (e.g., "What do you want to say to him?") before directing client attention to their internal experience in response to the imagined other (e.g., "What happens on the inside as you imagine him there, sneering at you?"). However, the guideline in EFTT is to direct attention to client internal experience before directing expression of that experience. Internal experience is the primary source of new information that can be used in the construction of new self-narratives. Expression is putting words to identified internal experience.

Attention to Internal Experience, Rather Than Stimulus Function,
of the Imagined Other

In the early steps of the resolution process, the imagined other is used strictly as a stimulus to evoke the old maladaptive pattern of thoughts, feelings, and reactions in the self so that the Same Old Story is available for exploration. Client empathy for the other is activated in a later phase when clients are closer to resolution. Once clients have had a chance to process and make sense of their own experience, they are in a better position to understand and empathize with the experience of the other. For many clients the Same Old maladaptive story explicitly involves understanding and making excuses for the other. Therapists can validate this as a personal strength and, at the same time, collaborate with the client to attend to his or her own experience. For example, "This is your strength. You are good at understanding others, but sometime this is at the expense of attention to your own feelings and needs. That is what we want to help you focus on in here. Does that make sense?"

Too Much Attention to Specific Content of Response of the Imagined Other

One of the steps in the IC process is for clients to imagine and sometimes enact the response of the imagined other to their expressed thoughts and feelings. Clients frequently will report the other's verbal and nonverbal response based on their history of perceived interactions with the other (e.g., "He would just walk away."). Rather than getting caught up in details of the content, it is important for therapists to identify and intensify the gist of the communicated message that clients react to—you are crazy, exaggerating, not important—and the effect this has on the client (e.g., "Ah, so this is how he shuts you down, renders you powerless."). This increases client awareness of the maladaptive aspects of the Same Old Story that need to change—the thoughts, feelings, and reactions that keep them stuck.

CONCLUSION

This chapter focused on the early phase of EFTT, with particular attention to (a) cultivating the alliance, empathic attunement, and heightened client experiencing; (b) listening for and addressing narrative-emotion Problem markers in terms of interventions and case conceptualization; and (c) introducing IC/EE reexperiencing procedures in Session 4. Together, these form the basis for all procedures used in the remainder of therapy. Promoting high-quality processes in the early phase sets the course for high-quality processes in the remainder of therapy. The following chapter describes process maps and intervention strategies used in the intensive analysis of two cases in the early phase of EFTT.

8

TWO INTENSIVE CASE ANALYSES: EARLY-PHASE EFTT

In this chapter we present an intensive case analysis of two recovered emotion-focused therapy for trauma (EFTT) clients and describe the steps involved in the process-diagnostic identification of narrative-emotion process markers and implementation of key EFTT interventions and process-guiding therapist responses. These contribute to case conceptualization and facilitate client movement to heightened emotional engagement and reflectivity in personal storytelling and imaginal confrontation (IC) and empathic exploration (EE) procedures designed to help clients resolve trauma-based "unfinished business" and promote self-narrative change. We define *recovery* in terms of clinically significant distress at pretreatment and significant symptomatic improvement at posttreatment on two dimensions: posttraumatic stress disorder (PTSD) symptoms and resolution of issues with particular abusive and/or neglectful others who were the focus of therapy. We chose a female client (Charlize) seen by a male therapist in the EFTT with the EE

http://dx.doi.org/10.1037/0000041-009
Narrative Processes in Emotion-Focused Therapy for Trauma, by S. C. Paivio and L. E. Angus

condition and a male client (Mark) seen by a female therapist in the EFTT with the IC condition. These cases were chosen because they represent very different client narrative and emotion-processing styles and therefore capacities for reflective, experientially focused engagement in therapy sessions.

Charlize's issues primarily concerned maladaptive sadness and longing for connection with her emotionally abusive and neglectful mother, with whom she had difficulty setting boundaries. This was her Same Old Story that she urgently wanted to change. Her early therapy sessions were characterized by engaging and exploring her internal struggles with conflicting emotions and desires—Competing Plotline Storytelling, which is described next—and then accessing primary adaptive anger to foster empowerment for the assertion of interpersonal boundaries—an Unexpected Outcomes Story—that was essential in helping her experience and construct a more adaptive self-narrative. The therapeutic relationship had a relaxed and intimate quality that is characteristic of EFTT, and Charlize was exceptionally responsive to therapist-expressed empathy. In turn, this strong empathic relational bond helped Charlize experience, explore, and integrate painful emotions emerging from the disclosure of traumatic memories of childhood abuse, in the context of Experiential Storytelling.

Establishing and maintaining an empathically focused therapeutic relationship was much more challenging with Mark, and a longer period of engagement was necessary to achieve recovery by treatment termination (20 vs. 16 sessions). Mark's main concern was the negative impact of maladaptive defensive anger, covering more vulnerable feelings of sadness and maladaptive shame that stemmed from severe emotional abuse from his mother and physical abuse by his father. His adult attachment style would be considered dismissive, and although he was able to identify and name feelings, he was extremely emotionally overcontrolled, as exemplified in his facial expressions and mode of narrative expression—Empty and Superficial Storytelling in early sessions. His EFTT therapist maintained a consistent focus on guiding and redirecting his attention to emergent, internally felt experiencing (e.g., Inchoate Storytelling) during therapy sessions. Accessing and expressing more vulnerable emotions, and disclosing painful personal memories—in essence, translating lived experiences into told stories—were important mechanisms of change in helping him construct a more adaptive, agentic, and compassionate self-narrative. For Mark, therapist process-directive responses and explicit emotion coaching were most effective in helping him to identify and explore his own emotional experiencing in sessions, and as such, his EFTT sessions had a less intimate and more task-oriented quality. Despite the clients' differences in narrative storytelling style and emotional expression, disclosing autobiographical trauma memories and allowing the emotional pain of abuse and neglect were essential for constructing a coherent trauma narrative that included a new, integrative understanding of who was to be held responsible for their abuse. Also important was a new, more agentic and compassionate view of self and self-identity narrative, integrating an awareness of how they had been wounded into their personal stories. Both clients reported benefitting from the process of disclosing and exploring painful emotional personal memories for the emergence of new emotional meanings, more satisfying relationships with significant others, and self-narrative change.

THE CASE OF CHARLIZE: EMPATHIC EXPLORATION

Charlize was an attractive woman in her mid-30s, a mature student, and married with two primary school-age children. She was adopted, and her adoptive parents separated when she was an adolescent. She has contact with both her birth mother and her adoptive father. At pretreatment, she identified issues of child sexual abuse at the hands of a babysitter as the primary focus for therapy and issues with her mother as secondary.

Session 1

During the first session, Charlize presented three important personal stories that are a part of her dominant self-narrative that becomes the focus of therapy. The first trauma story was the focus of her trauma narrative written just before the first session and processed with the therapist at the beginning of the session. This involved sexual abuse with penetration by a 12-year-old male babysitter beginning when she was age 4 years. The abuse continued for several years, and at first, she did not know it was wrong. Around the age of 9, she began to feel uncomfortable, that it was "dirty." Although she did not disclose the abuse to her mother, she asked instead if she could have another babysitter. The mother ignored her requests. She reported feeling angry at the babysitter ("How could anyone do that?!") and then at herself for not disclosing the abuse to her mother. She also felt neglected and unloved by her mother, whom she perceived as being more interested in drinking and boyfriends at the time of the abuse. She had sought out counseling from a local Sexual Assault Center prior to entering therapy, but she did not find it helpful.

Resolving issues around the sexual abuse was Charlize's primary reason for seeking therapy, and her therapist provided a rationale for reexperiencing trauma feelings and memories, addressed her fears (e.g., activating trauma symptoms), and assured her they would monitor her symptoms and go at her pace.

The second important story plotline for Charlize was her concern regarding unfinished business and ongoing relationship difficulties with her alcoholic mother. Charlize recalled several incidents in which the mother continued to make demands (e.g., for financial assistance), leaving Charlize feeling resentful but continuing to acquiesce. She saw her mother as self-centered, controlling ("always told me how to feel"), and invalidating ("She thinks we have a close relationship"), and she experienced herself as being "not seen or loved" and unable to assert personal boundaries with her mother. Although she expressed a deeply poignant wish "to bond" with her mother, and would get her hopes up when mother was nice to her, she was also aware that she constantly felt hurt and disappointed by her mother, leading to withdrawal and further resentment. As expressed in her Same Old Storytelling during early-phase sessions, Charlize felt intractably stuck in this maladaptive pattern of thoughts, feelings, and behavior with her mother.

The third important story plotline concerned a similar maladaptive (although not abusive) relational pattern with her husband. Charlize disclosed her memory of the moment when she told her husband about her childhood sexual abuse, and his response was anger at her mother, rather than sympathy or compassion for her, as the abused child. He also insisted that she tell her mother, which she did not want to do but acquiesced, and she was devastated when her mother sarcastically responded, "I hope you're not blaming me for this!" The therapist focused on her suppressed feelings and needs in the situation with her husband and invited elaboration.

> Therapist: So you wanted support, understanding; say more about your internal experience at the time.
>
> Client: I regret telling him, I feel scared to open up, I distrust him now.
>
> Therapist: This was a betrayal, like retraumatizing you.

The therapist identified the maladaptive relational pattern, the Same Old Story that Charlize wanted to change, and provided a rationale for an EFTT treatment approach: "These are situations where you feel one way but feel like you are not allowed to express. You suppress your feelings and go along with the wishes of others." A goal for therapy was to help Charlize understand and overcome her difficulties, asserting her own feelings and needs with both her mother and husband.

Problematic Narrative-Emotion Processes

The most obvious and dominant Problem marker was the repetitive nature of her Same Old Story that captured Charlize's maladaptive pattern of suppressing her own feelings and needs and acquiescing to the wishes of others, especially her mother. Identifying the core maladaptive emotion scheme that fueled her Same Old Storytelling was key to developing a process-diagnostic case conceptualization and provided a coherent rationale for engaging in EFTT interventions that would will help Charlize identify and assert healthy feelings and needs for new, rewarding story outcomes and construction of a more self-empowered self-narrative.

At the beginning of the first session, Charlize disclosed clear, vivid memories of her sexual abuse, and although she expressed emotion in words, the memories were narrated in a matter-of-fact manner with little expressed, emotional arousal. This kind of Empty Storytelling, where the emotional landscape or soundtrack of the story is somehow absent or missing, is frequently observed with clients in the first session when they are cautious and maintaining emotional control until they feel it is safe to let down their guard. On the outside, Charlize appeared strong, competent, and composed. Her therapist offered a process observation highlighting the disjunction between the poignancy of the story told and the absence of an emotional response: "I notice you describe a very painful experience but with an external calm." A client might hear this as a rather challenging, confrontational response, evoking feelings of being criticized and heightened self-consciousness, especially in the first session. For Charlize, however, her therapist's noticing a lack of emotional expressions seemed to be heard as an invitation to let down her guard with him, and as a consequence, she immediately engaged in deeper exploration of her feelings and meanings regarding the effects of abuse and neglect.

> *Client:* What bothers me is how I see myself now, the consequences of it, confusion, anger, distrust, hurt, mostly anger about how it affected my personality.
>
> *Therapist:* Such strong emotion, say more.
>
> *Client:* [*tears well up*] Life could have been different.
>
> *Therapist:* Sad about what could have been, what was taken away, like you were robbed [evocative empathy].
>
> *Client:* Yes, I should have been able to be a kid rather than the adult, carefree, not worried all the time. Now as an adult I feel like a child, confused, my thoughts all over the place, it bothers me.

This shift from an emotionally overcontrolled and constricted chronicling of events to a more emotionally alive, specific, and reflective narration of lived experiences—as a form of Experiential Storytelling—are good indicators of a readiness change. Additionally, her responsiveness to therapist-expressed empathy indicated a capacity to access and explore personal memories and emotions that can be used to construct a more adaptive self-narrative.

Transitional Narrative-Emotion Processes

Over the course of the first session, Charlize's storytelling involved several experiences of internal struggle or conflict between maladaptive thoughts and behaviors and healthy feelings and desires that are definitive of Competing

Plotline Storytelling and could be elaborated and explored to help challenge her "stuckness" in the Same Old Story pattern. A client's awareness of their role in these internal struggles, early in therapy, is another good prognostic indicator of the client's readiness for change. For example, when asked what she felt toward her abuser, she responded, "I am angry at him but also at myself. I should have done something," and then reflectively, "Why didn't I do something?" This self-reflective inquiry was followed by a voice of healthy adaptive outrage and strong emotion: "How could anyone do that?!" Later her self-reflective focus was on her own internal struggle between self-blame and anger at her mother for her neglect of her emotional needs as a young girl. Her therapist helped her to identify the competing, emotional plotlines of her internal struggles and validated healthy anger and outrage at others for abuse and not protecting her. Helping clients to access adaptive feelings of anger at both perpetrators of abuse and those caregivers who failed to intervene or provide protection helps to promote self-empowerment and their ability to assert interpersonal boundaries.

Another feature of Charlize's emotional and reflective processing difficulties was the expression of self-doubt and confusion about her perceptions, feelings, and needs. This is common among abuse survivors who have grown up in emotionally unresponsive attachment relationships. As Charlize stated, "I am always second guessing myself, am I overreacting, should I let it go, it's confusing, frustrating." The therapist empathically responded to and validated the pain and confusion of always questioning herself, which evoked tears and heightened feelings of sadness for Charlize. Helping her approach and allow emotional pain permitted Charlize to construct a more compassionate understanding of herself, in relation to the painful, traumatic memories of her childhood. It is important to note that her therapist reassured her that "in therapy we will help you get at and clarify all those feelings," thus providing a rationale for disclosing and emotionally exploring trauma memories in therapy.

During her first therapy session, her therapist frequently directed Charlize's attention to her emotional experiencing, in the context of her Same Old Storytelling, with open questions such as "What are you feeling right now as you talk about this?" Helping her become aware of, symbolize, and explore feelings that emerged in the context of traumatic memory disclosures or Same Old Storytelling deepened in-session experiencing, reflection, and the articulation of new meaning that, in turn, opened the door to more assertive, adaptive feelings and needs. These directly challenged her Same Old Story, the pattern of acquiescence ("I feel a lot of sadness, I want to be myself, not a happy façade, a mask to suit the situation.") and withdrawal in personal relationships. Here again, the therapist validated her desire to be her "true self" and identified this as a goal for therapeutic change.

As part of EFTT protocol, the therapist also explicitly asked the client about her hopes for herself ("I want to be a better wife and mother, but I want to do it for me too, know who Charlize is, think clearer, be more decisive."), and hopes for therapy ("I want to focus on real issues, not just relaxation techniques or something, not just handle my reactions but change my thinking."). The therapist reinforced her hopes and desires for the future and reassured her that this would be the focus of therapy. This set the stage for expectations regarding self-narrative change.

Initial Case Conceptualization

Expressed in the themes emerging from her repetitive Same Old Storytelling about her mother and husband, in early-phase sessions it became clear that Charlize was preoccupied with maintaining an attachment relationships and fearful of abandonment at the same time (fearful, preoccupied attachment style). Although she experienced shame and self-blame for not disclosing the sexual abuse to her mother, the extent to which Charlize also felt worthless or unlovable (shame-based sense of self) was unclear. What was clear was that she experienced herself as a "puppet" controlled by others, suppressing her own feelings and needs to acquiesce to the needs of significant others (e.g., babysitter, mother, and husband). As a result, she perceived her husband and mother, in particular, as inattentive to her feelings and needs and unsupportive of her emotional needs for validation, security, and protection. This is the core theme of her maladaptive emotion scheme that fueled her Same Old Storytelling in early-phase sessions and will become the focus of therapeutic change.

In terms of strengths, it was evident in her early-phase sessions that Charlize was readily responsive to therapist empathic responses and had access to healthy feelings and needs (anger, sadness, need to be valued, for authenticity, assertiveness) that are essential to challenge and change her maladaptive emotion scheme. She also had an awareness of how her own fears and concerns made it difficult for her to assert her own needs and a strong capacity for self-reflective engagement and depth of experiencing in early therapy sessions. Key narrative-emotional processing difficulties and task markers included unresolved issues with the babysitter and mother (Same Old Storytelling), as well as confusion and self-doubt concerning her feelings and needs that resulted in a frustrating lack of assertiveness (Competing Plotline Storytelling) with others. Implications for intervention include principles of fostering the disclosure of painful trauma memories (reexperiencing sexual abuse); focusing to clarify internal experience; accessing healthy, agentic emotions; and engagement in EE interventions to resolve issues with her mother.

Sessions 2 and 3

Past and present issues with her mother and current issues with her husband (the Same Old Story), as well as sadness about the loss of her true self through abuse and neglect, became the primary focus for Sessions 2 and 3. Charlize's core unmet need was to feel valued—she had longed for that her whole life (healthy resources) and had difficulties asking for what she needed from others.

At the beginning of Session 3, Charlize reported early gains in her relationship with her husband (Unexpected Outcome Storytelling), wherein she stated that her husband had become more affectionate toward her, and that while she enjoyed his newfound attentiveness, she was also puzzled by feelings of annoyance and wanting to push him away, all at the same time. Charlize's emotional ambivalence toward her husband's affection is a key indicator of Competing Plotline Storytelling, suggesting that her Same Old Story of her relationship with her husband was in transition. As demonstrated by her therapist, this was a marker for further reflective, empathic exploration:

> *Client:* Strange, I've wanted that for so long and now that I have it, I push him away.
>
> *Therapist:* Say more about strange. What's your understanding of your reaction?
>
> *Client:* I don't know, maybe I don't quite trust that it will last, the rug pulled out from under my feet.

The emergence of early change narratives—that is, Unexpected Outcome Storytelling—likely has good prognostic implications for successful therapy if, as in the case of Charlize, the therapist helps the client to notice, narrate, and reflect on the possible impact of this change as a challenge to the Same Old Stories and as a platform for self-narrative change. When clients report positive Unexpected Outcomes happening in their lives at an early point in therapy, it suggests that they are already taking steps toward addressing core needs in primary relationships and experiencing more satisfying emotional outcomes that are, in turn, the basis for a new view of self and future self-narrative change. Indeed, as we see with Charlize, her Same Old Stories of her husband are no longer a primary focus in the mid- or working-phase sessions, whereas the significant emotional gains she has experienced in her marital relationship do become a focus for self-narrative change in final-phase sessions.

Session 4

Because Charlize was randomly assigned to the EE condition, in the context of an EFTT treatment trial her therapist introduced the EE reexperiencing procedure for the first time during Session 4. Although there was no reason to assume she would not have benefitted from engaging in EFTT with IC interventions, as noted earlier, she responded particularly well to an empathically responsive therapeutic alliance with her therapist that helped her to access and reflect on painful trauma memories and emotions, for deepened reflection and new meaning making. In Session 4, the therapeutic relationship had a relaxed and intimate quality (e.g., her therapist sat facing her, very close, their knees almost touching), which is compatible with her needs for connection and attachment style. The session began with Charlize retelling the story of what happened when she first told her husband about her childhood sexual abuse—her angry reaction in response to his lack of understanding about her emotional needs and her subsequent withdrawal from him. The therapist then identified the Same Old Story of Charlize's maladaptive relational pattern of anger and withdrawal with both husband and mother in the past and noted how this same pattern was happening with her mother now, as a key indicator of unfinished business.

Accessing Adaptive Feelings and Needs to Help Shift the Same Old Story

The marker for introducing an EE intervention dialogue with mother was Charlize's complaint about her mother's repeated pattern of neglect. The therapist empathically responded to her implied anger with a focus on self-empowerment. This could challenge the old pattern of nonassertiveness that kept her stuck in her Same Old Story of longing for connection but experiencing dashed hopes and angry withdrawal. He validated her sense of being caught in a frustrating emotional trap and suggested that an in-depth exploration of her competing feelings of wanting closeness and yet feeling strong dissatisfaction with her mother's inability to emotionally care for her was important. He encouraged Charlize to explore and further differentiate her feelings of dissatisfaction and neglect, in the context of childhood memories.

> *Therapist:* You were cheated, did not have a good mother. Think back to those experiences with your mother as a child [evoke specific autobiographical memory]. Say more about what you were angry about.
>
> *Client:* Her lies, pretending we have a great relationship, always do as I say, never paying attention to my wishes.

Then she collapsed into powerlessness, described herself as repeatedly giving in, feeling hurt and angry, and behaviorally withdrawing. In essence, she was enacting in the session, the maladaptive relational patterns evidenced in her Same Old Storytelling.

Rather than focus on the maladaptive plotline of shame, powerlessness, and withdrawal, her therapist redirected Charlize's attention to the other emotional plotline—adaptive anger in response to neglect—to promote self-empowerment.

> *Therapist:* You give in but you feel angry, then you feel bad on the inside for not saying anything.
>
> *Client:* I hope things will change but I feel trapped, manipulated.

Here again, rather than respond to the maladaptive powerlessness, the therapist focused on the importance of her healthy unmet needs.

> *Therapist:* What would you want to say to your mother if you could? What did you need from your mother as a child?
>
> *Client:* I wanted to be the most important thing in her life. If I would have been "the apple of her eye" the abuse would not have happened or maybe not lasted as long.

Validating her need to be loved and valued, her therapist offered a new, more coherent and compassionate understanding of the conflicting emotions that Charlize experienced in relationship with her mother, when he empathically responded, "Feeling sad for that little girl and angry at mother for her neglect." Later in the session, he again responded to emergent process indicators of adaptive anger, as an agentic push for change in the stuck pattern of her same old storytelling, but again sadness was activated.

> *Client:* Always do as I say.
>
> *Therapist:* You want to say STOP, listen to me!
>
> *Client:* I don't know. I want her to want me.

Charlize's response was indicative of a core sense of self as sad and unloved and still clinging, hoping, trying to get core needs met from her mother. This is classic unfinished business and what keeps her stuck. Letting go of the unrealistic expectations regarding her mother will be one step in the path toward resolution (Degree of Resolution Scale [DRS] Level 6; Singh, 1994; described in Chapter 4 and the Appendix) that sets the stage for construction of a more adaptive self-narrative. It is important to note that Charlize also reflected on her feelings of love, protection, and nurturing toward her own children, putting their needs first, and wondered out loud, "How could she [mother] be so selfish? I don't understand why." This narrative incoherence and the struggle to make sense of her feelings and the behaviors and intentions of others are typical of unresolved trauma. Accordingly, EFTT interventions should validate a client's need to understand, to help narrate a coherent integration of actions, intentions, and emotions that turns questions into statements of feelings and needs (e.g., "It's hard to understand how a mother could be so selfish. You needed her to put your feelings first. All children need this.").

Over the course of therapy as clients become more clear and confident in expressing their feelings and needs, a clearer, more differentiated understanding of the other and a new more coherent narrative will emerge.

Thus far, personal stories and concerns regarding sexual abuse had not emerged or been a focus of therapy with Charlize. However, at the beginning of Session 5, she reported that during the previous week, she had been having terrifying nightmares about her 3-year-old daughter being abused. Her therapist connected her nightmares to unresolved issues concerning her own abuse and suggested addressing and processing those childhood traumatic memories in her therapy session. Consistent with guidelines for reprocessing traumatic memories of childhood abuse, he first asked her to recall a specific incident and then directed her attention to sensorial details of the event to evoke an emotionally engaged narration of the events of what happened to facilitate enhanced narrative coherence and emotional self-regulation. Charlize recalled vivid details of the room in which the abuse took place, the smell of the babysitter's jacket, and his coercive comments. The therapist also directed her attention to her internal experience before, during, and after the event (Experiential Story) and empathically highlighted her feelings of dread anticipating his arrival, repulsion about the abuse, and powerlessness to make it stop. He also asked what she would want to say to the perpetrator now, as an adult, if she could (accessing adaptive anger to shift the self-narrative).

Client: How could you do that? You knew it was wrong.

Therapist: Wrong. Say more.

Client: I was naïve and innocent and you took advantage of me, and you got away with it, no consequences.

Therapist: Angry that he got away with it. But you paid a price.

Client: Yes, the worst part is he damaged my ability to trust.

She then shifted into an expression of compassionate sadness, for herself as young girl, and her own loss of innocence.

At the end of the session, she reported feeling "really strong" after confronting her abuse experience and recognized her achievements despite her abuse experience. During the following session, Charlize reported an "emotional transformation" since disclosure and emotional reexperiencing of her childhood sexual abuse in the previous session. In this new, unexpected outcome story, she reported no longer having nightmares, being able to think about the abuse without feeling ashamed, no longer worrying if others believe her or not, and feeling more calm and warm with her own children. Noticing and highlighting the importance of this Unexpected Outcome Story for Charlize, her therapist then asked her to account for these changes, to understand how this important shift in her view of herself, and her childhood abuse, had happened. Charlize responded that reexperiencing the abuse "was difficult but a release." Disclosing and expressing her feelings "were helpful in clarifying things, realizing the abuse was not my fault, I felt bad because I knew it was wrong but didn't stop it. I realize now I was a child, not in control, and afraid to speak up." Thus reexperiencing herself as a powerless, frightened child, and accessing adaptive anger at the perpetrator and compassion for self, contributed to the construction of a new self-narrative in which she felt more confident and clearly held the perpetrator accountable for harm (this is DRS Level 7). Again, this early change is a strong indicator of good outcome. She no longer wished to focus on sexual abuse but on issues with her mother. This marks the end of Phase 1 with Charlize.

Refined Case Conceptualization

By the end of Session 4, a core maladaptive emotion scheme of sadness, loneliness, and abandonment repeatedly emerged in the context of Charlize's Same Old Storytelling about her mother. She had access to adaptive anger and associated meanings, but her dominant emotional experience was sadness (rather than anger) and unmet needs for connection, to be "the apple of her [mother's] eye." Her predominant narrative style was composed, personal, and emotionally alive with moderate levels of Experiencing and Reflectivity. Nonetheless, she struggled to accept her own feelings of having been emotionally neglected by her mother, and she frequently collapsed into resignation and powerlessness, stuck in her same old relational pattern. In the midphase of EFTT sessions, her therapist continued to help Charlize identify and express her feelings and needs as a child and, in current relationships, to feel entitled to unmet needs for validation, protection, and prizing, allowing emotional pain and grieving losses, expressing anger, and asserting her boundaries with mother.

THE CASE OF MARK: IMAGINAL CONFRONTATION

Mark was in his mid-30s, a well-educated, intelligent man, employed as an engineer. He had two teenage stepchildren and one 5-year-old biological daughter. He had a history of depression. He sought therapy to deal with hatred toward his mother and disrespect toward women, in general, as well as anger toward himself for being like his mother. On the DRS at pretreatment, the relationship with his mother was identified as the primary focus of therapy and the relationship with his father as secondary. As in the case of Charlize, therapy focused equally on past issues with his mother and current issues with his mother and the rest of his family (whom he perceived as nonsupportive and invalidating of his childhood "abuse"), as well as in his marriage, which was rocky.

Session 1

During Session 1, Mark recalled several incidents of emotional and physical abuse. He returned to one trauma memory, in particular, over the course of therapy, a trauma that he wrote about prior to the first session. This involved having to beg his mother's forgiveness on his hands and knees for hours for what he described as normal adolescent behavior, "as if I was the worst kid in the world, and I believed her." He then was strapped with a belt by his father at the insistence of his mother and recalled pleading with his father not to do it. He viewed his mother as a "monster" and his father and brothers as nonsupportive and kowtowing to her.

Mark's other dominant personal story concerned his chronic defensive anger in current relationships, particularly with his wife and children (although he offered few details of his behavior). He attributed this to his experiences with his mother. His wife recently accused him of being just like his mother (cold, selfish, a know-it-all, never admitting he is wrong) and insisted that he needed to change. The impetus for seeking therapy was Mark's realization that she was right: "I'm the same asshole as my mother." When probed by the therapist, he said he felt "sad to realize this" about himself, that he was pushing the people he loved away with his defensiveness, conveying a key maladaptive emotional plotline of his negative view of self and Same Old Story.

Narrative-Emotion Process Problem Markers

During Session 1 Mark painted a vivid picture of what it was like for him growing up and used metaphors to describe his internal experience, but with a focus on details of the environment. He was able to intellectually reflect on his experience and identify feelings (he did not appear to be alexithymic), but he described incidents of severe emotional and physical abuse in a monotone, with no arousal in his voice or facial expression (Empty Storytelling), and his posture was one of deliberate cool aloofness, leaning back in his chair with one leg crossed over the other. Mark's extreme emotional overcontrol made him difficult to empathically read. Unlike the client Charlize, presented previously, Mark's emotional overcontrol was extreme and emotionally avoidant, and Empty and Same Old Storytelling markers were prominent throughout the first session. The therapist did not directly identify this as a problem, as that might have left him feeling criticized and more self-conscious and would have risked creating an alliance rupture. This was consistent with EFTT protocol for the first session. It also appeared that Mark was more responsive to questions about—and explicit directives to attend to and elaborate on—his inner felt feelings and emotions rather than to expressed empathy. Empathic responses were nonetheless essential and were best offered to communicate understanding and promote elaboration after Mark identified feelings. Therapist empathic understanding responses helped Mark to coconstruct a more emotionally alive self-narrative. Facilitating shifts from Empty and Superficial Storytelling to more Experiential Storytelling is consistent with EFTT protocol. Helping Mark to become more emotionally engaged with his trauma memory and personal storytelling disclosure was a gradual process requiring patience, persistence, realistic expectations for change on the part of the therapist, and a balance between accepting and changing the client's emotional processing style.

Mark also was stuck in maladaptive patterns of secondary defensive anger with limited access to vulnerable experience. He hated his mother, had problems with anger in general, and disrespected women. He described himself as "not a nice guy" who pushed others away. This was the Same Old Story he wanted to change. When the therapist asked how his disrespect for women would affect their relationship, he denied it would be a problem because it was not a personal relationship. (Indeed, the relationship was task oriented and lacked the intimate quality observed in therapy with Charlize.) He recognized that the pattern of anger stemmed from his experiences with his mother and that some of his anger was defensive, and he acknowledged vulnerable experiences and needs. When asked, Mark said he felt sad and empty to realize what he was like with his kids and sad to realize he was exactly like his mother. Again, however, these vulnerable feelings and needs were acknowledged with little emotional arousal (Empty Storytelling). There was a big disconnect between the content and quality of his narrative.

Narrative-Emotion Transition Markers

Mark's storytelling during Session 1 revealed several internal struggles between contrasting maladaptive and healthy emotions and behaviors. Competing Plotline markers included struggles between adaptive anger at abuse and guilt about, and suppression of, anger toward his parents, and between defensive anger, pushing others away and wanting to connect, and sadness at hurting loved ones that indicated access to primary adaptive emotional responses and early readiness for change. For example, at the beginning of the session, he said that he hated his mother. His therapist validated this emotional reaction and then process-directed his attention to current emotional experience.

> *Therapist:* Very strong emotion. What's it like for you to say you hate your mother? Let it register.
>
> *Client:* I hate her. I want to connect with her but I can't, I won't let her in.
>
> *Therapist:* Protecting yourself—like I deserve respect?
>
> *Client:* I feel guilty, they are old. I was brought up to have respect for your parents.

Although Mark's personal stories focused primarily on maladaptive rejecting anger, an example of his capacity to access and reflect on vulnerable experience happened at the end of the first session. He told the story of his wife telling him that he was selfish, that he had issues with women because of his mother, and that he was (tragically) just like his mother and needed to change.

> Therapist: What was it like for you to get that feedback from your wife?
>
> Client: I was all anger at first, defensive, then I hit rock bottom, do you know what I mean?
>
> Therapist: Tell me what you mean.
>
> Client: Just sad and empty to realize what I am like, especially with my kids. I have improved but I have a long way to go. The most traumatic thing in life is realizing I'm the same asshole as my mother.
>
> Therapist: Devastating.
>
> Client: Hurting the people I love.
>
> Therapist: I don't want to be like that.
>
> Client: Exactly.
>
> Therapist: Seems like you can still feel the weight of that sadness.

Here his vocal quality was momentarily internally, emotionally focused in a Reflective Storytelling mode, and his therapist empathically responded to the emergence of adaptive emotion to reinforce his desire to change, shift the punishing Same Old Story pattern of maladaptive, defensive anger.

At the end of the first session, Mark's therapist asked him about his experience of the session.

> Client: It was like breaking a fish tank, it all comes spilling out.
>
> Therapist: Ah, so much to tell.
>
> Client: Yes, so much baggage.

Mark's response highlighted the discrepancy between the experiential impact of his internal awareness of having opened up and his external presentation of extreme emotional constriction. This is consistent with research (Gottman, Coan, Carrere, & Swanson, 1998) on men in couples therapy whose external calm is at odds with extremely high physiological arousal. It also was indicative of his valuing of disclosure. His therapist then provided information about the process of therapy: "We will focus on all those feelings and memories from the past so you can move beyond them, so they don't impact the present, so you can heal." Mark agrees that this will be helpful.

Initial Case Conceptualization

Mark's core maladaptive emotion scheme, as repetitively represented in his Same Old Storytelling, was shame covered by defensive anger. In the context of his maladaptive view of himself, conveyed in his Same Old Storytelling, he perceived himself as "not a nice guy," "an asshole just like my mother." Mark perceived others (his mother and family) as controlling, hurtful, humiliating, and nonsupportive, and he pushed others away as self-protection. His adult attachment style would be considered primarily dismissive. This is the Same Old Story that emerged from unresolved trauma issues and suppressed feelings about his mother for severe emotional abuse, and to a lesser extent his father and brothers for not validating and supporting him during his childhood. His dominant emotional processing difficulty was overcontrol of emotional experience, particularly vulnerable feelings of shame and sadness. He could identify and label different emotions—suggesting that he was not alexithymic—but his personal storytelling and emotional expression was flat, devoid of emotional arousal, and not experientially alive (Empty Storytelling marker). He had the capacity for reflection, but this was mostly at an intellectual level (Superficial Storytelling). However, Mark's storytelling also revealed several internal conflicts or competing emotional plotlines with access to healthy, adaptive, and agentic feelings and needs (e.g., sadness, need to connect) that could be used to shift the negative emotional plotlines and hold of the Same Old Story. Therefore, the first task in therapy was to reduce emotional overcontrol, which could (a) negatively impact all other therapeutic tasks, (b) interfere with empathic attunement and connection in the therapeutic relationship (the bond), and (c) impede emotional processing and recovery from trauma for resolution of past and current relationship issues. Narrative-emotion process shifts from Problem to Transition markers facilitate a sense of increased emotional coherence that allows reflective engagement and meaning making that are indicative of readiness for change.

Sessions 2 and 3

Sessions 2 and 3 with Mark focused on his pattern of reactive anger in current relationships and his negative view of self (Same Old Storytelling). For example, he described an incident of being "too harsh" and critical with his stepdaughter, just like his mother. The therapist directed his attention to healthy values and unmet needs: "How do you want to be with your daughter? What did you want as a child besides harsh criticism?" This intervention helped him to access his shame and regret about his behavior, sadness at pushing loved ones away, and desire to change, which are healthy resources that can help shift the maladaptive pattern and negative emotional plotlines of defensive anger. Mark recalled another incident of automatic anger with his wife and daughter. The therapist asked him what it was like for him to consider his behavior. Mark responded, "I felt embarrassed to behave like that in public with my wife. I feel sad to realize what I am like with my kids." Although Mark's storytelling remained overcontrolled, this was an excellent example of accessing Competing Plotlines Transition Storytelling markers and externalizing the client's internal struggle against his dominant maladaptive Same Old Story and maladaptive view of self. The therapist empathized and fleshed out both sides of the struggle, with a focus on highlighting healthy wants and needs for increased awareness and motivation.

> *Therapist:* Devastating, the last thing you want is to hurt the people you love, automatic anger, regret. How do you want to be?
>
> *Client:* Not push others away, to connect, not be alone.
>
> *Therapist:* Ah, not alone, but automatic anger interferes. Can you recall the situation with your daughter, what was going on inside?
>
> *Client:* I felt hurt, not respected; as usual, I expected something that I didn't get [Same Old Story], but I forgot she is only 15 [Competing Plotline Storytelling marker].

Here his therapist chose to focus on understanding the problem rather than the pain of feeling alone and healthy longings to connect. Nonetheless, the intervention effectively increased narrative specificity, self-awareness, and supported collaboration on therapeutic goals.

> *Therapist:* I see how important it is for you to change the things that push others away. It takes a lot of courage to admit you are wrong and to try to change. We need to understand the thoughts and feelings that interfere with making the changes you want.

Here she reinforced his motivation and readiness for change.

Similarly, Session 3 focused on Mark's view of himself as an "ugly person" like his mother and on his regrets concerning his selfishness toward his wife during her pregnancy as an example of his disrespect for women. He recalled several specific incidents (disclosure of autobiographical memories) that connected his behavior to experiences with his mother, then questioned how he could understand the origins of his problems but could not change them (Reflective Storytelling). His therapist used this as an opportunity to provide a treatment rationale: "You need to go back and feel the feelings. It's so hurtful to have your mother not care. These things are locked in on a feeling level. I will help you keep focusing on your feelings. There is a need for emotional reprocessing of these old wounds." Mark acknowledged this but leaned further back in his chair, examined his nails, maintained his flat, cool vocal quality (Empty Storytelling). It was clear he was uncomfortable with this emphasis on expression of his emotional experience. The therapist validated that this would be challenging and painful at times but reiterated that it was new learning and was how he would be able to make the changes he wants.

In these sessions, the therapist was actively directing his attention to what was happening for him inside, in terms of emotions, intentions, and expectations. A challenge when working with clients like Mark, who are intellectual, cool, and distant, is focusing on problem solving and emotion coaching at the expense of empathizing with client pain. Another challenge is to balance being in sync with and respectful of the client's more cognitive emotional processing style while gradually deepening emotional engagement.

Session 4

Mark began Session 4 by acknowledging that he did not express his anger well, that he bottles it up. The therapist reflected and connected his unexpressed anger to unresolved issues with his mother. Mark understood this connection but questioned, "Why can't I let it go? Why do I feel guilty about my hatred toward them? Why do I feel obliged to keep seeing them?" The therapist reflected both sides of the struggle encapsulated in this Competing Plotline marker and invited further exploration.

> *Therapist:* All this anger but still there's this pull, say more.

> *Client:* They have power over me.

This was the marker for introducing IC.

Accessing Autobiographical Trauma Memory and Adaptive Emotion

The therapist said, "Ah, power over you, power to shut you down it seems. I want to invite you to express your anger." She brought out the empty chair, asked him to imagine his parents and tell them what he was angry about. Mark immediately responded with blame and complaint and rejecting anger expressed directly to his imagined parents (DRS Level 1). He was moderately engaged in the procedure, made eye contact with imagined others, used I–you language, and expressed feeling words, but again his Empty Storytelling quality lacked emotional arousal. This was a perfect in-session example of bottled up anger—the problem he identified at the beginning of the session. The challenge continued to be to help Mark shift into a more emotionally engaged stance. The therapist asked how he felt when he said these things to his parents, and he acknowledged anger but then collapsed into resignation ("There's no point. They won't listen."). Again, this is the emergence of a Competing Plotline marker, and his therapist decided to bypass the negative plotline of resignation (DRS Level 2) and instead asked him to recall and disclose a specific autobiographical memory from his childhood that was connected to his feelings of anger. This was the beginning of a shift from Empty Storytelling to a more productive, emotionally alive process, Experiential Storytelling, in which the feeling, actions, and meanings of his trauma memory became coherently integrated as he narrated what happened.

Mark recalled the core trauma story he told during Session 1 of having to beg his mother for forgiveness, on his hands and knees, for hours.

> *Client:* I felt like I was charged with a murder, going to jail.
>
> *Therapist:* No way out, convicted, powerless. Tell Mom, what did that do to you, make her understand. Pay attention to your body, put words to your experience [explicit emotion coaching, guidance].

At first Mark described his experience in general terms but the therapist persisted: "Tell her what it did to you, all that harsh criticism. It's important." This process-guiding response invited Mark to engage at a deeper level of experiencing and exploration of meaning, in the context of the Reflective Storytelling marker. He said, "I have lack of confidence, little emotion, everything is bottled up, I have no respect for women, I can't be myself because I'm afraid of being wrong, like there's something wrong with me, because of you I have no confidence." This was the first time that Mark clearly acknowledged maladaptive fear as a central part of his maladaptive self-narrative. The therapist asked him to tell his mother how he felt about that. He replied, "Robbed. You did terrible things to your kid. I have no respect for you." Here the therapist empathically responded to his emotional pain, rather than his anger, to help elicit a more compassionate response to his experience as a little boy: "You hurt me deeply. Tell her what was most hurtful." But Mark's dominant emotional experience was anger at maltreatment.

> *Client:* I felt like I was a rotten kid and stupid. Is there anything worse you can do to a kid? You treated me like a piece of dirt, you scarred me.
>
> *Therapist:* How do you feel, now, saying that?
>
> *Client:* I want to grab her by the throat and say shut the f—k up.

He again collapsed into resignation. Throughout this process, his vocal quality was flat and his facial expression was blank. The therapist asked him what was going on in his body. Mark replied, "All uptight, sweating, heart racing." This is another example of the discrepancy between his internal experience and outward presentation, and it highlights the importance of therapist process-guiding inquiry to help him accurately symbolize his emotional experience. His therapist then identified and focused on adaptive anger at maltreatment as the healthy side of the struggle: "A lot going on inside, being stuffed, so angry at her for good reason, for treating you so badly. We will continue to help you express that anger rather than stuff it."

Later in the session, Mark's therapist focused on more vulnerable feelings that emerged from his trauma memory disclosure and IC dialogue with his parents. Consistent with EFTT protocol, this was expressed in interaction with his therapist rather than the imagined abusive other.

Therapist: What did you feel as a child?

Client: As a child I felt abandoned, helpless.

Therapist: Say more about that sense of helplessness.

Client: Like someone pushed you off a cliff and there was nothing you could do but fall.

Therapist: All alone, how awful for you, Mark.

This communication of compassion for his suffering was important because it strengthened the therapeutic bond and helped the client to feel truly seen and supported by his therapist. Mark then responded, "It's mostly all hate." To help move the resolution process forward and shift from secondary anger and Same Old Storytelling of blame and complaint, his therapist focused on promoting entitlement to unmet needs and accessing a new, primary adaptive emotional plotline.

Therapist: All that pain turned into hate. Like, I didn't deserve to be treated like that. I deserved to be treated like a human being.

Client: Exactly. [Mark's vocal quality was momentarily inwardly focused as if he was experiencing the impact of the therapist's words.]

Reflecting on the experience of having confronted his mother in the empty chair, Mark said he liked it but admitted that he was "saying stuff but not from my heart." He was aware that this was missing and implied that this was something he would like to change. The therapist validated his perceptions and identified emotional overcontrol as a learned way of coping that interfered with his ability to be authentic in current relationships and to resolve past issues. She suggested that the next phase of therapy would continue to focus on helping him deepen his experiencing, step-by-step, connect his head and heart, for enhanced narrative-emotion integration.

Refined Case Conceptualization

Despite his cool, detached stance, Mark's Same Old Story plotline revealed that he lacked confidence and viewed himself as defective, "an ugly person" like his mother, who was afraid to be himself for fear of being wrong and criticized. This partly accounted for his emotional overcontrol evidenced in Empty Storytelling, which he acknowledged was a problem. As evidenced in his poignant trauma memories, Mark had felt alone, abandoned, and unloved as a child and was still seeking acknowledgment of harm from his parents. He also acknowledged adaptive sadness and regret about pushing loved ones away and unmet needs for love, connection, authenticity—indicators of a new, emerging Competing Plotline that challenged the secondary anger, resentment, and blame of his Same Old Story. He used vivid metaphors to describe his emotional experience in the context of Reflective Storytelling, which provided a window into his inner world, and he had the capacity to reflect on his experience. He was motivated and engaged in the process of self-exploration. Phase 2 would focus on helping Mark to explore and change his negative view of self, to allow emotional pain, and to feel entitled to unmet needs, thereby coconstructing a more emotionally alive, coherent, and compassionate self-narrative.

CONCLUSION

In this chapter we observed the importance of therapist process-diagnostic assessment of client narrative-emotion processing difficulties and interventions to enhance more productive processing in the early phase of EFTT. These cases illustrate different approaches to effective EFTT intervention, with different client processing difficulties. In Chapter 9 we describe the middle phase of EFTT, which focuses on addressing client difficulties that emerged in early sessions. Then, in Chapter 10, we continue to follow Charlize and Mark through the middle phase of their therapies.

9

PROMOTING SELF-DEVELOPMENT: MIDDLE-PHASE EFTT

The preceding chapter introduced two individual clients whom we continue to follow over the course of therapy (Chapters 10 and 12). In this chapter we describe the diversity of narrative-emotion processing difficulties and interventions used, particularly in the middle phase of emotion-focused therapy for trauma (EFTT). Midphase EFTT consists of active work on core self-related problems, painful emotions, and client Same Old Storytelling that often emerge during initial imaginal confrontation (IC) and empathic exploration (EE) reexperiencing procedures. Key issues may include feeling overwhelmed by trauma feelings and memories; repeated collapse into resignation and powerlessness; limited awareness of or access to painful emotions; avoidance, suppression, and interruption of emotional experience and expression; minimization of harm; and difficulty feeling entitled to unmet needs. It is important to address these self-related problems, as they often are blocks to

http://dx.doi.org/10.1037/0000041-010
Narrative Processes in Emotion-Focused Therapy for Trauma, by S. C. Paivio and L. E. Angus

trauma recovery, resolution of issues with perpetrators, and emergence of new emotional plotlines that contribute to significant self-narrative change.

Accordingly, the middle phase of EFTT consists of (a) process-diagnosis assessment of prominent narrative-emotion process (NEP) markers for the facilitation of shifts from Problem to Transition and Change Storytelling modes and (b) the implementation of process-guided tasks and procedures that are designed to increase emotion and experiential awareness and narrative coherence, and to reduce fear and avoidance of emotion experience as well as shame and self-blame, for increased self-awareness, self-esteem, and self-confidence. Additionally, the emergence of primary adaptive emotions, often in the context of IC/EE dialogues, challenges the negative emotional plotlines of the clients' Same Old Storytelling and supports the implementation of new actions and the coconstruction of a more agentic, compassionate self-identity narrative. To facilitate shifts from problem to more adaptive markers by late-phase sessions, NEP Problem Storytelling markers continue to be an explicit focus of therapeutic intervention in the middle phase of EFTT. This focus is supported by recent research findings (Bryntwick, Angus, Paivio, Carpenter, & Macaulay, 2014; Carpenter, Angus, Paivio, & Bryntwick, 2016), suggesting that successful EFTT involves a client shift from problem-focused storytelling in early-phase sessions to the emergence of more frequent and dominant healthier emotional plotlines that contain adaptive emotions, needs, and action tendencies, as well as a search for—and exploration of— affective meaning and self-coherence, indicating a readiness for change. These are evidenced in NEP Transition markers such as Competing Plotline, Experiential, Inchoate, and Reflective Storytelling modes. Intervention with NEP Transitional Storytelling markers was described in Chapter 5 and is briefly reviewed in the next section.

INTERVENTION WITH TRANSITION MARKERS

First, NEP research findings indicate that Transition markers occurred most frequently in middle-phase EFTT sessions for clients who recovered from trauma symptoms and resolved issues with perpetrators by treatment termination (Bryntwick et al., 2014; Carpenter et al., 2016). Therefore, key treatment goals in midphase therapy include (a) increasing client reflection and awareness (Reflective and Inchoate Storytelling) and integration of emotional meaning into their trauma story (Experiential Storytelling) and (b) accessing and expressing new adaptive emotional plotlines (Competing Plotline Storytelling) that hold perpetrators responsible for their actions and reduce maladaptive shame and self-blame. This adaptive information destabilizes clients' maladaptive Same Old Stories for the emergence of new views of self and self-understanding. It is important to note that NEP Transition markers set the stage for self-narrative change observed in the disclosure of Unexpected Outcome and Discovery Storytelling Change markers that predominate in late-phase EFTT sessions (Bryntwick et al., 2014; Carpenter et al., 2016).

EXPERIENTIAL STORYTELLING MARKERS

With the empathic support and encouragement of the therapist, Experiential Storytelling involves the intentional exploration of specific autobiographical memories of either (a) past traumatic events that contributed to the development of a client's core maladaptive emotion scheme or (b) more recent, troubling events wherein the maladaptive scheme was activated in the context of interpersonal relationships. Interventions help clients to access and describe a detailed, vivid image of the unfolding narrative scene to activate an emotional reexperiencing, rather than simply a retelling, of trauma memories in therapy sessions. To promote an integrative reexperiencing of the trauma memory, therapist responses focus on directing clients' attention to the feelings, sensations, and expectations that emerge in the context of narrating their stories for heightened emotional differentiation and narrative coherence that support further reflective self-exploration, new meaning making, and self-narrative change.

Basic intervention guidelines include the following:

- Bring the scene or situation alive to evoke the emotion structure. Encourage the client to provide vivid sensorial descriptions that are personal and specific.
- Direct attention to internal experience during the situation— bodily experience, thoughts, perceptions, and feelings. Help the client to regulate emotion as necessary—intensify or decrease.
- Direct attention to presently felt adult experience, their reaction to and reflection on the experience, and question feelings and perceptions at the time.

For example, in her response to her therapist's empathic support to disclose the memories that are "etched so deeply in her mind," Monica begins to disclose her painful childhood memory of discovering the body of her mother, who had committed suicide, in the family home. In the following therapy session sequence, her therapist empathically supports Monica as she discloses these events and elaborates their emotional impact. Her therapist uses a series of process-guiding responses to help Monica coconstruct a detailed unfolding of the sequence of events that frame the suicide scene for heightened narrative coherence and to differentiate specific emotions, intentions, and appraisals experienced in the context of the scene for new meaning making.

Client: The night she killed herself. It's so clear, I can remember everything.

Therapist: Just like it happened yesterday . . .

Client: I was walking toward the house, and um, it was quiet and I walk up the sidewalk and open the front door very carefully and listen, still nothing, just the sound in my eardrums [experiential awareness].

Therapist: This deafening silence [empathic evocative reflection].

Client: So quiet, and I'm thinking this is really berserk, really crazy, because usually my brother and sister would be there.

Therapist: Mmm.

Client: And I remember walking in and still nothing, and thinking this is really funny, and I took my boots off and I went down into kitchen and I saw my mother's foot first and—I was in absolute shock and not knowing what to do.

Therapist: And your heart almost stopped [evocative empathy].

Client: And I started shouting because I thought my sister was supposed to be there and I started screaming for my sister and I was frightened to call anybody because you know your own business stays within the four walls of your house so . . .

Therapist: Sure.

Client: I'm sure it was only a minute but it seemed like 10 hours.

Therapist: So then you walked in and saw what had actually happened [therapist invites a return to elaboration of unfolding plotline for heightened narrative coherence].

Client: I tried waking her up, and I'm just shaking her and shaking her and trying to wake her up, and thinking you know, oh God, what do I do, who do I call, what do I do?

Therapist: Mmm, the horror of it.

Client: So the first thing I did, I called my uncle, and he came over, and of course when he came in, my heart also goes out to him because I can't imagine myself now walking in on a situation like that.

In this sequence both the client and therapist collaborate in a coconstructed account of the unfolding trauma scene in the context of a narrative storytelling structure that now includes a beginning, middle, and end. Additionally, a clear scene and setting is provided along with the internal bodily felt experiences of the protagonist. For the first time, an experientially integrated, coherent narrative of her trauma memory begins to take shape for Monica. Finally, in the context of Experiential Storytelling, it is important to note that both client and therapist contributed to a coelaboration of emotions, intentions, and expectations that the client experienced at the time of her mother's suicide.

Another example is the client Richard, who had been molested by a priest, as described in a previous chapter and volume on EFTT (Paivio & Pascual-Leone, 2010). Richard could not understand why he did not disclose the abuse or quit the church, and the therapist's initially conceptualizing this as self-blame was not helpful. Rather, effective intervention involved helping him to reexperience a situation when he left the priest and sat by himself in a playground weighing his options, trying to figure out what to do. He reexperienced himself as a trapped, powerless boy, with no good options except to try and avoid the priest as best he could. This helped him construct a more coherent narrative that made sense of his behavior at the time.

Another marker for initiating reexperiencing procedures is painful recent situations in which the core maladaptive sense of self was evoked. An example is a client who was in therapy to deal with social anxiety stemming from severe emotional abuse and degradation by a highly critical and demanding father. At the beginning of one session, she recalled being at an event with her husband's colleagues when she was overwhelmed by feeling like a complete loser, small and insignificant, uninteresting, and shrinking away, just like she had as a child with her father (Same Old Story). Intervention involved having the client disclose and reexperience her autobiographical memory of the recent social event, provide external details of the situation, as well as her thoughts, feelings, sensations and perceptions before and during the event. She recalled feeling self-conscious about her clothes; she was underdressed, must look like "a hick," then worrying that she would not have anything interesting to say or be able to keep the conversation going, and so on. Eventually, she said, "Why do I always feel like I have to be scintillating? Like what's wrong with just being average?" This questioning or challenging of the Same Old Story emerged from reexperiencing the situation in which her core maladaptive emotion scheme involving fear and shame was activated. This leads to further exploration to help her answer these questions and construct a new self-narrative, which included increased self-acceptance and confidence.

INCHOATE STORYTELLING MARKERS

Inchoate Storytelling is identified when clients are engaged in a halting, emergent experiential search for words to articulate their inner felt experiences in therapy sessions. Inchoate Storytelling often emerges in context of role-play interventions and the emergence of Reflective and Experiential Storytelling modes. Interventions with Inchoate Storytelling involve a collaborative, coconstructive search for the right words to symbolize and describe emergent primary adaptive emotions, needs, and action tendencies that support the discovery of new views of self and self-narrative change. This type of storytelling is distinctly different from problem-focused markers described in the preceding chapter, in which clients provide nonverbal indicators of the emerging painful emotions that they try to suppress, avoid, or dissociate from. Alternatively, Inchoate Storytelling can also emerge in the context of experiential focusing interventions that help clients focus on an unclear bodily felt sense and construction of new meaning (Gendlin, 1997). We describe an example of this next.

REFLECTIVE STORYTELLING

Reflective Storytelling involves exploration of the meaning of clients' experience—causes, interpretations, effects on self. Reflective Storytelling markers are indicators of higher levels of experiencing, in which clients are constructing new meaning in the process of exploring problems about the self. Reflective Storytelling functions as a check-in on the client's understanding of experience as it currently stands, including emerging emotions, interpretations, connections between events, and meaning. This moves the process along by revealing points of conflict or confusion and missing information, perhaps evoking the disclosure of a specific autobiographical memory and/or inviting further self-reflectivity and meaning making. By inviting the client to put pieces together but with some reflective distance, this storytelling mode reveals "what else is missing or incoherent," which acts to string together and catalyze shifts between other Transition and Change markers. Therapist interventions involve empathic responding and questions to help scaffold the client's search for meaning and coconstruct a new self-narrative.

The following is an example of shifting from Competing Plotline to Inchoate and Reflective Storytelling and the emergence of self-narrative change. This occurred in Session 11 with a client who had been emotionally abused and neglected by her alcoholic mother. She began by telling the story of an argument with one of her daughters and trying to understand the appropriate way to respond to her—should she let it go or confront her daughter (Competing Plotline)? In the context of this narrative, the therapist shifts the focus to exploring issues with her mother and shifts the process to more Reflective Storytelling.

Therapist: So it's like struggling, I don't know which way to go [identifies Competing Plotline]. So what if your mom said something to you like you say to your kids. You would probably have pushed her away still even though she tried to get close because, what? I don't trust these tries to be intimate [evocative empathy].

Client: That's really good because [pause, thoughtful, reflective] any steps she would have taken toward me I would have pushed her away because . . .

In the following excerpt, the therapist invites exploration and helps the client shift to exploring and accessing new emotional experience in the context of further Reflective Storytelling.

Therapist: OK, so what could she do, or not do, that would make you want to draw closer to her?

Client: Not need me [thoughtful, exploratory, searching internal experience]. But I mean she couldn't have done anything, because she took up all the space.

Therapist: Mm hm, how did she do that? [promote specificity and further exploration].

Client: It was a feeling thing, this neediness.

Therapist: So there was a neediness, like wanting something? What did she do exactly? [silence, thoughtful]. I know it's hard to put into words . . .

Client: Wow, words for this! Because she didn't *do* anything. She was always saying how beautiful I was and how smart I was, and I liked that, but hearing it was [pause, searching], it's like she's too focused on me or something? [pause, shaking head, searching inside] How did she fill up all that space? So that it would make me turn away?

This is Inchoate Storytelling. The therapist is attentive, following, offering minimal encouragers as the client searches.

Client: It's like her whole being . . . the only thing I can come up with is I didn't like who she was [silence, client sustains an internal focus].

Therapist: If we stick with the things you have identified, it's almost like in every gesture you felt this neediness coming from her, and you felt this desire to create space?

Here the therapist is providing guidance, scaffolding the clients search for words and inviting the client to shift to a Reflective Storytelling mode.

Client: Yes, it was like first I was going to be a . . .

Therapist: Sounds like . . . molding your identity or . . . intrusive . . .

Client: Very, it would be like her trying to be me, trying to get in my back and move my arms and my head and . . .

Therapist: Just control everything you do.

At this point the coconstructive process results in emerging self-narrative change and Discovery Storytelling.

Client: Yes! So that's controlling, getting in and directing, of course it is. I never put that word to it. So this is what I mean how I never had a chance to know how I felt, be myself.

PROMOTING REFLECTIVE STORYTELLING IN EXPERIENTIAL FOCUSING PROCEDURE

Recall that the Client Experiencing Scale (Klein, Mathieu-Coughlan, & Keisler, 1986) identifies steps in shifting problem narratives that are external and behaviorally focused, to those containing more personal and affective material, to those that are increasingly exploratory and reflective. The highest level experiencing involves constructing new meaning evident in Discovery Storytelling narratives.

Experiential focusing (Gendlin, 1997) is a semistructured procedure designed to facilitate this shift and deepening of experiencing. The process begins with client confusion or lack of clarity about experience, then focuses on bodily felt sense, a search for the right words to describe this felt sense, then exploring the meaning of accurately labeled experience and constructing a coherent narrative that makes sense of the experience. This can be taught to clients with emotion awareness skills deficits observed in Empty Storytelling. Alternately, the principle of focusing can be used in the narrative coconstruction process throughout therapy; principles of intervention for deepening experiencing were presented in Chapter 6. Numerous instructions for conducting focusing are available through a Google search and can be tailored to meet individual client needs. Here we focus on features that are common across these variations.

Steps in the Focusing Procedure

The basic focusing procedure is characterized by the following five steps, which result in increased self-awareness and coconstruction of a coherent narrative concerning previously unclear or confusing experience.

1. *Invite the client to explore.* The client is unclear or confused about internal experience; for example, the client feels upset but is not clear what it is about, and there is vague experience with no

narrative content. Intervention involves an invitation to "Let's try to understand what that's all about."

2. *Focus on bodily felt sense.* Help the client find a comfortable position, relax, take a few deep breaths, close his or her eyes or rest his or her gaze on a fixed point. Ask the client to focus on their bodily felt sense, "Go inside. Where in your body do you feel those feelings, your chest or belly for example? Perhaps put your hand on that place. Stay with that bodily felt sense."

3. *Search for symbols.* Explore possible labels or symbols to describe the experience. Encourage an attitude of patient waiting for words or symbols to emerge. "Is there a word or symbol that emerges from that feeling? Don't force anything. Let your body speak." This can involve explicitly encouraging the client to "stay out of your head, let your body speak, if your body could speak what it telling you." The narrative is Inchoate, disjointed, searching. Therapist empathic responses scaffold the search process.

4. *Check the fit.* Check the fit of labels or symbols until the right words to describe the experience are found. This is like the "tip of the tongue" experience followed by relief once the right words are found. The therapist helps the client to accept the experience and the label, whatever emerges, without judgment.

5. *Reflect on meaning.* The final stage in the focusing process involves fleshing out and reflecting on the meaning of the accurately identified internal experience so that it makes sense (Discovery Storytelling). The therapist helps the client to coconstruct a coherent narrative.

An example of using the structured focusing procedure in EFTT took place with a client who had a history of emotional and physical abuse by her father and husband. She constantly pressured herself to achieve, came to therapy with "packaged" problems to look like a good client, found it difficult to identify her feelings, and engaged in intellectual Empty Storytelling, The therapist suggested the focusing procedure to increase her ability to identify feelings in the moment and directed her to focus on her bodily experience. At first the client focused on the soft, relaxed breathing in her belly, but this quickly shifted to worry that she felt nothing in her chest. The therapist encouraged her to put the worry aside for the moment and just observe her chest ("Did it stay the same, or change?"). The client then noticed a feeling of warmth and recalled the warmth of therapeutic touch she experienced when she was being treated for breast cancer. The therapist asked her not to go into the memory but rather to stay with this "healing warmth" and what it was telling her. The client said it was telling her she was okay, everything was alright, and it was a feeling of being "alive." The therapist repeated these words and encouraged her to stay with, savor, and speak from the new experience. Quickly the client interrupted her experience and began pressuring herself, "This is childish, a waste of time, I should be doing something . . ." Thus the focusing process shifted from Inchoate Storytelling to Discovery of an experience of well-being, to a Competing Plotline Story—the client's core struggle between adaptive well-being and pressuring herself to do more. Further therapeutic work involved starting sessions with the focusing procedure to increase the client's ability to attend to her internal experience in the moment, as well as repeatedly activating this core struggle through the use of a two-chair dialogue intervention and strengthening the adaptive side of the struggle, the part of her that needed to feel okay and savor the feeling of being "alive."

COMPETING PLOTLINE STORYTELLING MARKER

Competing Plotline Story indicators can include conflict, struggle, or tension between an old maladaptive pattern of thoughts, thoughts, feelings, and behaviors and the emergence of healthy resources—feelings, needs, action tendencies, and perceptions of self and others. These healthy resources challenge and destabilize the dominant Same Old Story and negative view of self (e.g., damaged, too needy, blameworthy, worthless, unlovable) for the emergence of new, more satisfying ways of being in the world and view of self. Competing Plotlines Storytelling markers capture the emotional and narrative incoherence frequently expressed by complex trauma clients.

Recent research findings have indicated a significantly higher predominance of Competing Plotline markers in mid/working phase sessions for recovered EFTT clients compared with unrecovered clients who had a higher proportion of Problem Empty Storytelling markers in midphase sessions (Carpenter et al., 2016). This suggests that the emergence of this storytelling mode can be an indicator of client readiness for change and implementation of two-chair and IC/EE dialogue interventions to strengthen the healthy side of the conflict. This is especially so when a client's new, more agentic voice of protest against abuse and maltreatment, "I really want to leave and walk out that door, and he will never touch me again," is noticed and focused on by a therapist for further elaboration, heightened emotional engagement, and new meaning making. Hager (1992) suggested that client confusion, anxiety, and ambivalence may be a sign of in-session productivity. This may explain why the recovered clients evinced a higher proportion of this marker in the working phase of therapy, in contrast to the unchanged clients, who may not have engaged as productively in midphase therapy because of a propensity to emotionally avoid and withdraw.

Accordingly, EFTT intervention for Completing Plotline markers involves helping clients identify the core conflict or struggle expressed in their storytelling and directing their attention to (and empathically supporting) the expression of new adaptive emotional responses, needs, and actions; it challenges the emotional "truth" of clients' repetitive maladaptive narratives and sets the stage for articulation of a new view of self (Discovery Storytelling) and new story outcomes, particularly resolution of issues with significant others (Unexpected Outcome).

An example of an intervention with a Competing Plotline marker was observed in therapy with the client Marianne,[1] who volunteered to participate in a single demonstration session of EFTT. This session was produced by the American Psychological Association (APA, 2013). Marianne had been exposed to severe domestic violence in her early years, which included her father beating her mother, threatening to murder the family, and using guns. The client was mute for several years as a child and held back in school, indicating severe trauma exposure. At the time of the session, she was functioning well but still experiencing distress and symptoms of posttraumatic stress disorder (flashback, nightmares) when she was reminded of these experiences. At the beginning of the session, she stated that she struggled with a conflict: Should she sweep her feelings under the rug or process them? This competing emotional plotline indicated that there was a part of her that believed she should process and not ignore her feelings.

Although Marianne initially told the story of her childhood experiences in a matter-of-fact, detached manner (Empty Storytelling), her feelings became increasingly close to the surface and her use of metaphors gave access to her inner world. For example, tears welled in her eyes as she described herself as a "little girl in a dungeon" and recalled a recurring nightmare of her mother being eaten by a shark. The therapist empathically responded, "Very scary and sad, still affects you." The client then deliberately suppressed emerging tears and minimized the harm: "I don't want to cry. It could be worse because I was protected. My mother left the marriage, and I have a good life today." Effective intervention involved helping her to allow the painful feelings she has begun to approach, first by validating the struggle to suppress and then by encouraging expression of her "true self." The process of helping her to allow emotional pain is presented later in this chapter. Once allowed and tolerated, new information about how one has been wounded can be processed and integrated into a new self-narrative in which the trauma

---

[1]For the purposes of this book, the client's name has been changed to protect her identity.

is accepted as part of who she is. The quality of her early narrative processes, with immediate access to adaptive resources, suggests that Marianne would be a good candidate for short-term EFFT.

Another example of Competing Plotlines Storytelling was described in Chapter 8 on the case of Charlize, who found herself experiencing a confusing array of emotions in relation to her husband's new expression of affection and caring toward her during the past week.

> Client: I was feeling like, "Why am I feeling angry when [my husband is] around, when that's what I've always wanted?"
>
> Therapist: Yes, something I've been asking for all along.
>
> Client: Yes. Isn't that strange?

Charlize expressed puzzlement and surprise about her own reaction to her husband's affectionate desire to be physically close to her, and her therapist responded empathically, highlighted her emotional reaction, and invited a shift to reflective exploration and differentiation of that new feeling.

> Therapist: Strange?
>
> Client: That I would feel kind of annoyed.
>
> Therapist: Maybe there is something like "I'm not used to this, even though this is what I wanted"?
>
> Client: Mhm. I was also trying to . . . sort of protect myself too, you know? How long is this going to last? Am I going to set myself up for disappointment again?

In her inquiry, Charlize externalized the voice of the Same Old Story that expressed her fears of being let down again, in terms of having her emotional needs met, and at the same time revealed the emergence of a new emotional plotline and action tendency: "But when it continued, I relaxed a little bit." Her therapist immediately identified her expression of a new, primary adaptive emotion and action tendency as the emergence of a Competing Plotline Story marker and highlighted both the emotional meaning of her new adaptive response ("The other side of it, really getting excited, happy about what you're experiencing.") and the fears that those feelings evoke, and needing to protect herself, in the context of the negative plotlines of her childhood Same Old Story of being let down once again.

> Therapist: But there is a nagging feeling of . . .
>
> Client: I was just cautious.
>
> Therapist: I might lose this? That's pulling you in a different direction from feeling good about things.

Guidelines for implementing specific EFTT procedures facilitating client engagement in productive NEP Transition markers, especially during the middle phase of EFTT, are described next. Procedures include two-chair dialogues, reexperiencing and restorying trauma memories, allowing emotional pain, and accessing self-soothing in conjunction with IC/EE interventions.

COMPETING PLOTLINE STORYTELLING MARKERS AND TWO-CHAIR DIALOGUES

Two-chair dialogues are used in EFTT to resolve internal conflicts or struggles between a dominant maladaptive part of self and a less dominant, healthy, experiencing part of self—key indicators of Competing Plotline Transition markers. For example, self-criticism involves a conflict between negative beliefs about self that erode self-esteem that were observed in the Same Old Story and healthy rebellion or protest against these beliefs (e.g., "I don't deserve that harsh criticism.") and need for self-respect. The goal is to support the part of self that does not believe the self-criticism and constructs a more adaptive self-narrative. Another conflict is self-interruption, which involves a struggle to suppress emerging adaptive feelings of anger or sadness. The goal is to support the expression of the healthy experiencing side of the new emotional plotline, the adaptive feelings and needs, to construct a more coherent and emotionally alive self-narrative.

Effective intervention with all competing emotional plotlines involves first accurately identifying the essential conflict or struggle in the client's narrative—for example, is the client eroding his or her self-esteem, making himself or herself feel afraid or anxious, or invalidating or squashing self-experience. Self-doubt and self-interruption are easily observed as competing emotional plotlines—healthy feelings and perceptions emerge in the client's storytelling and are immediately squashed, suppressed, or invalidated. Self-criticism and anxiety, on the other hand, may not initially be observed as a conflict, but rather as negative and maladaptive beliefs about self and others that are part of the core maladaptive emotion scheme that emerges in the Same Old Story. Two-chair dialogues are used to activate the alternative healthy part of self, the part of self that does not believe the criticism, that finds it unfair, untrue, or too extreme, and to shift the Same Old Story into a Competing Plotline with the potential for change. Once again, the goal is to strengthen the healthy part of self so that an alternate side of the story can be integrated into a new narrative.

Two-chair dialogues are helpful when there are specific criticisms or fears, but not so helpful when one needs to explore and change a core or deeply engrained shame-based sense of self as defective, worthless, unlovable, or dirty. Intensifying these extremely damaging and painful messages to self can be retraumatizing, and the core sense of self frequently is not associated with specific self-critical messages (see Chapter 5 on emotion typology). This core self-organization is best restructured through reexperiencing procedures and memory work.

Steps that are common to all two-chair intervention processes, regardless of the nature of the conflict or struggle, are outlined next. It is important to note, as is observed in the case of Charlize in the following chapter, that these steps guide the process, with or without the use of chairs. Criteria for promoting high-quality engagement in two-chair dialogues are the same as those for engagement in IC presented in Chapter 8. These include psychological contact between parts of the self (i.e., looking at and directing expression to the other chair, use of I–you language), spontaneous elaboration and meaning exploration, and emotional experience and expression.

Steps in the Process of Two-Chair Dialogues

The following nine steps act as guidelines for conducting two-chair dialogues regardless of the specific internal conflict or struggle that is the focus of intervention.

1. *Structure the dialogue.* Structure the dialogue between parts of self in two chairs facing each other. Begin with the maladaptive part of self that gives voice to the maladaptive Same Old Story plotline.
2. *Express the negative side of the story.* In this step, the client is encouraged to express maladaptive self-appraisals and feelings about the self (e.g., anger, contempt, distrust) directly to the less dominant experiencing part of self. Intensity and specificity are increased by providing examples of situations that support the maladaptive perspective. The goal is to increase awareness of the harsh criticism or fearful suppression in the maladaptive self-narrative and to increase awareness of agency in producing bad feelings of shame, guilt, or being stifled, for example, in the less dominant experiencing part of self.
3. *Experience and express the impact of the negative perspective.* In this step, intervention directs the client's attention to the experiential responses of the emerging, adaptive emotional plotline (the subdominant part of self). The goal is to increase awareness of the negative effects of maladaptive beliefs and feelings toward self and to express the negative impact of that voice, to the dominant side, "make him or her (the dominant part of yourself) understand." Give this side a voice.

4. *Intensify negative messages.* At this step in the process, interventions intensify or exaggerate the negative messages of the dominant self to evoke a reaction in the experiencing self, an alternative healthy response—new emotional plotline—that will challenge or shift the maladaptive self-narrative, for example, rebellion or protest against the self-criticism or suppression of self-experience. This can be accomplished by heightening client awareness of nonverbal aspects of the negative message, such as a sneer of contempt or finger wagging, and the extremity of the maladaptive perspective (e.g., "Never express your feelings, better to stay locked up inside." and "Don't take a risk, it would kill you to fail.").

5. *Deeply experience and express the new perspective.* It is essential to help the client really feel or experience the truth of this new alternative way of viewing the self; it is not simply an intellectual affirmation. This new perspective, this side of the argument, is then communicated to the dominant part of self. As in all EFTT interventions, expression emerges from experience. One question that emerges is what to do when a healthy part of self does not spontaneously emerge, when there is no competing plotline. This can be particularly troubling at the end of a session or therapy when you do not want the client to be overwhelmed by bad feelings. In these instances, the therapist can ask, for example, "Is there any little part of you that does not believe," "How would a friend react if they heard you saying that to yourself?" or "What would you say to a child who held those negative beliefs about and feelings toward self?" The goal is to strengthen that alternative voice.

6. *Express the need of experiencing self.* At this step, the client is encouraged to express the heartfelt need of the healthy part of self, for example, for self-esteem, confidence, or expression to the other side (e.g., "What do you want/need from this part of yourself?"). Interventions help the client to elaborate on the importance of this more adaptive perspective, the positive effects on self (e.g., "Make him understand how important this is to you.") and specify ways in which the dominant side can meet the need, be supportive.

7. *Promote understanding of both sides of the story.* The next step is to promote understanding of both sides of the client's Competing Plotline Story. Often the dominant maladaptive part of the self-narrative will shift to represent values and standards, for example, a desire to protect or motivate self.

8. *Negotiate a new interaction and self-narrative.* The final step in resolving the conflict involves negotiating a new interaction between parts of self, co-constructing a new, more adaptive, integrative self-narrative about self that includes adaptive experience (feelings and meanings and actions). This now becomes a new Discovery Story, a key indicator of NEP change. Therapist empathic responses help the client coconstruct this new self-narrative. Interventions also help the client to bridge to possible situations outside of therapy when the maladaptive voice emerges and to develop strategies for how to handle, stand up to, or challenge the old maladaptive narrative (Same Old Story).

9. *Switch to IC/EE.* When the dominant maladaptive side of the self is an internalized negative other or perpetrator, the client can be encouraged to assertively express a new perspective or view of self to the imagined negative other.

TWO-CHAIR DIALOGUE FOR COMPETING PLOTLINE INVOLVING SELF-CRITICISM

An example of Competing Plotline Storytelling involving harsh self-criticism and the implementation of a two-chair intervention was observed with the client Kristen,[2] who volunteered to participate in a single demonstration session of EFTT. This video is available from the American Psychological Association (2015). Kristen had a history of sexual molestation and emotional abuse by her father. She managed to leave home at age 16 but still had recurring traumatic memories of being locked in a closet, as well as nightmares, and continued to feel guilty about leaving her sister behind, even though she eventually was able to get her sister out of the home and take her father to court. This guilt is part of the Same Old Story, and by helping Kristen to access and express more adaptive emotions, we facilitate a transition to a new Competing Emotional Plotline, and the explicit assertion of unmet needs and that support a new view of self. The following is an abbreviated transcript from the published tape. The first step is to structure the dialogue.

> *Therapist:* One of the most common, and tragic, outcomes is victims feel guilty and responsible. It might be useful for us to work on that and help you come to terms with those feelings ["Yes"]. I am going to suggest you carry on a dialogue between two parts of yourself, the part that makes you feel guilty, says

---

[2] For the purposes of this book, the client's name has been changed to protect her identity.

certain things like "you should have protected her" and the other part that feels bad, guilty. We'll start over here with the guilt-producing part [*directs client to switch chairs*]. Here's Kristen who was not able to protect her sister [*points to experiencing chair*], and from here [critic chair] what do you say to make yourself feel guilty? You should have . . . ?

Here the client directed her response to the therapist, who then directed her to make contact with the other part of self to promote awareness of agency.

Therapist: Do it to her so you experience how it works inside you. You should . . .

The following sequence illustrates therapist empathic responding and process-directives to help increase Kristen's awareness of maladaptive feelings and beliefs about herself in the context of Same Old Storytelling.

Client: You should have told someone, shouldn't have left.

Therapist: So if you hadn't left, these things wouldn't have happened to your sister. Say more about what you should have done [promote specificity].

Client: [*sighs*] You should have fought back, you could have stopped him.

Therapist: How do you feel toward her, this part of yourself, that she didn't fight back?

Client: I'm angry.

Therapist: Angry.

Client: Yes, You should have been able to stand up for your family.

Here the client's tone of voice is chastising, and she is pointing her finger at the other part of herself in the other chair as she talks. The therapists directed her attention to these nonverbal expressions to increase awareness of the affective quality of her self-criticism and help evoke an adaptive reaction in the other side of self.

Therapist: Notice your tone of voice is kind of lecturing and you're finger-pointing?

Client: Yes [*laughs*].

Therapist: You get it?

Client: Yes.

In the following sequence, therapist process directives helped elicit the painful reaction of Kristen's experiencing self and promoted client agency by helping her to feel the impact of maladaptive feelings and beliefs directed at herself.

Therapist: So come over here [points to experiencing chair]. How do you feel hearing that you should have done something?

Client: It's just like my dad saying that. I feel like I'm not worthwhile [eyes tear up], just weak, like a "nobody," like I'm just not worth it [here the interjected critic, the core maladaptive emotion scheme in the Same Old Story is activated].

Therapist: OK, so when you say those things to me [points to critic chair], I feel weak and worthless, like a "nobody"?

Client: I feel bad and I agree with you.

Therapist: I feel like it's true.

In the following sequence, the therapist is intensifying the maladaptive message directed toward herself to activate an alternative healthy response and articulation of a new primary adaptive emotional plotline.

Therapist: OK, come over here again [points to critic chair]. Do it some more. Make her feel guilty. You're weak . . .

Client: You're not worth anything, you're stupid, you're . . . [long pause]

Therapist: What's happening [hand on heart].

Client: I hear his voice [weeps]. And then I remember all the things he used to say to me.

Therapist: You hear your father's voice and this hurts, makes you cry. So you have learned to say these things to yourself ["Mm hmm"]. It's like your father in your head, beating you up, putting you down ["Mm hmm"].

The following sequence illustrates directing attention to and promoting client full experience of the healthy reactions, the alternative to the maladaptive self-narrative, and communication of this experience to the other part of self. The therapist then deliberately coaches healthy protest to shift the maladaptive self-narrative.

Therapist: Come over here [points to experiencing chair]. What do you want to say to those put-downs, the father in your head?

Client: Well, it's not true.

Therapist: Stay with that. Tell him, this part of yourself, what is true.

Client: I am strong.

Therapist: Tell all the ways in which you are strong, make him understand.

Here the therapist was promoting specificity in the storytelling to increase emotional engagement. The client recounted several examples of the client's strength, and the therapist directed her attention to her internal experience recalling these situations. "Can you really feel the truth of that?" In terms of promoting change, it is critically important that clients fully experience these internally generated challenges for them to be integrated into a new self-narrative. This is a distinguishing feature of EFT compared with a cognitive–behavioral therapy approach to self-criticism in which challenges to maladaptive cognitions are generated top down and clients are encouraged to experience the truth of these challenges outside the session.

Just as in the initial IC/EE procedure, clients typically do not complete all the steps in the two-chair dialogue process outlined previously. Instead, clients repeatedly cycle through the steps in subsequent sessions, moving closer toward resolution of the conflict and full integration of healthy resources. Nonetheless, it is important to bring a satisfactory close to the process at the end of each session. This involves processing the client's experience of the procedure and bridging to the future. For many clients, the first two-chair intervention will simply heighten awareness of their painful self-criticism. Effective intervention involves reassuring them that this is an important beginning that will contribute to reducing self-criticism in subsequent sessions. Homework can involve observing their internal experience when that critical voice emerges between sessions. The session is closed with appropriate attention to emotion-regulation capacity between sessions as needed. Importantly, procedures that heighten self-critical processes are not appropriate for clients who have no access to adaptive resources or are suicidal.

In Kristen's case, at the end of the session she said she did not realize how much her father's voice was still in her head—this was her new learning (Discovery Story). When asked how she was going to handle situations when she heard that critical voice, Kristen said she would recall all the things she said in session, about being strong. The therapist supported her strategy and encouraged her to not only recall the words and know it in her head, but also to feel it in her heart: "This is where it will take root." In an extended course of EFTT, this dialogue and process would need to be repeated for the client to fully integrate, at a deeply experiential level, the new feelings and beliefs into a new self-narrative. Therapy with Kristen would likely move into an IC with her father.

TWO-CHAIR DIALOGUE FOR COMPETING PLOTLINE INVOLVING SELF-INTERRUPTION

An example of working with self-interruptive processes occurred with the client Violet, who had difficulty confronting her emotionally abusive mother in IC. Initially, remembering her mother's cruel verbal abuse evoked feelings of hurt, anger, and sadness. When asked to stay in touch with her sadness and to elaborate, she shut down and interrupted her experience: "I draw a blank, feel like I am pushing it away." Her narrative now involved an obvious struggle between two parts of the self, a Competing Plotline between emerging feelings and suppression or avoidance of this experience. The therapist identified the struggle between parts of self—"so many deep feelings, but part of you is pushing it away"—and structured a two-chair dialogue to explore the conflict and help Violet allow healthy anger and sadness and construct a self-narrative that includes her strong feelings. The following excerpt illustrates therapist process directives to access the negative messages of the dominant self and use of evocative empathy to exaggerate the negative message and potentially evoke an adaptive reaction, the healthy side of the emotional plotline.

Therapist: What do you say to this part of you that feels, how do you push it away?

Client: Don't go there . . . pretend it didn't happen.

Therapist: Pretend, be a phony. Why, tell her why she should not go there.

Client: It's scary.

Therapist: Scary. Tell her the bad things that will happen if she expresses her feelings [elicits specificity].

Client: You will feel weak . . . it scares me that she will know what I am saying here.

Therapist: So do not speak your truth.

Client: It's too hard, easier to pretend.

The following except again illustrates intervention to intensify the negative messages to evoke a reaction, alternative adaptive feelings and needs, in the experiencing self, then helping the client to express this new experience and perspective to the interrupting part of self.

Therapist: You don't want to feel vulnerable. So don't let it out. Never open up about your feelings

Client: It sounds awful!

Therapist: So the other part of you says it sounds awful. Switch chairs. Tell her what's awful about never speaking your truth.

Client: It doesn't make sense to not talk about it, bottling it up.

Therapist: Tell her the benefits of talking about it [specificity].

Client: You will get it off your chest.

> *Therapist:* How does it feel to bottle up [integrate affect into this side of the story]?
>
> *Client:* I don't like feeling all tense and bottled up. I want to get it off my chest. I would feel lighter.
>
> *Therapist:* So better to express.

This is a marker for switching back to IC with her mother, encouraging the expression of previously interrupted experience. Typical of the early phase of interpersonal resolution, Violet expressed blame and complaint to her imagined mother: "You're like a child . . ." The therapist differentiated this reaction and helped Violet express adaptive anger. She encouraged her to recall a specific event with her mother, an autobiographical memory, to deepen her emotional engagement. Violet recalled an incident in which her mother cruelly insulted and degraded her younger sister, called her fat, and insisted she eat out of the dog bowl.

> *Therapist:* Tell Mom how you feel remembering her cruelty.
>
> *Client:* You have no right to talk to her that way . . . it's so damaging . . . you should want the best for your kids . . . you are a bully.

The therapist supported her increased assertiveness and promoted increased sense of entitlement to unmet needs.

In processing the therapy experience at the end of the session, Violet acknowledged she had a lot more to say, that she did not want to keep living in the past, wanted to be herself: "I won't let her bully me anymore." This was the beginning of increased awareness of authentic feelings and needs to construct a new narrative involving assertive expression, from the heart. With clients like Violet, working through self-interruptive processes and reengagement in IC typically continues over several sessions.

ALLOWING EMOTIONAL PAIN TO CONSTRUCT EXPERIENTIAL AND REFLECTIVE NARRATIVES

An early step in the process of approaching emotional pain involves work with Empty Stories or Competing Plotline Stories in which clients deliberately suppress or interrupt painful emotion that is in conscious awareness. Intervention principles (see Chapter 6) to help clients allow painful emotional experience include the following: use gradual exposure, affirm vulnerability, provide encouragement and support, offer evocative empathic responses followed by deepening experiencing in the exploration phase. The goal is to help the client construct a new narrative about self (and others) that includes painful affect and associated meaning, an understanding of how one has been wounded, and implications for healing. As such, the painful experience does not dominate but is integrated into one's life story (this is part of who I am). Allowing emotional pain and self-soothing (described in a later section) often go hand in hand because, once allowed, the client must have access to self-soothing resources to help him or her tolerate the pain.

The process of allowing emotional pain has been documented through observational research (Greenberg & Safran, 1987) and qualitative research on clients' experience of allowing emotional pain (Bolger, 1999; Greenberg & Bolger, 2001). Convergence of these research findings resulted in the following steps and intervention that were originally presented in the EFTT treatment manual by Paivio and Pascual-Leone (2010).

Steps in the Process of Allowing Emotional Pain

The following are steps in the process of helping clients to allow previously suppressed or avoided painful emotional experience so that the meaning of the painful emotion can be understood and integrated into a more coherent self-narrative. The process of helping clients to allow emotional pain is not a specific intervention, but rather occurs over the course of therapy in the context of storytelling and different specific interventions or procedures.

1. *Approach*. Clients gradually approach painful experience. This is a process of gradual exposure beginning in early therapy sessions with disclosure of situations involving, for example, rejection, humiliation, or loss that may be Empty of emotional arousal. Intervention involves provision of safety and evocative empathy to increase arousal and activation of the emotion scheme and shift the client to Competing Plotline Storytelling. Interventions also validate client fear when they deflect away from experiencing emotional pain.

2. *Allow*. At some point (once they feel safe and rebel against the constriction), clients make a conscious decision to relinquish emotional overcontrol and allow painful feelings to wash over them. At this point, arousal levels are high. Interventions provide encouragement and support and empathic affirmation of their vulnerability in the process. This permits more Experiential Storytelling in the next step.

3. *Tolerate*. Clients can quickly shift away from emotional pain. However, they need to be able to tolerate the experience to explore and understand its meaning and begin to construct a new self-narrative. Interventions provide encouragement and

support to help the client stay in touch with the painful experience. Soothing empathic responses help reduce emotional arousal to optimal levels that permit emotionally engaged meaning exploration.

4. *Explore meaning.* Helping clients to explore and come to understand the meaning and significance of painful experiences involves identifying the causes of the pain, the unmet attachment needs, and the effects of painful events on self and relationships. This involves deepening experiencing in Reflective and Discovery Storytelling.

5. *Acknowledge those responsible.* In EFTT, those responsible for causing emotional pain always include perpetrators of abuse and neglect. However, clients also can acknowledge how they have contributed to causing their own pain—for example, clients whose alcohol abuse has destroyed their relationships and their health, or the client Mark, presented in the preceding chapter, whose defensive anger contributed to his marital difficulties.

6. *Switch to IC/EE.* The ultimate goal in helping clients to allow the emotional pain of issues concerning childhood abuse and neglect is to help them feel strong enough to imaginally confront others responsible and construct a new narrative in which they hold perpetrators, rather than self, appropriately responsible for harm. This is observed in Unexpected Outcome Storytelling.

A Clinical Example of Allowing Emotional Pain

Marianne (APA, 2013), who was presented earlier, initially struggled between a desire to express her feelings, be free, and be authentic versus exercising control and self-interruption. Intervention aimed at shifting this Competing Plotline Story to one that completely integrates her authentic emotional experience by allowing pain and accessing self-soothing resources. In the following excerpt, the therapist affirmed Marianne's vulnerability in approaching painful memories of herself as a child and validated her struggle to suppress her feelings. At the same time, she provided encouragement and support to relinquish overcontrol, as well as evocative empathy and process directives to activate the emotion scheme and access her painful feelings and unmet needs as a child. The excerpt begins with accessing a specific autobiographic memory to help the client emotionally engage.

Therapist: Is there a specific memory or event you would like to focus on?

Client: When I picture myself, it's like just a little girl in a dungeon.

Therapist: In a dungeon, that's a very sad image.

Client:	[wipes tear] There's worse.
Therapist:	Yes, there's worse, but it's not a way you want your little girl to be raised, in a dungeon [the client shakes her head]. Can you speak from what it was like for you?

Here Marianne was trying to suppress her tears. The therapist validated her struggle but focused on accessing the healthy side of the competing plot-line. She helped the client express her sadness by specifying all the things she missed out on as a child and empathically responding to those losses.

Therapist:	I know it's hard, you're trying to hold back, but if you can try and get in touch with that little girl, Marianne, in a dungeon. What is she feeling, feeling lonely?
Client:	Helpless, you said it before.
Therapist:	Helpless, yes, totally helpless, just shut out and helpless and alone.
Client:	[suppressing tears] I'm sorry I don't like to cry.
Therapist:	I know you don't want to cry but . . . just a lot of tears for that little girl; she missed out on a lot [client silently weeps]. What did you miss the most do you think?
Client:	[wiping tears] I think those happy childhood memories, you know that people talk about.
Therapist:	Yes, children should be happy, carefree, and have all kinds of happy memories. You got gypped.
Client:	My mom and dad, they tried.
Therapist:	They tried and your strength is in understanding where they are coming from. But it doesn't change the pain that you went through. It's important.
Client:	Yes [wiping eyes with tissue].
Therapist:	You missed out on some precious things.

Once Marianne had allowed the pain of her childhood memories, even momentarily, she also accessed a healthy response of holding her father responsible. Therapist empathic responses supported and encouraged this new assertive expression.

Client:	I'm just angry. . . . It's like I feel responsible for it.
Therapist:	Well, how unfair!
Client:	Like you did that.
Therapist:	Yes, you did that and now I feel responsible for it.

In later sessions, Marianne would be encouraged to engage in IC or EE with her imagined father to further integrate this new perspective.

ACCESSING SELF-SOOTHING TO CONSTRUCT
A MORE COMPASSIONATE SELF-NARRATIVE

For clients to safely experience previously avoided painful emotions, they must have the resources, both external and internal, to cope with them. The capacity to feel compassion for and soothe oneself is one such resource. The procedure involves imagining and experiencing the effect of soothing responses of significant others, for example, an attachment figure, friend, adult self, or the therapist. When clients have difficulty imagining soothing responses (Empty Story), the therapist needs to model these and provide considerable guidance.

The following are steps in the process of helping clients first to activate painful feelings and needs and then to access self-soothing resources that can be used to help tolerate this distressing and painful experience. This process can take place in a two-chair dialogue between the adult and recalled child self, which can be highly evocative, or the steps can be followed without the use of chairs.

1. *Evoke autobiographical memory.* The first step involves directives and evocative empathic responses, based on the therapist's knowledge of the client, to evoke specific autobiographical memories of the self as a vulnerable needy child. Clients can be asked to imagine and describe themselves in another chair—"Can you see her over there, sad little thing?"

2. *Direct attention to internal experience.* In this step the therapist directs the client's attention to the lived experience of the child, his or her feelings of sadness, loneliness, feeling unwanted, worthless, or afraid, in the context of the remembered narrative scene (Experiential Storytelling). Therapist empathic responses help to evoke and scaffold the client's painful feelings—"There she is over there, little Sarah, wishing she had a different mother."

3. *Identify unmet needs.* This step involves identifying the unmet needs of the self as a child in the situation (e.g., for love, protection) that emerge from evoked painful emotional experience. The therapist can offer empathic conjectures and prompts to help the client symbolize needs—"What do you think she needed? Someone to love her, tell her she was beautiful?" An important part

of the process is to <u>increase the client's sense of entitlement to unmet needs</u>. For example:

Therapist: Yes, she deserved to have childhood innocence . . .

Client: Yes that was taken away long ago. And she didn't deserve to have it go on and on.

Therapist: Yes, she deserved a break for God's sake, too much for such a little person!

4. *Respond to need.* Here the client is encouraged and supported in responding to their unmet needs as a child, from the current adult perspective—"What would you like to say to her, now, as an adult? What do you think she needs to hear?" This can include expressing compassion for the client's suffering, nurturing, or comforting. Here again, therapists can offer empathic conjectures based on their knowledge of the client's story and prompts to help clients with limited experience of having been nurtured and soothed to symbolize responses. It can be highly evocative to model and help clients express soothing action tendencies, such as stroking the chair.

5. *Experience the effect of the soothing response.* Just as in all EFTT interventions, change occurs from deeply experiencing new healthy feelings, needs, action tendencies, and perspectives so that these new healthy resources can be integrated into a new, adaptive self-narrative. In this instance, interventions direct client attention to, and help them express the positive impact of, their self-soothing responses in Unexpected Outcome Storytelling—"Stay with that. Put words to your feelings—so warm and secure?"

6. *Carry into the present.* In the final step client and therapist identify how this process can be used in present situations. Clients are asked to anticipate possible situations in which painful feelings and memories would be evoked and are helped to strategize how they will handle them, how they will access these new healthy resources, and possibly anticipate the reactions of others. This is part of helping to integrate the new outcome into a new self-narrative.

The following example presents the processes of accessing self-soothing resources that followed the process of Marianne allowing emotional pain, described previously. Later in the session, Marianne described her struggle and desire to be more open with her feelings—the other side of the Competing Plotline. The therapist supported the emergence of this healthy side of the narrative and helped her access autobiographical memories of herself as a child.

Therapist: No, it's not right that being open feels unsafe. But you know that is the legacy of your environment, growing up with all that fear. It's like you still carry that with you.

Client: I want to just let it go.

Therapist: So you want to learn to express your feelings, weep for that little girl in the dungeon, who spent so many years down there.

Client: [nods] Yes, but how do you go about doing it? I'm at a loss.

Therapist: Well, I could suggest maybe you could put that little girl right there [pats client chair beside her]. How do you feel imagining little Marianne beside you?

Client: [weepy, internally focused] Sad little thing.

Marianne explicitly stated at the beginning of the session that she did not want to do chair work, which is quite consistent with her fear of intense emotional experience. This is a good example of responding to client needs and the effective use of the self-soothing procedure without the use of chair work. Rather, the therapist asked her to imagine herself as a child sitting beside her in her own chair. In the following excerpt, the therapist offered prompts to help Marianne articulate self-soothing responses and then directed her to attend to the experiential impact of these responses to reinforce motivation to freely experience and express her suppressed feelings of sadness and rage for all she had been exposed to as a child. Thus she helped her coconstruct a more experientially alive and compassionate self-narrative.

Therapist: Do you want to comfort her?

Client: [weeps] Very much, I would very much like to. Just keep her safe.

Therapist: Keep her safe, yes.

Client: So she can express any emotion, if she wants to scream, if she wants to cry.

Therapist: And what would you say? It's okay? ["Mmm hmm"] I'll take care of you?

Client: And no one will be offended and no one will be hurt, just go ahead. That would be great.

Therapist: That would be great. Can you feel how great that would be? How much she needed that? How much you still need that?

Client: [nods] If I could just let it out and not be judged or . . .

Therapist: Yes, that's what you need more than anything.

Marianne then described her struggle to "open the door" and express her feelings, her anger at herself for not being able to do it, and her anger at her family for making her so fearful. The therapist explicitly supported the healthy side of the competing emotional plotline, anger and a sense of entitlement to unmet needs, to help her construct a more self-empowered self-narrative and move forward in the process of resolving abuse issues with her father.

> *Therapist:* I suggest you stay away from anger at yourself for not being able to do it. That little girl should be angry at her father for not protecting her [*the client nods*]. You did not deserve that. You deserved, like all children, a safe environment.
>
> *Client:* Yes, that's my goal to just one day open that door firsthand and just be carefree. That would be fantastic to be able to do that.

Imagining and soothing herself as a child increased the client's awareness of unmet needs and motivation to get these needs for authentic emotional expression met. In a longer course of therapy Marianne would participate in IC/EE to assertively express anger toward her father and hold him accountable for harm, thus further reducing fear of expression and helping to integrate these healthy resources into a new narrative concerning self, others, and traumatic events.

With greater access to adaptive feelings and meanings through Competing Plotline, Experiential Storytelling, and Reflective Storytelling, clients feel stronger and more confident. They are better able to resolve issues concerning perpetrators and construct more adaptive narratives concerning self and others. The following chapter illustrates intervention in the middle phase of EFTT with Charlize and Mark.

10

TWO INTENSIVE CASE ANALYSES: MIDDLE-PHASE EFTT

In keeping with the emotion-focused therapy for trauma (EFTT) clinical model, the middle phase of therapy with the clients Charlize and Mark primarily focused on exploring internal struggles, accessing and symbolizing new emotional responses for further reflection, and asserting core needs and adaptive actions to strengthen the subdominant healthy "voice" of client self-narratives. During this working phase of therapy, client maladaptive processes are repeatedly activated and worked through.

CHARLIZE

The middle phase of EFTT with Charlize focused primarily on helping her to allow and understand the pain of unmet attachment needs and to begin to assert her interpersonal boundaries with her mother.

http://dx.doi.org/10.1037/0000041-011
Narrative Processes in Emotion-Focused Therapy for Trauma, by S. C. Paivio and L. E. Angus

Session 9

During her midtreatment review in Session 9, Charlize reported that disclosing and reexperiencing her memory of sexual abuse (Experiential Storytelling) during Session 6 was the most helpful aspect of therapy to date. She stated that she was no longer angry at the babysitter or herself and now found herself rarely recalling her experiences of sexual abuse. She also reported positive, unexpected outcomes in her marital relationship in terms of having experienced more physical and emotion intimacy with her husband in recent weeks. Hearing the disclosure of Unexpected Outcome Storytelling as an important indicator of client relational and self-narrative change, her therapist asked her to recall and describe the specific circumstances of these important new developments in her marital relationship and to reflect on the emotional impact of those experiences for her and how these were different from her relationship with her husband in the recent past. Therapist interventions focusing on the emotional impact of key change events, and their importance for the client, facilitate the articulation of a new, more adaptive and compassionate view of self and others that is the basis for Discovery Storytelling and self-narrative reconstruction.

Despite her experience of positive intrapersonal and interpersonal changes, especially in her relationship with her husband, Charlize reported that she continued to have difficulties speaking her mind and establishing boundaries with her mother and wanted to focus on this concern in the remaining therapy sessions. Accordingly, the focus of Session 10 was Charlize's disclosure of feeling profoundly stuck in two simultaneous, conflicting emotional plotlines—anger and sadness—in her relationship with her mother and the constant push–pull of longing for connection with her mother while simultaneously pushing her mother away.

Session 10

At the beginning of the session, she recalled and described in detail several specific autobiographical memories that highlighted her mother's erratic behavior and physical and emotional abuse—spankings, welts on her legs, and sometimes cruel punishments. For instance, Charlize recounted the time that her mother insisted that Charlize euthanize their beloved cat because she was leaving home at age 16, and Charlize acquiesced out of fear. These are examples of the maladaptive relational pattern with her mother, and initially her story was conveyed with little emotion or self-reflection.

To deepen Charlize's emotional engagement with her memories of childhood neglect and help empower her to hold her mother accountable, her therapist initiated an empathic exploration (EE) dialogue with mother. He directed

Charlize to try and focus her attention on feelings of anger toward her mother's cruel actions and behaviors, the unfairness and pain, but Charlize collapsed into feelings of helplessness, saying, "I just can't get over those feelings of anger and sadness. It's confusing." Rather than continue with the interpersonal dialogue, her therapist redirected her attention to her own competing emotions, desires, and action tendencies of wanting closeness with her mother and at the same time wanting to push her mother away, that is, Competing Emotional Plotline Storytelling: Charlize: "One minute I am angry at her manipulation and irresponsibility, I want to cut ties with her. The next, I get all excited and happy if she says anything nice about me or my kids. It's exhausting, I'm walking on eggshells with her, I don't know why I care about her so much." Although Charlize understood intellectually that her mother wouldn't or couldn't change, she still clung to the wish that somehow, someway, it was still possible that they would be able to emotionally "bond." Allowing and accepting the pain of the loss of her wish to bond, and the possibility that it might come true, would be an important part of the healing process.

Although one part of Charlize wanted to be able to clearly express her feelings to her mother and appropriately assert her own personal boundaries, she easily slipped into hopeless resignation about being able to do so: "It doesn't matter what I say, she will just belittle it, say I am just overreacting, blame it on my hormones or whatever." This collapse to an earlier step in the resolution process (Degree of Resolution Scale [DRS] Level 2; Singh, 1994) is typical, as clients reiteratively cycle thorough steps in the process. In response to Charlize's collapse back into externalizing blame and emotional invalidation, her therapist first validated her feeling of hopeless resignation and focused their inquiry on the importance of understanding both sides of the conflict. He started with the bodily felt feeling of having a "lump in her throat," longing to be close to her mother, and hoping her mother will change. This would be an important focus of later sessions. As Greenberg (2002) suggested, you need to fully arrive at an emotion before it can be changed—that is, you need to "leave the station."

Session 11

The dominant focus for Session 11 was Charlize's painful disclosure that she had always felt like an outsider in her extended family-of-origin relationships and how difficult it was for her to fully allow the pain of this awareness (Competing Plotline Storytelling) and the meanings that it may have for her finally finding a relationship in which she can be loved and belong to a family. Charlize: "I feel like a visitor everywhere . . . like I always have to be careful not to overstay my welcome . . . an outcast" (Same Old Story). The therapist focused on her healthy interpersonal need to belong, to experience closer, deeper relationships with her family. Charlize acknowledged her wish for connection but stopped herself from exploring the meaning of these feelings for her when she stated, "Maybe I'm just too dramatic, never satisfied." Here she struggled to feel entitled to these unmet needs (Competing Plotline Storytelling).

A shifting back and forth between more poignant Experiential Storytelling disclosures, inward focus, approaching pain, then interrupting and suppressing painful experience continued throughout the session. Her eyes were downcast, her voice was wistful, but there were no tears. Charlize related, "I feel bad saying these things, choked up in my throat. I feel like a spoiled brat for wanting close relationships that aren't going to happen." Despite Charlize's dismissive belittling of her own longing for emotional connection, her therapist explicitly encouraged her to stay with her feelings of longing and to explore in the session "what they said to her." In response, Charlize's Reflective Storytelling became more emotionally engaged as she approached and began to allow the pain of her unmet needs (Inchoate Storytelling).

> *Therapist:* What is that choked-up feeling?
>
> *Client:* Sad.
>
> *Therapist:* Say more.
>
> *Client:* It's like it's too late, I missed the boat, I won't get what I want from either my biological or raised mother, I won't get that bond.
>
> *Therapist:* That's important, your sadness, those are big losses to come to grips with, very painful. These feelings are not resolved. Say more about your need for deeper relationships.
>
> *Client:* I want to feel close, comfortable.
>
> *Therapist:* Stay with those feelings, your pain and sadness, and what they tell you.
>
> *Client:* I feel choked up again hearing you say those words.

This is a new understanding of how she has been wounded and of core unmet needs that need to be integrated into new self-narrative.

Session 12

The dominant narrative during Session 12 concerned Charlize's struggle to understand a disturbing and puzzling outburst of angry, resentful feelings toward her husband that happened between sessions and their possible connection to the emergence and painful awareness of her core unmet needs for mother–daughter bonding in the previous therapy session. As Charlize recounted the circumstances of her emotional outburst, she noted that she had felt needy, vulnerable, and lonely after her therapy session, and her husband, who was at home, had been preoccupied with other concerns and did not notice her downcast state. This situation can be understood as evoking her core maladaptive emotion scheme, the Same Old Story ("unfinished business") with her mother now activated in a new relational context with her husband. However, Charlize did not understand or connect her reaction to unmet attachment needs and regretted "hurting him, saying rotten things."

There are only four more sessions of therapy left, and hence her therapist became more process directive in his responses to Charlize in a bid to help facilitate an emotional plotline shift from resignation to anger to challenge her maladaptive relational pattern and move the resolution process forward. Accordingly, her therapist focused on helping her to understand the relational context of her angry outburst and her negative reactions to her husband.

> *Therapist:* What was behind that reaction?
>
> *Client:* Anger, I felt like a volcano, lashing out, out of control.

This is an excellent example of an Unstoried Emotion marker and, as such, her therapist helped her to construct a coherent narrative, to contextualize and bring meaning to her strong emotional reactions, for heightened narrative coherence and emotional self-regulation.

> *Therapist:* Put words to it, what was that volcano about?
>
> *Client:* He wasn't giving me the attention I wanted, he wanted me to tend to him, like his haircut was more important than sitting down with me, giving me a hug.

The therapist asked explicitly if she had connected her need to be "tended to" to an increased awareness of painful unmet needs in her previous session.

> *Client:* Yes, striving for connection. I needed him and he wasn't there, but he is there for me lots of the time, strange.

The therapist then explicitly connected her puzzling angry reaction to her husband with the maladaptive pattern of her relationship with mother for the coconstruction of an emotionally integrated, coherent narrative and new self-understanding.

> *Therapist:* Not so strange, you have a lot of emotional issues with mother that are not resolved, that spill out with him. You need to work these through, get these emotions out and process them. It's frightening, but you need to stare them in the eyes, this will give you clarity, help put them to rest. Does this fit?
>
> *Client:* I never had a chance to work them through [*pause*]. I hate that I'm still going through this adolescent process. It bugs me.

Therapist: So you shouldn't be going through this? You sound like your mother!

Client: Yes [*both laugh*].

It was clear that in that moment a new, shared understanding of Charlize's voice of resignation and her frustrating return to the Same Old Story had emerged in the session—and with it, an emergent new view of self and readiness for change. It was at this pivotal point in the session that her therapist then asked her to express her unmet needs to her imagined mother, in the context of an EE dialogue, to increase her sense of entitlement to unmet needs.

Therapist: What would you want to say to her?

Client: I wanted her to be there, to have a real relationship.

Therapist: Say more, what would that look like?

Client: I never felt like a person, always like an appendage; treated like an object.

Therapist: What did you need?

Client: I needed to feel special, by her actions, not just words.

After this new, more empowered assertion of core needs, Charlize once again collapsed into the voice of self-criticism, self-doubt, and self-invalidation. Her therapist now redirected Charlize's attention to the voice of the competing plotline of emotional invalidation and belittling criticism, and to be the critic. Charlize said, "I sound like a spoiled brat, grow up, move on. There's something wrong with me." The stinging impact of these harsh judgments brought tears to her eyes, and her therapist empathically deepened those feelings.

Therapist: It hurts to hear that, speak from that side.

Client: I shouldn't let trivial things bother me—but it's not trivial.

Therapist: Say more about it's not trivial—this is incredibly important not to brush it aside.

Here the therapist's process direction supported the coconstruction of a new self-narrative in which Charlize felt deserving of having her attachment needs met.

The turning point in therapy in terms of resolving issues with mother occurred at the end of Session 12. The narrative quality shifted from incoherence and Inchoate Storytelling (searching for words) to allowing emotional pain (Experiential Story) and Reflective and Discovery Storytelling. Initially, Charlize was surprised by the depth of pain around unmet attachment needs. She could not understand all the thoughts and feelings that had emerged in the context of her imaginal conversation with her mother (narrative incoherence).

Her therapist then focused on helping Charlize to make sense of her experience and shifted into more empathically based, Reflective Storytelling inquiry and the coconstruction of new meaning.

Therapist: You never have been down this path before, so deep.

Client: I used to feel confident. I never realized all this stuff.

Therapist: It's rocked your world because now you are aware of all those unmet needs, it's taken away your confidence?

Client: When I was younger I didn't have these feelings or maybe pay attention to them.

Therapist: Yes, as a child, core painful emotions were avoided or ignored, but they affect you nonetheless, the pain has been carried with you for a long time. You deserved love, closeness, to feel safe.

In his response, the therapist identified and validated the importance of integrating new, unexpected outcomes and self-understandings that challenge core assumptions of the Same Old Storytelling patterns for the emergence of a new, more coherent self-narrative.

The therapist reintroduced an EE dialogue with the mother to heighten Charlize's sense of entitlement to have unmet needs met and move the resolution process forward to DRS Level 4: "Did you deserve to get your deepest needs met with mom? [Yes.] Say that to her. What would you say?" Charlize clearly expressed her entitlement to unmet needs: "I needed to feel safe, loved, wanted as a child, I deserved to have my deepest needs met." Her therapist then asked how her how she felt while expressing her need for love, and Charlize replied that she felt quiet, calm, relaxed. Noting the emergence of an important new experience of self, her therapist process diagnostically invited Charlize to reflect on this new feeling, to promote Reflective Storytelling.

Therapist: Say more.

Client: I understand that episode with my husband, my behavior of getting close and withdrawing. It's from insecurity with my mother.

Therapist: Yes, lack of trust in your most important relationship, desperately wanting closeness, then fear and pull back.

Client: I want to realize not everyone is like my mother.

Therapist: It's hard because, my sense is you had an extremely emotionally abusive relationship with your mother.

Client: [tears well up] It's hard to hear that, it's hard to hear the truth [allowing pain, Inchoate Storytelling]. It hurts so much because she's my mother and she was supposed to be there.

Therapist: Very painful, hard to be confronted with it.

Client: It hurts but at least I'm no longer pushing it under the rug.

Therapist: Face it, call it like it is.

At the conclusion of the session, Charlize wondered about her ability to handle the strong emotional impact of her new, painful awareness of her experience of childhood neglect, outside of the therapy hour. Although her therapist empathically validated her experience of emotional pain, he also provided hopeful encouragement: "My sense is you will be able to manage your feelings just like you did after the deep feelings when processing sexual abuse." The client looked relieved and thanked him.

MARK

The middle phase of therapy with Mark included two-chair work with "Dr. No," the part of himself that stopped him from expressing his feelings and opinions (self-interruption) and undermined his confidence. His spontaneous naming of this part of himself externalized the problem and was used as an evocative "handle" for future coconstruction of a more positive self-narrative in the context of Discovery Storytelling markers.

Session 6

Session 6 began with Mark's complaint that his mother's "rubbing out" of his feelings and perspectives had stood in the way of his achieving his potential professionally and in relationships. The therapist suggested that he had "internalized her beliefs and actions and now it's you that rubs out your confidence and courage" and structured a two-chair dialogue to address the Competing Plotlines of his harsh inner self-critic (Dr. No) and his healthy voice of protest that needed to break free.

Mark immediately understood the struggle between the two parts of himself. From the perspective of Dr. No, he told himself not to say anything because he would look stupid, be criticized, rejected, and end up feeling bad, hurt. From the experiencing self and voice of healthy protest, he initially felt beaten down and agreed with Dr. No. The therapist asked him for specific examples of situations—shifting to narrative specificity for heightened emotional engagement and impact—in which Dr. No "rubbed him out" and he disclosed personal memories from his workplace. From the experiencing chair, he said he wanted to be able to share his opinions, and the therapist helped him identify the potential benefits of doing so. Therapist: "Tell Dr. No what would be good about sharing your opinions."

Mark was able to identify several examples of situations in which his unexpressed opinions would actually have been beneficial to the company. When processing his experience of participating in the two-chair procedure, the therapist provided an important rationale for directly addressing the Competing Plotlines of his two parts of self in future sessions: "Our job will be to make Dr. No smaller and the part of you that wants to share larger." Mark expressed enthusiasm about the possibility of increasing his self-confidence and the idea that he might have some control over this—an important adaptive, agentic, emotional plotline that challenged the negative expectations, and withdrawal, of his Same Old Story. He also realized this was learned in his childhood but was now part of him (Reflective Storytelling). His expression of a desire for personal agency and change was indicative of readiness for change and prognostic of good outcome.

Sessions 9 and 10

At the midtreatment review, Mark said this work with Dr. No had been the most helpful in this therapy sessions, so far. During Sessions 9 and 10, he also reported several new Unexpected Outcome Stories about his less reactive behavior with his family and feeling less guilt about not respecting his mother. In response to these storytelling markers of therapeutic change, his therapist directed Mark's attention to the importance of these new emotional plotlines and action tendencies and empathically guided exploration of the emotions, intentions, and expectations that guided his new actions and that highlighted his contributions to making positive changes happen in his own life.

Session 11

During Session 11, Mark again returned to the core trauma memory narrative of being strapped by his father. This memory was now narrated as a deeper, more experiential story (Experiential Storytelling) with some indication of feeling more deserving of having important personal needs met (DRS Level 4).

> Client: I have kids, how could anyone do that? I didn't deserve that.
>
> Therapist: No, you did not! How did you feel at the time?
>
> Client: I was crying, yelling, begging, pleading like I was going to be shot.

Here Mark describes his feelings in behavioral terms, but his use of vivid metaphor is a window into his internal experience that helps the therapist empathically respond.

Therapist:	Begging for your life.
Client:	Then begging my mother's forgiveness. I had to kneel in front of her for something trivial, begging my mother's forgiveness for hours, and she refusing to forgive—"You don't mean it, you don't care about us, you're just using us." The whole time she's lying down on the couch, looking at the TV.
Therapist:	What is Mother's tone? Come over here [*points to empty chair*]. Can you enact your mother?
Client:	[*switches chairs*] She's hard, unforgiving—you are a bad kid. Then she turns and watches TV.

He described this scene in a monotone (Empty Storytelling), and in response, his therapist helped him shift into a more emotionally alive mode of Experiential Storytelling by posing a key question.

Therapist:	What is your reaction, how did you feel on the inside?
Client:	The hole in my heart is getting deeper and deeper—"I'm not using you."
Therapist:	Hole in your heart?
Client:	My mother is degrading me. I feel empty, like I am useless, a piece of shit. I felt like I really am . . . I would go upstairs and cry . . .
Therapist:	So sad, so hurt.
Client:	Brokenhearted that my mother hated me.

Mark is internally focused, in touch with his emotional pain, as he expressed the poignant emotional meaning of his trauma story and the devastating impact on his sense of self as a child.

Later, when processing the imaginal confrontation (IC) with his parents (reprocessing trauma feelings and memories), Mark continued in Reflective Storytelling.

Client:	I felt like I wasn't worth too much, then it turned to hatred and contempt for her, disrespect for her, and lying to her . . . When I was younger I used to do everything wrong, now I can't be wrong.
Therapist:	Now you can't tolerate that.

Mark was thoughtful, internally focused, and connected his childhood experiences with his mother to his disrespect for women and the origins of his negative view of self and Same Old Story plotlines.

Client:	I don't trust women. I think I am going to be screwed over. I end up treating others like they treated me.
Therapist:	Can you be specific? How do you treat others?
Client:	Talking down, pompous. How can I be like someone I hate [Reflective]?
Therapist:	This really bothers you, stay with that.
Client:	I hate my mother and I'm scared of women, of what they can do, so I keep my guard up, don't give them any breaks, I don't trust. Hate has rubbed off on everybody. My mother never showed me any love or told me she loved me. There was a serious lack of love in the house. I didn't know how to love until my daughter was born.

The therapist then directed Mark to reflect on his emerging bodily felt feelings and emotions (Inchoate Storytelling marker) to facilitate the emergence of adaptive sadness implied in his story about the love missing in his life.

Therapist:	What is your feeling as we talk?
Client:	Sad about what I missed out on [internally focused Inchoate Storytelling].
Therapist:	Say more.
Client:	Relationships, sharing myself.
Therapist:	I needed that.
Client:	Not respecting women or being able to love, having a relationship is the biggest thing a man could miss.
Therapist:	What's it been like all these years?
Client:	Very lonely, I couldn't give, always twisting things around, always scared of being screwed.
Therapist:	Very lonely, a big loss.

Session 12

The turning point in therapy occurs during Session 12, in which the full experience and expression of adaptive anger and sadness accesses new meaning (Reflective Storytelling) to aid the process of resolving issues with perpetrators and constructing a new self-narrative. The session began with a focus on his marriage and disrespect toward women.

Client:	I haven't been my wife's best friend, I keep distant because of how my mother treated me, and I see my dad, he is her puppet. I am scared of being a wimp like him.

Therapist:	So if you let her in, you will become like that? How did your dad become a puppet, what did he do? [specificity]
Client:	He did what he was told, he had no mind of his own. Now when there is a woman above me I get very negative. I think she doesn't deserve this.
Therapist:	So you feel contempt toward them. How do you want to be?
Client:	I want to be equals. Free from all that baggage.
Therapist:	Ah, yes, all that residual fear and anger.

His therapist then introduced an IC with his father and through her process-guided inquiry facilitated a shift to Experiential Storytelling.

Therapist:	What memory comes up for you as I bring out the chair?
Client:	Mother accused me of all kinds of things and he never stood up for me. He was always disappointed in me.
Therapist:	Disappointed, say more. Talk from your body not your head. What's going on as you think about that?
Client:	I'm in knots, frustration. He knows I did nothing wrong and he said nothing.
Therapist:	Stay in the memory.
Client:	My mother is ranting and raving.
Therapist:	Switch, be your mother [evoke memory more vividly, stimulus to evoke response], rant and rave, how did she sound? Do it, what is it like?
Client:	Her voice is like a knife in your back.

Mark then collapsed, stating, "I can't do this very well," which heralded the emerging of a Competing Plotline marker. His therapist bypassed this self-critical interruption and kept him focused on the experience of imagining his mother.

Therapist:	No, no, that's a block, you're doing fine, keep going, mother ranting and raving. What are you feeling imagining her? Really check inside, stay here [hand on heart], whatever it is.
Client:	I feel bad, I believe I am bad. I asked my brother to stand up for me and he did nothing. My father did the same thing.
Therapist:	Ah, you're bad. Put your father in the chair, what did you want to say to him?

Client:	You know I didn't do anything, why don't you stop her, help me, I didn't do it.
Therapist:	Switch to father, how does he respond?
Client:	He's not listening to me, just says, "Why are you such a bad kid?" [therapist asks him to switch chairs].
Client:	Please believe me, like I'm begging . . .

His therapist acknowledged his feelings of fear and powerlessness at the time and then directed his attention to presently felt experience.

Therapist:	Tell him what you're angry about.
Client:	You never stood up for me, you only looked out for yourself, I'm not important.
Therapist:	That's wrong. Tell him.
Client:	I would never do that to my kids. You stunk as a father [turns to therapist]. The f—king ignorance of this man!

Mark shifted to disclosing more stories of his father blaming him, dismissing and derogating his talents, and the therapist worked to keep him emotionally engaged.

Therapist:	Tell Father how angry you are about all his derogation.
Client:	I hate your guts for . . . for . . . for . . . You stole my confidence, I ended up hating everybody, I thought I was a bad kid, it held me back.
Therapist:	Tell him I hold you responsible for these things.
Client:	It was f—king terrible.
Therapist:	Heartbreaking [shift to vulnerable experience].
Client:	If I did that to my kids it would be like pulling out their heart.
Therapist:	Tell him what you wanted, needed instead.
Client:	To listen to me, stand up for me.
Therapist:	Protect me.
Client:	But you never did, you're just a spineless wimp, you degraded me just like her, infected me with your negative attitude [turns to therapist]. He can't listen, he's programmed that way.
Therapist:	How do you feel?

Client:	Tired, disappointed, sad.
Therapist:	Yes, so much sadness for yourself, you missed out on so much.
Client:	He chose my mother over me. I suppose he had to, but it was not the right decision for me.
Therapist:	Yes, very sad, devastating, he did not choose you.

The clear expression of anger and sadness during this IC contributes to Mark's construction of a more differentiated perspective of his father and increased awareness of his own emotional pain and how he has been wounded. These can be integrated into a more coherent and compassionate self-narrative (DRS Levels 4 and 5) in the late phase of therapy.

11

RESOLVING ISSUES WITH PERPETRATORS AND NEW STORY OUTCOMES: LATE-PHASE EFTT

The late phase of emotion-focused therapy for trauma (EFTT) focuses on facilitating and consolidating emotional transformation, self-narrative coherence, and resolution of core conflicts emerging from trauma story reexperiencing and interventions in the final therapy sessions. As intrapersonal blocks to narrative disclosure and emotional reexperiencing are reduced, and with the support of therapist marker-guided interventions, clients are increasingly able to access and express adaptive anger and sadness, explore associated meanings, and feel more entitled to and deserving of unmet needs. Their perceptions of self, other, and traumatic memories become more coherent and emotionally meaningful for the coconstruction of a new self-identify narrative. More specifically, the quality and focus of client storytelling begins to shift wherein key indicators of narrative-emotion process (NEP) Change markers begin to emerge in late-phase EFTT sessions, especially for clients who achieve recovery by treatment termination (Bryntwick, Angus, Paivio, Carpenter, & Macaulay, 2014; Carpenter, Angus, Paivio, & Bryntwick, 2016).

http://dx.doi.org/10.1037/0000041-012
Narrative Processes in Emotion-Focused Therapy for Trauma, by S. C. Paivio and L. E. Angus

It appears that when EFTT clients begin to narrate and reflect on positive intra- and interpersonal shifts in emotional responses, actions, and needs, a new, more agentic view of self begins to emerge. In particular, achieving resolution in two-chair dialogues and imaginal confrontation (IC) and empathic exploration (EE) interventions, wherein new adaptive emotional plotlines transform a client's Same Old Story, NEP research findings highlight the critical role of EFTT process-guiding responses that notice and support client narration and reflection on salient intra/interpersonal change events (Unexpected Outcome Storytelling). This is the basis for the articulation of a new, more agentic and empowered view of self as a coherent self-narrative change (Discovery Storytelling). As discussed previously, McAdams and Janis (2004) suggested that an internalized self–narrative may have as much impact on guiding actions and behavior as dispositional traits. Accordingly, when EFTT therapists help their clients to coconstruct a new, more agentic and compassionate self-identity narrative, wherein adaptive emotional plotlines now influence future actions, expectations, hopes, and goals, they are supporting enduring client change.

RESEARCH ON LATE-PHASE NARRATIVE CHANGE PROCESSES AND TREATMENT OUTCOMES

Results of several studies documenting improvements in narrative quality over the course of EFTT were presented in earlier chapters. Findings regarding late-phase and posttreatment outcome are reviewed briefly here to highlight the qualities of narrative-emotion change in EFTT. For example, Mundorf and Paivio (2011) examined qualitative dimensions of client trauma narratives written before the first and last sessions of EFTT. Results comparing late with early narratives indicated greater use of positive emotion words, greater focus on the present and the future, less incoherence (i.e., dysfluency, incomplete sentences, unclear meaning), and deeper levels of experiencing (exploration of feelings and meanings) in late narratives. Results also indicated that increased depth of experiencing from early to late narratives was associated with reduced trauma symptoms and resolution of abuse issues. These findings support the EFTT model of change and narrative restructuring presented in this volume. Accordingly, client stories, particularly those of clients who benefitted the most, become more coherent, experiential, and reflective toward the end of therapy, and they have a new and more positive and future-oriented focus that would be observed during in-session Unexpected Outcome and Discovery Storytelling.

Interestingly, Mundorf and Paivio (2011) did not find a decrease in the use of negative emotion words in late written narratives. This is consistent with EFTT theory that stories about traumatic events told at the end of therapy would include uninhibited references to the negative emotions involved. This also is consistent with findings (Ralston, 2006) that the extent of client self-reported alexithymia, characterized by emotion awareness deficits, significantly decreased by the end of EFTT. At the beginning of therapy, 80% of clients met criteria for alexithymia, and this dropped to 20% by the end of therapy, suggesting greater access to emotional experience in late narratives.

In terms of in-session narrative processes, Mundorf (2013) conducted a qualitative analysis of client in-session self-narratives over the course of EFTT. These were stories in which clients were talking about their experience and perceptions of self. Three major content themes that emerged in late sessions concerned (a) an increased sense of authenticity and being true to oneself, (b) feeling more in control of one's life choices, and (c) increased self-acceptance. These would be evident in Unexpected Outcome and Discovery Stories told in the late phase of therapy. Good examples of these kinds of changes will be seen in the cases of Charlize and Mark presented in Chapter 12.

Two recent studies examined emotional processes in self-related and trauma narratives during early and late sessions of EFTT (Khayyat-Abuaita, 2015; Nussbaum, 2014). Results of both studies indicated more productive emotional process in late sessions, that is, more expressions of assertive anger, grief, acceptance, and relief. Again, these findings are consistent with Unexpected Outcome Storytelling. The following are examples of client changes reported in the Khayyat-Abuaita (2015) study. A case example that represents the increase in productive emotional experience is the client Richard, presented in earlier chapters, who had been sexually molested by a priest. During an early session he stated, "I have so much anger towards him. That is the most degrading thing. I still don't understand why I didn't do something; he was close to my family . . . I always blamed myself. Why did I go back to the church?" This is the Same Old maladaptive Story of shame and self-blame. In comparison, during a late session he expressed assertive anger as he stated: "Darkness came over my life, it started the day you molested me. I questioned myself. I realized that it was not my fault. You are 100% to blame." This is a Discovery Story. On the other hand, this client frequently continued to express rejecting and blaming anger during late sessions, stating: "Until the day I die I will have hatred towards you. May you spend eternity in hell." This is consistent with findings that clients who benefit from EFTT evidence a decrease in, but not absence of, Transitional narrative processes late in therapy, in this case, emotionally alive Experiential Storytelling.

Khayyat-Abuaita (2015) also presented two case examples that demonstrate the difference in emotional processes in good and poor treatment outcome cases. The first good outcome example is a client who experienced physical abuse by his stepfather. During an early trauma narrative, he stated,

"Dad measured food before going to bed, everything was his. If anything was down, we would be beat . . . It would go on until you wouldn't feel anymore . . . you grow up thinking this is the way it is, so you don't know any different. I think it hurt more when we started realizing . . . that's my disappointment in myself, not realizing things sooner." This is the Same Old Story involving global distress, fear/shame, and self-blame. In contrast, during a late narrative, he expressed assertive anger as he stated, "Now I don't think I deserved it. There was no reason for it, nobody deserved it, I didn't deserve it. I couldn't make sense of it, it has nothing do with me . . . the realization that there was no sense to anything done . . . I am fine, it's not me, it was never me. I beat myself up for all my life." This is an example of a Discovery Story that the therapist would attend to and explore further.

The second example (Khayyat-Abuaita, 2015) represents a poor outcome case of a client who experienced physical abuse and neglect by her stepmother. During an early trauma narrative, she expressed global distress and fear/shame as she stated, "I was scared of her, I was terrified of this woman . . . she's controlling, she's got to dominate. I hated it, I wanted to die, I wish I was never born . . . I was worthless to her, she only put up with me because she married my dad, I hated it there." This is the Same Old Story involving fear, powerlessness, and victimization. Similarly, during a late trauma narrative she stated, "I was basically an outsider, I was stupid, I did everything wrong . . . I want to be myself, I will never be like you, you are an ugly terrible person . . . everything makes me feel that I am stupid. I needed help and I never got it . . . she would say I was never good enough for her." Here we see no change in the Same Old Story involving experiences of fear/shame, negative self-evaluations, and victimization for this client who made only moderate treatment gains.

Khayyat-Abuaita (2015) provided the following case example to demonstrate the sequence of change in affective processes during trauma narratives over the course of therapy. This good outcome client experienced childhood neglect by her mother. During an early session, she stated, "I have been going through the motions for the last 20 years. Before that, I think I believed I wasn't real" and "I was treated bad, going to school hungry, dirty, laughed at, picked on. She didn't care, she was mean, not a nice person, yucky . . . I don't think I want that mother, I don't want her near me." This is the Same Old Story with rejecting anger and global maladaptive perceptions of self and other. Later in the session the client explored negative evaluations of herself and expressed unmet needs: "You told me I was worthless and I was nothing. I can't see myself as anything more than nothing . . . I needed somebody to love me." This is an emerging Competing Plotline with views of self as worthless but some access to adaptive resources that the therapist can highlight and then push for increased sense of entitlement to unmet needs. In a late-trauma narrative, this increased sense of entitlement to decent treatment and assertive anger emerges in an Unexpected Outcome Story: "Everything you did was unacceptable . . . I have the right to distance myself from you . . . God has other plans for me. I don't want any part of this, I deserve better."

These case examples are consistent with narrative-emotion marker research by Angus and colleagues (Angus Narrative-Emotion Marker Lab, 2015) indicating the importance of therapist process-guiding interventions facilitating client shifts to both NEP Transition and Change markers to promote and consolidate self-narrative change. Research has also indicated a significant increase in the frequency of NEP Change markers in late sessions of EFTT for the most improved EFTT clients (Bryntwick et al., 2014; Carpenter et al., 2016).

More specifically, Carpenter et al. (2016) found a medium effect size wherein recovered clients expressed nearly 10 times more Unexpected Outcome Story than the unchanged group overall, along with a significant stage by outcome interaction. Unexpected Outcome Story is defined as client narratives expressing new and positive ways of being in the world. Through the process of accessing and exploring emotion and creating a coherent narrative, the client is able to create new understandings of the self, others, and the world (Angus & Greenberg, 2011; Paivio & Pascual-Leone, 2010). This new understanding may provide the impetus for new behaviors, emotional responses, and/or thought patterns outside of therapy. The following example is from Session 14 of the client Charlize, whose case we have been following in earlier chapters. Charlize: "I'm feeling good . . . because this is new for me, to depend to that extent on someone that has to take care of me and my children while I do what I want to do" [laughs].

Whereas relatively low proportions of Unexpected Outcome Story were evidenced for both outcome groups across the early and middle stages of therapy in the Carpenter et al. (2016) study, recovered EFTT clients expressed approximately 15 times more Unexpected Outcome Story markers than the unchanged clients in the late stage of therapy. Not surprisingly, the gains made by the recovered sample within therapy are likely to be articulated toward the late stage of therapy. Similarly, Matos, Santos, Gonçalves, and Martins (2009) found that new experiences were significantly higher in recovered clients than in unchanged clients in a sample of women who experienced partner violence and received individual narrative therapy. As such, converging research findings suggest that Unexpected Outcome Stories are a marker of productive change in psychotherapy across client populations.

Carpenter et al. (2016) also reported a significant increase in Discovery Storytelling for recovered clients from the middle to the late stage of EFTT, with recovered clients expressing approximately 15 times more Discovery Storytelling markers, at the late stage of therapy, compared with unchanged clients. Discovery Storytelling is coded when a client articulates a new understanding or reconceptualization of the self emerging from exploration. Another example from Session 14 with Charlize illustrates this point: "I never thought I would be able to feel this way, at peace and at ease in myself. Before I always seemed so tense and on edge, and my emotions were scattered all over the place . . . now I feel like I'm all in one piece."

Providing additional empirical support for this finding, Margola, Faachin, Molgora, and Revenson (2010) examined the written narratives of students coping with the unexpected death of a classmate. The study showed that at 4-month follow-up, participants who recovered from the trauma demonstrated insight, causation, and movement toward integrating the trauma into their worldview. Similarly, it is likely the case that significantly higher proportions of Discovery and Unexpected Outcome Change markers indicate that an important step in the EFTT change process is clients' capacity to access and coconstruct new meaning and new understandings of the self and traumatic events in their late-phase EFTT sessions.

INTERVENTION WITH NEP CHANGE MARKERS

To review, NEP research findings (Bryntwick, Angus, Paivio, Carpenter, & Macaulay, 2014; Carpenter et al., 2016) suggest that effective EFTT therapists help clients to express painful emotions (Inchoate Storytelling) for further reflection (Reflective Storytelling) and the emergence of new adaptive emotional plotlines (Inchoate Storytelling) in midphase sessions. Heightened narrative coherence and client self-reflection are further facilitated by a narrative retelling of troubling events that aids in the identification of specific situational contexts, and cues, to organize, contain, and explain distressing emotional experiences (Experiential Storytelling) in midphase therapy sessions. Additionally, the NEP Transition marker, Competing Plotline Storytelling, highlights client reports of shifts or changes in their Same Old Stories and the experience of new, more adaptive emotions and action tendencies, often in the context of IC/EE and two-chair interventions. EFTT therapists can then help clients to coconstruct a new view of self that highlights their role as agents of present and future change and preferred story outcomes. These new views of self, others, and traumatic events are evident in NEP Change narratives that emerge in the late phase of EFTT. We review the following Change subtypes that were presented in earlier chapters on assessment and intervention specifically in the context of late-phase sessions.

Unexpected Outcome Storytelling

In agreement with a narrative therapy approach (White, 2007), we believe it is important for EFTT therapists to help clients identify and elaborate unique narratives—or what we term Unexpected Outcome Stories—that challenge the underlying negative expectations and assumptions of clients' Same Old Stories and problem-focused self-narratives. Limitations of clients' Same Old Storytelling are explored and challenged by the identification and elaboration of new positive outcome stories that highlight clients' adaptive capacities to form deep and satisfying interpersonal relationships as well as to meet important goals and achievement outcomes. Sensing and "seeing" new possibilities for the resolution of problematic life concerns, in turn, engenders a hopeful expectancy for change and a heightened willingness to take action in the world.

Importantly, stories that represent positive Unexpected Outcomes destabilize the negative expectations of a client's Same Old Story and provoke a radical reauthoring of the client's self-narrative along more agentic and compassionate emotional plotlines. The emergence of NEP Unexpected Outcome Storytelling markers helps EFTT therapists to notice, and further elaborate, clients' expression of surprise, excitement, contentment, or inner peace in response to experiencing new emotional responses in the context of EFTT procedures, and/or taking positive action, and fulfilling unmet needs and goals, in their daily lives. Accordingly, it is of critical importance that EFTT therapists are responsive to the emergence of NEP Unexpected Outcome Change markers, in late-phase sessions, for the facilitation of heightened client meaning making and the articulation of self-narrative identity reconstruction—this is a Discovery Storytelling Change marker.

The following are indicators of Unexpected Outcome Storytelling. Clients themselves may notice (a) encouraging differences in their own behavior or psychological and emotional well-being, or such differences may be brought to their attention by a significant other(s); (b) articulation of a new sense or experience of the self in the world, including concomitant cognitions, emotions, and bodily sensations; (c) comparisons between past and present behavior, emotional responses of surprise or delight, or thought patterns as indicated by phrases such as "whereas before . . ."; and (d) clients' expressions of surprise, excitement, contentment, or inner peace. Paralinguistic cues such as frequent smiling, laughing, or deep satisfied breathing by a client may also indicate the emergence of a new outcome story.

In terms of EFTT specifically, clients report feeling greater self-esteem, stronger, and able to assert interpersonal boundaries; they may report surprise and relief at these changes. During IC/EE they are better able to stand up to and confront the other and to tell their own "truth." They perceive the imagined other more realistically, as less powerful, more human, and life-sized. They let go of expectations regarding the other, are no longer seeking an apology or to get their needs met from the other. Clients report "I don't care anymore," "I'm no longer angry," or "I feel sorry for him." They hold the other, rather than self, appropriately responsible for harm. Interventions encourage clients to elaborate on their reports of change, directing their attention to their internal experience during the new experience or in the present as they are telling the story. This process is identical to the process of exploring maladaptive or negative experiences in earlier phases of therapy. Therapists validate the importance of and share the client's excitement about these changes, promote client agency in contributing to the new outcome (what did they do or think differently), and connect to possible or desired future events.

At markers of Unexpected Outcome, it is helpful if EFTT therapists notice and heighten clients' experience of positive difference and change. They encourage the client to elaborate and amplify what happened to create a full account of the newness and draw out and emphasize clients' contributions and agency in the change. This is all done in a curious, inquiring manner as exemplified next.

> Client: The good thing is that like right now I don't feel responsible for this person who moved out . . . there was always the split of well, should I care or should I make an attempt to contact him . . . I always feel responsible for other people and like mothering them and making sure they are okay and so on, and I'm really tired of it, it's not up to me . . . to worry about it anymore.
>
> Therapist: Well, it sounds like the alarm bells went off and you knew what you wanted and needed and you did something about it . . .
>
> Client: And not feeling guilty about it.
>
> Therapist: Yes, that's the part, you're happy that you did it, you're not feeling guilty about it.
>
> Client: Oh, yes, that's really, really great.

This client identified new, more satisfying emotional outcomes occurring in the context of interpersonal situations that would have caused feelings of anxiety and distress in the past. The attuned and responsive therapist skillfully affirmed the importance of this new development in the client's life by reflecting the actions she took and linking them with the positive emotional outcomes.

Another unexpected story outcome marker was identified in Session 16, when this same client recollected a positive and unanticipated experience that she had during a recent job interview: "It was just really surprising and amazing to notice that . . . I just . . . took a completely different approach to answering the question and presenting what's important to me . . . I was very pleased with myself."

In this example, the client indicated her surprise and amazement over her performance and seemed to feel an invigorating sense of accomplishment. She additionally acknowledged pride in her achievement. This statement helped to cement the unexpected event as something meaningful and noteworthy.

Unexpected Outcome Storytelling was also found to play an important contributing role for the facilitation of self-narrative change, and recovery from complex trauma, in the case of Charlize. In the following excerpt the therapist helps to consolidate that change.

> Client: [*voice quivering*] Usually I don't like depending on people like that. I'm the one carrying everybody. And now I'm being carried financially and it's different. And I'm feeling okay about it and . . . I'm sensitive about it [*tears*].
>
> Therapist: So the ability to be vulnerable, to depend on other people and feel that that's legitimate.
>
> Client: Yes, that's good! These are not sad tears [*laughs*].
>
> Therapist: Say more about that, because that's an incredible feeling that you just described, and that's new.
>
> Client: It is!

Discovery Storytelling

As noted by McLeod (2004) and White (2007), personal stories organize clients' most significant lived experiences into meaningful episodes that are imbued with specific cultural expectations. Although a range of cultural themes exist within any given society, many of the stories are "constrictive and blaming" (White, 2007) when it comes to providing a personal account of a troubling life experience or interpersonal relationship. Self-identity narratives that omit important aspects of lived experience and cannot comfortably house the ambivalences and complexities that reside in all people are the most constrictive and restrictive, and they often lead clients to seek out psychotherapy in the first place. As such, adaptive, self-narrative reconstruction—in which all aspects of the self can peacefully coexist within a story, complex enough to account for the full range of emotions, events, and interpersonal relationships—is an important therapeutic goal in EFTT.

Discovery or self-identity change stories are identified when clients describe a positive transformation in the overall narrative plotline of their life story and perhaps most important, their view of self. Indicators are: (a) clients express experiencing or seeing themselves in a new, positive light and/or (b) engage in identity reconceptualization in which they reflect on current positive changes in their views of self, actions, and feelings by contrasting them with past maladaptive interpersonal patterns and emotional plotlines. In the context of client Discovery Storytelling, EFTT therapists help clients to explore the significance of the new view of self for future life possibilities and choices and coconstruction of a new, more differentiated, agentic and compassionate self-narrative. Clear elaboration of Unexpected Outcome Stories leads to new heightened awareness and integration of personal strengths, hopes, and future possibilities. Accordingly, the capacity to narrativize, understand, and integrate our most important life stories is key to adaptive identity development and the establishment of a differentiated, coherent view of self—for example, a Discovery Storytelling marker evidenced in the client Lisa's final therapy sessions, wherein she explored her new experience of emotional transformation and emergence of a new view of self.

> Client: Yes, get back into my feelings, because the awareness I know is there now and before I never knew it existed [*laughs*]. So I realize I'm an individual and I have the right to vent my feelings and what I think is right or good for me, and that's been the improvement of the therapy.
>
> Therapist: Yes, really finding your feet.
>
> Client: Yes, as an individual, before I thought I was glued to him [*laughs*], I didn't have an existence and now I do and that's a good feeling.

Lisa clearly made contrasts between her previous self and her present self, elaborating the change process beneath, clear indicators of Discovery Storytelling and self-narrative change.

Another example comes from the client Jan who gave voice to a new feeling of entitlement to look after her own needs and who was no longer feeling the overwhelming desire to please others, irrespective of the personal costs (maladaptive Same Old Story), in the therapy session. Again, therapist responses support and reinforce this change for further elaboration and consolidation.

> Client: I'm the perfect caregiver and caretaker when it comes to other people, and I have known it for some time, but just by saying that and thinking a little bit about it, it's all of sudden, like no, I should be first before anybody else comes, and it's almost like shifting gears, like getting used to that . . . so I feel really excited about it.
>
> Therapist: Yes, it sounds really exciting . . . to feel more centered in yourself, and somehow to know that you do come first and to be able to act on that . . .

Although both client and therapist contributed to the coconstruction of a new view of self, the therapist also evocatively heightened her client's emotional experience of excitement that conveyed the importance of this new development for the client. In response to the therapist's evocative and supportive empathic response, the client then expressed the important emotional impact and consequences of her self-identity transformation. In this instance, the client also made reference to new bodily feelings associated with her new experience of self, and the therapist captured her affective experience through metaphor.

Client: And it's just . . . like discovering a completely new world.

Therapist: It's like a new dimension that you were never really . . . tuned into . . .

Client: It's just such a relief to get away from that, and I can feel like I just get so much more energy . . . a lot less tension for sure.

Therapist: You're just sort of in yourself, like a deep breath is.

Client: Yes, absolutely . . . it's just like, "Where have you been?"

Another example of the important interplay between Unexpected Outcome and Discovery Storytelling for self-narrative coconstruction is Charlize, whose final phase EFTT is presented in the next chapter. Charlize spontaneously disclosed her positive experience of EFTT, at the end of Session 15, in an extended interplay of Unexpected Outcome and Discovery Storytelling that was empathically supported and facilitated by process-guiding therapeutic responses.

Client: I didn't expect this type of progress. I expected some kind of technique for handling my emotions. Now it's subconscious, automatic rather than having to sit down, breathe, count to 10, think, analyze. Now I just [*snaps her fingers, smiles*; Unexpected Outcome Storytelling].

Therapist: Very natural, just a part of you.

Client: I never got in tune with my thoughts, feelings, physical feelings, like now. This is an exhaling experience, I'm free now. Those fears are gone, things are not compounded like they used to be, drama after drama. I can deal with the drama one at a time as they come, less stress for me. I feel more of a whole person [she is inwardly focused, thoughtful, slow, talking from her internal experience]. I feel like I have the ability to fulfill my dreams, my goals [Discovery Storytelling].

Therapist: You are surprised at what you accomplished in this process, in a very short time, not just symptom reduction but real growth.

Client: It's funny how a simple thing like naming my feelings can really make a connection, things retained in my brain and my body.

> *Therapist:* Very powerful, you're right, the act itself is simple, but it's not so easy to find the right words to describe your experience.
>
> *Client:* It's kind of like taking a desk of scattered papers all over the place and now organizing them, as far as emotions are concerned, everything has its own file now in my brain. It's more manageable [*laughs*].
>
> *Therapist:* I like how you describe this, a very good image of your experience.

Charlize continued to describe feelings of increased self-esteem, using her ability to accept rather than dismiss her husband's compliments as an example.

Through the process of accessing, exploring, and verbally symbolizing emotion, the client is able to create a new understanding of the self, others, and the world (Angus & Greenberg, 2011; Paivio & Pascual-Leone, 2010). Clients who achieve the goals of EFTT, such as tolerance of painful emotions and self-soothing, assertiveness against the self-critic, and confidence in interpersonal relationships, would be more likely to experience positive changes in their way of being in the world and interacting with others (Unexpected Outcome Stories). A new view of the self, others, and the world (Discovery Storytelling), in turn, provides a further impetus for new behaviors, emotional responses, and/or thought patterns outside of therapy and sustained positive change after therapy termination.

FINAL STAGE IN THE RESOLUTION PROCESS (IC/EE)

Late steps in the processes and procedures of EFTT frequently involve reengaging the client in IC/EE. In two-chair dialogues involving self-criticism, for example, clients frequently access the internalized voice of an abusive or neglectful parent. We saw this in the example of Kristen who immediately recognized the "father in her head" as she was blaming herself for being weak and not protecting her sister. Later sessions could involve more two-chair work, but eventually, resolution of abuse issues would take place in the context of IC with the imagined father. Similarly, Competing Plotline Stories involving self-interruption of emotional experience frequently emerges in the context of confronting perpetrators during IC. This was observed with Violet, described in the preceding chapter. Once interruptive processes are reduced, the client is encouraged to reengage in IC and express the interrupted experience to the imagined other, thereby moving forward in the trauma resolution process. Similarly, the final step in allowing painful emotional experience described in Chapter 9 typically involves identifying and confronting those responsible for harm in IC or EE.

The last stage in EFTT begins with experience and uninhibited expression of adaptive emotion, usually anger and sadness, as a new emotional plotline, and the exploration and expression of associated meaning and unmet needs, as evidenced in Reflective Storytelling inquiries. This is Level 4 on the Degree of Resolution Scale (DRS; Singh, 1994) presented in earlier chapters and the Appendix. Emotional experience and expression are the catalysts for self-narrative change as the meanings associated with previously avoided adaptive anger at maltreatment and sadness at loss are accessed and become available for integration into a new sense of self and new narrative. Once these new adaptive internal resources are accessed, the resolution process moves quickly forward. Therapists help clients articulate what they resent, specify what made and still makes them angry and why, what they missed or missed out on, the effects of abuse and neglect on self, and how life would have been better if their needs had been met. Therapists help clients construct stories about past experiences with the other that are specific and imbued with emotion and emotional meaning.

This is followed by increased sense of entitlement to unmet needs at DRS Level 5 in the late phase of therapy. In stories about and dialogues with the imagined other, therapists help clients shift from "I want" to "I deserve" and "I insist." Gradually, the client's narratives contain views of self with legitimate wants and needs that are clearly and assertively expressed. Interventions during DRS Levels 4 and 5 also elicit client perceptions of the other and reactions of the imagined other to new client assertions. Interventions promote reflection on meaning as more adaptive views of self as deserving emerge in these Unexpected Outcome Stories. Finally, at DRS Level 6, interventions support more adaptive perceptions of self as separate, autonomous, empowered, and able to assert interpersonal boundaries, as well as more differentiated and realistic perspectives of significant others that emerge in Unexpected Outcome and Discovery Stories. These stories include letting go of the past and clearly holding abusive/neglectful others, rather than self, responsible for harm.

Client Examples of Final IC/EE

The end of therapy (usually Session 14 or 15) includes a final IC/EE with the significant other(s) who has been the focus of therapy. The client is encouraged to compare his or her experience of engaging in this procedure and confronting imagined perpetrators now with what it was like at the beginning of therapy. This New Outcome Story is thoroughly explored.

Anger promotes assertiveness, self-empowerment, and interpersonal boundary definition. Sadness promotes grieving and acceptance of loss, letting go, and compassion toward self and others. Just as in the initial IC/EE described in Chapter 7, different types of resolution and changes in perceptions of self and significant others are observed in the final IC/EE. For example, Monica, whose mother committed suicide, imagined her mother taking full responsibility for the devastation she caused; Monica was then was able to forgive her mother. This resolution resulted from several IC procedures over the course of therapy in which the therapist validated and helped her express anger toward her imagined mother for her "unspeakable" act, as well as sessions that helped her process current difficulties with her siblings, all of which she attributed to the trauma of her mother's suicide.

Interventions during the final IC helped Monica acknowledge all she had missed and grieve these losses ("Yes, this is where it hurts. Tell her all that you have missed."), as well as directives to recall specific autobiographical memories that exemplified her mother's love. At the end of this final IC dialogue, when asked how she felt recalling these positive experiences with her mother (a critical step in self soothing), Monica reported that she felt warm and secure in a way she had not felt since her mother's death. She now saw her mother as loving, rather than uncaring, and her mother's suicide as an act of desperation, rather than as selfishness and a desire to escape from her children. This was her coherent Unexpected Outcome Story in which she finally made sense of traumatic events that had been incomprehensible and had haunted her all her life. Resolution and New Outcomes in the form of forgiveness are important in healing emotional injuries with primary attachment figures, and this is more likely to occur when clients can imagine the other being genuinely remorseful and repentant. Forgiveness may not be possible or even desirable in cases involving malevolent or disturbed others who are not seen as capable of or willing to fully acknowledge harm. In these instances, Unexpected Outcomes involve increased self-empowerment rather than forgiveness, increased separation from the other, and fully holding them accountable for harm.

For example, the client Richard, who had been molested by a priest, had focused primarily on making sense of his inability to stop or disclose the abuse as a boy. Interventions involving two-chair dialogues focused on resolving self-critical processes (Competing Plotlines), and reexperiencing himself as a powerless, frightened boy before, during, and following episodes of molestation (Experiential Story). Toward the end of therapy, he wrote a letter to the priest, which was like a "victim impact statement." It is important to note that the therapist asked him to read the letter out loud in the session and to attend to his internal experience while doing so. He reported feeling anxious at first, but stronger, fully understanding his inability as a boy to disclose the abuse and fully holding the priest accountable for harm (New Outcome Story). This was followed by a final confrontation of the imagined priest in which Richard fully expressed his anger at profound maltreatment. The prevalence and devastation of childhood abuse by priests has been a focus of much attention in the media in recent years, for example, the placement and sexual and physical abuse of children in Indian Residential Schools in Canada. Part of the struggle for these individuals and their families has been the lack of acknowledgment of harm on the parts of church and government authorities. This is a form of revictimization. However, healing involves helping these clients to fully hold individuals and the institutions responsible for harm, whether or not they apologize. A final IC can involve imagining "the church" or the Pope in the other chair.

For another client, Kim, who was dealing with sexual molestation by her uncle, reexperiencing the abuse and confronting her uncle during IC took place during an early session. The remainder of therapy focused primarily on current issues with her parents, who invalidated the abuse, and on increasing her awareness of and reducing her own internalized invalidation (Competing Plotline and Discovery Storytelling). It is not uncommon for clients to focus more on issues with neglectful or invalidating primary attachment figures rather than on issues with more distant abusive others. We have seen this in the case of Charlize, whom we described in earlier chapters. The final IC with Kim was with her parents, in which she was able to assert her boundaries with them and focus more on ways in which she could meet her needs for support and validation in other relationships in the future.

Other clients presented in earlier chapters and elsewhere evidenced other forms of resolution. For example, Lisa, with posttraumatic stress disorder (PTSD) from physical abuse by a stepmother, was first described by Paivio and Shimp (1998). The middle phase of therapy focused on two-chair work to help her allow vulnerable experience (Competing Plotlines) and a behavioral technique for reprocessing terrifying nightmares that involved reexperiencing the nightmare in session and renarrating a more satisfactory ending in which she stood up to her stepmother (Experiential Story). Two-chair dialogues also helped her explore her fear of intimacy and of disclosing the abuse to others. During a final IC in the last session of therapy, interventions helped her to fully experience and express her anger ("Keep going, tell her more about why you hate her. It's important to say exactly what you are so furious about.") and allow herself to weep for what she had suffered ("Yes, such a lot of feelings. It's okay, let it come, you've held this in a long time."). This was the first time Lisa allowed herself to cry in therapy. In processing the therapy experience, she said that although she would not wish her abuse on anyone, she felt that she was a stronger and more compassionate person for having endured it and worked it through. This New Outcome Story is an example of posttraumatic growth (Tadeski, Park, & Calhoun, 1998), in which clients move beyond symptom reduction to feel that they are better off than they were before the trauma. Lisa's directions for the future entailed her dreams of becoming a lawyer and helping maltreated children.

Another client, who had been severe physically abused by his grandfather, had been unable to imagine the grandfather acknowledging harm and any wrongdoing, and he was thus unable to let go of his own blaming and rejecting anger and move on in the resolution process. He was stuck in the Same Old Story of himself as victim to a perceived globally malevolent other. Helpful intervention in the final IC involved shifting from what he imagined his grandfather would say in response to his accusations, to imagining what he would feel on the inside, up in heaven, if he knew how the client felt. Typical of IC protocol, imagining perpetrators in early sessions functions purely as a stimulus to evoke responses in the self. Only in later sessions, when clients have expressed their own feelings, are they asked to imagine the internal experience of the other. In this case, the intervention elicited client empathic resources and a New Outcome Story in which he imagined that although his grandfather in real life would be too proud to apologize, his grandfather in heaven would regret his behavior.

Still another example of resolution observed in Unexpected Outcome Stories is a client who grew up in an alcoholic home where he had been physically and sexually abused by numerous members of his family, and who also abused his siblings. Healing involved working through guilt (Competing Plotline), coming to understand his experience as a child, and constructing a more self-compassionate self-narrative (Discoveries), as well as an IC to apologize and ask for his siblings' forgiveness. He imagined that they would forgive him. Toward the end of therapy he was able to apologize and ask for their forgiveness in real life, which they freely gave. This was a profound New Outcome Story, which enabled him to move forward and forgive his parents during a final IC. This client came to understand that they, too, had been victims, and if they could have changed things they would have (Discovery Story).

Termination

Preparation for termination begins in late sessions. EFTT is a time-limited model so that clients typically initially contracted for 16 or 20 sessions and most clients are ready to end at that time. For clients who could benefit from a longer course of therapy, termination can be difficult, and they may need considerable support. For example, Matt, whose primary problems concerned defensive anger, became angry when, at the beginning of Session 14, the therapist reminded him that they had only two more sessions. Over the course of therapy, Matt and the therapist had developed a strong collaborative relationship focused on helping him experience and express more vulnerable experience. He had made considerable gains in this area, and by Session 12 he was able to cry and allow himself to experience his profound sadness and loneliness. At termination, however, Matt accused the therapist of not caring about him. Although he responded positively to the therapist's interpretation that he was angry about therapy ending and apologized for his outburst, a longer course of therapy would have been better for him. This would have allowed him more time to completely resolve intra- and interpersonal issues and give him control over when therapy ended. Unfortunately, this is the situation in many cases where clinics offer only time-limited therapy. Analyses of EFTT sessions with clients such as Matt, who made more modest treatment gains (e.g., reduced PTSD but unresolved in terms of issues with perpetrators), indicated a higher frequency of Transitional narratives in the late phase of therapy (Carpenter et al., 2016). This suggests they were still in the process of constructing more adaptive, experiential, and reflective self-narratives and could benefit from a longer course of therapy to resolve intra-personal issues, move on to resolving issues with perpetrators, and fully integrate the self-narrative changes they had begun to make.

EFTT protocol for therapy termination (Paivio & Pascual-Leone, 2010) is as follows. Prior to the last session, clients are asked to write another trauma narrative that can be processed with the therapist during the last session in terms of any observed changes from their written story in the first session. The final session also involves mutual feedback. The therapist invites the client to talk about important changes in views of self and others, thoughts, behavior, current relationships, level of functioning, as well as progress in terms of goal attainment. They also are asked about helpful and hindering aspects of therapy. The therapist directs client attention to internal experience as they are telling these New Unexpected Outcome Stories, to enhance client awareness of agency in contributing to their described changes and consolidate self-narrative change in the context of Discovery Storytelling markers. The therapist provides feedback on observed client processes and positive changes in processes during sessions. This could include their regular attendance and commitment to change, and their struggle and willingness to confront and work through painful material, for example. It is important that therapists also acknowledge and validate whatever degree of resolution the client has achieved, including validating client disappointment with limited gains. Together, they create a bridge to the future, as described in the two intensive case analyses that follow in Chapter 12.

12

TWO INTENSIVE CASE ANALYSES: LATE-PHASE EFTT

The late phase of emotion-focused therapy for trauma (EFTT) with clients Charlize and Mark evidenced transformative changes in their narrative and emotion processes. Both shifted from Transitional, Competing Plotline, and Inchoate Storytelling to more Reflective Storytelling. Both achieved full resolution of their issues with abusive and neglectful others who were the focus of therapy, which included profound changes in their views of self and others and in their current relationships. These were evident in Unexpected Outcome and Discovery Stories.

CHARLIZE

Late-phase sessions with Charlize began with a further exploration of her fears of standing up to her mother and then shifted to the disclosure of stories focused on her engaging in new, assertive actions with her mother

http://dx.doi.org/10.1037/0000041-013
Narrative Processes in Emotion-Focused Therapy for Trauma, by S. C. Paivio and L. E. Angus

(Unexpected Outcome Storytelling). Her therapist played a significant role in helping Charlize to identify, describe, and reflect on the importance and meaning of her new emotions and actions with her mother in these therapy sessions and supported the articulation of a new view of self and the coconstruction of her new self-identity narrative (Discovery Storytelling).

Session 13

Session 13 began with Charlize again exploring her desire for connection with her family and at the same time finding herself pulling back from contact with them. When Charlize struggled to find the right words (Inchoate Storytelling) in the session, her therapist empathically highlighted her most poignant feelings.

> *Therapist:* Afraid you are not wanted.
>
> *Client:* A burden. I am not part of the family, the history. I am a guest, it's time to go.
>
> *Therapist:* Say more, how that feels.
>
> *Client:* It feels uncomfortable, distant, time to leave.
>
> *Therapist:* Some agonizing feeling, lonely?
>
> *Client:* Not lonely, detached, not part of them, an oddball.
>
> *Therapist:* It's somehow connected to your mother, wanting her and never knowing when she would decide to toss you away. Let's go back to a memory of a situation with mother.

Demonstrating a process-diagnostic understanding of the essential interrelationship between emotion and narrative processes, her therapist attempted to deepen Charlize's emotional engagement with her Same Old Story memories (of feeling excluded by her family) by having her remember and describe a specific autobiographical memory. Charlize recalled an incident in which her mother had wanted her to take care of her grandmother's belongings.

> *Client:* But it was for her, my missing my grandmother is not heard. Sometimes when she asks me for things I hope we will get close, but I am always disappointed. This has happened all my life. She opens up to me, is vulnerable, but it's just a false sense of getting close to her. That's not going to happen.
>
> *Therapist:* Maybe we will bond, getting your hopes up.
>
> *Client:* My job is to take care of her. That's it.
>
> *Therapist:* Time's up! Just *chop!* Gone!

Client:	No bond. So now with everybody, I go to a certain point then pull back, I end it [shifting into more Reflective Storytelling].
Therapist:	To avoid the pain of being left on your own.
Client:	Sort of rejected.
Therapist:	Rejected, say more about how that affects you [*Charlize struggles to explain*].
Client:	It's hard to describe.
Therapist:	How do you feel now?
Client:	Choked up, lack of bond with my mother, just used, nothing for me. [*The therapist reflects her pain.*]
Client:	Yes, but hoping, it eats away at me [*voice quivers, pause*] but I can't withdraw completely from her.
Therapist:	Can't let go of the hope.

Charlize's therapist then helped direct her attention to specifying her fears about setting boundaries with her mother and possibly risking losing her completely.

Therapist:	So better to hold back.
Client:	[*quickly*] No, better to say, at least I will know where I stand. At least things will change. I need to bite the bullet, but I'm also afraid I will not express myself properly.

It is important to note that a new perspective and experiential sense of urgency emerged for Charlize that directly challenged the feared outcomes of her Same Old Story of abandonment and neglect. In essence, the Same Old Story became a narrative with Competing Plotlines and the possibility of new, more agentic actions and satisfying emotional outcomes. Again, her therapist validated her understandable fears but supported and highlighted the singular importance of new feelings, needs, and perspectives that had emerged in the context of her exploring her emotional experience: "This therapy is the first time you have been able to express your feelings, and the goal of increasing clarity in therapy is so you can feel more confident about expressing your feelings in real life."

Session 14

The following session focused on the disclosure, and reflective exploration, of situations in which Charlize implemented new behaviors with both her mother (e.g., asserting boundaries) and husband (e.g., not reacting to his negative comments). This was an excellent example of how EFTT therapist process-directive work with Unexpected Outcome Storytelling is more than simply acknowledging a client's report of new change. Rather, it entails a deliberate exploration of the experiential impact and meaning of achieving new emotional outcomes, which directly challenge the assumptions of the maladaptive Same Old Story, for the reflective articulation of a new view of self and coconstruction of a more differentiated and compassionate self-narrative.

Charlize began the session by telling the story of saying no to her mother's recent requests for a favor. Her therapist noticed that Charlize had not only taken new actions (Unexpected Storytelling) but also clearly understood the important significance of this event for the emergence of a new view of self (Discovery Storytelling). As such, he invited Charlize to then fully describe how it happened, how it felt (Experiential Storytelling), and what it meant to her (Reflective Storytelling).

> *Therapist:* Let's go there. What happened that you were able to say no when before you struggled?
>
> *Client:* Yes, I always did. Now I am not going to rearrange my life any more to handle her problems. And she didn't argue or complain at all. I was pretty pleased. I set my priorities and my boundaries there. Two thumbs up!
>
> *Therapist:* Exciting, you were clear, knowing what you want. And people around you are responding. What's your understanding of that?
>
> *Client:* Because I am saying it. The problem was I was keeping things inside, no one knew what was bothering me or where the boundaries were and now they see.
>
> *Therapist:* So being able to say where you stand is critical [reflects her new understanding].
>
> *Client:* I felt confident, strong, respected . . . my only fear is if I have no legitimate reason to say no to her. That's where the real test will be.

Again, the competing emotional plotline of fearful, self-silencing Same Old Story emerged, and again her therapist decided to more fully emotionally engage and understand the impediments to her ability to assert herself with her mother. This was done, in the context of a specific autobiographical memory narrative, with the intentional goal of strengthening Charlize's capacity to implement new actions and behaviors.

> *Therapist:* Let's look at that. Imagine a situation [*client ponders*]. Let's say the one when she insisted you take your grandmother's utensils and you now say no [access autobiographical memory to increase emotional engagement].

Client:	It's a control struggle for me.
Therapist:	Control over your own decisions is critical to you.
Client:	I want what I say to be taken seriously and not just pushed aside. I'm an adult.
Therapist:	So it's not really about the utensils, it's about being sucked into giving up control. What are your needs at that moment, to be respected, not taken lightly?
Client:	I want to be in control of what I want to do and that's it.

This was a clear marker for the introduction of an empathic exploration (EE) intervention in the session and the enactment and coconstruction of a new narrative, with new emotional outcomes, with her mother.

Therapist:	That sounds legitimate to me [validation]. How would you say that to her, imagine her in that situation?
Client:	[pause] Please respect my wishes, I do not want them.
Therapist:	I'm in charge ["Right"]. I know what I want and don't want. What else about guarding your boundaries?
Client:	Please take what I say seriously, take my choices seriously.
Therapist:	It's my choice. What I think is important ["Yes"]. So would mother react?
Client:	Oh, excuuuuse me! That's it, and then I would get upset at her digs [evokes maladaptive emotion scheme, Same Old Story].
Therapist:	She is digging, carving a hole in your boundaries.

This intentional use of evocative empathy successfully evoked an alternative healthy protest, a new storyline, from Charlize.

Client:	Wait a minute. I'm allowing that to happen!
Therapist:	So now?
Client:	I would not allow that to happen. I would ignore her or say "grow up"—respectfully, of course [they both laugh].
Therapist:	So you don't want to get into a power struggle with her.
Client:	Right. I don't want to be rude, that's just not me.
Therapist:	So she says, "excuuuuse me" [stimulus] and you feel the dig, how do you react?
Client:	Come on Ma. I'm a grown woman. Please respect my wishes. I'm not doing it to hurt you. I'm doing it so you respect my choices.

At this point the therapist directed Charlize's attention to her presently felt experience of having asserted her boundaries with her imagined mother.

Therapist: What's going on for you?

Client: I feel really good.

Therapist: Can you be more specific about that feeling because that's a very important feeling because you were stuck for a long time [supports elaboration of new Unexpected Outcome Storytelling beyond simply a report].

Client: I have no anger, no turmoil, no conflict.

Therapist: You kind of like yourself.

Client: Yes. [*giggles*] I feel like I'm in control right now, in control of my emotions, in control of my decisions.

In processing her EE dialogue, her therapist promoted reflection on her new experience of herself, for further self-narrative coconstruction (Discovery Storytelling) that emerged in the context of self-assertion.

Therapist: If you were to describe what's different, where did this new confidence come from?

Client: Because I am able to verbalize and am actually sure of my feelings, not all over the place . . . I have to keep doing it, condition myself.

Therapist: So that kind of experience needs to be reinforced. So what you are really saying is . . . It's all about what's important to you ["Mm hmm"], and you want to do it respectfully, not cut her off.

Client: Yes, she's my mother, I'm not just going to cut her out, but I won't have to if she knows my boundaries . . . I know my identity . . . I'm learning more about me.

Therapist: That's exciting.

Client: What's more exciting is to know my body signals, feelings, and what I should do about them.

Therapist: Tell me about some of those signals [direct attention to internal experience, explore experience].

Client: Like today when she asked for money, usually I feel guilty, sad, upset. Today I was calm, inclined to help, and when my husband was saying how I shouldn't give her money, I was getting upset but I was aware, processed the information from my body, and I did it quickly, I didn't have to think about it for hours.

Therapist: So you listened to your body, this allowed you to be in control, not all hurt ["Yes"]. That's incredible. I'm so excited to hear that. That's exactly what we're trying to do here, increase awareness [shared excitement about new learning].

The therapist then asked Charlize to anticipate future situations to further elaborate and consolidate her new self-narrative. Toward the end of the session, the client teared up as she talked about finding herself able to trust and feel safe enough in her relationship with her husband to depend on him, another Unexpected Outcome Story.

Client: That's a first. Someone is taking care of me. I can be open, vulnerable. I don't have to be responsible all the time.

Therapist: That's very powerful, what you are discovering about yourself.

Her therapist highlighted the poignant sense of joy and relief that she experienced in the context of finding herself able to let go of her fears and take a risk to trust and depend on someone else for the first time. A direct challenge to the assumptions and fears that have fueled the maladaptive patterns of her Same Old Storytelling, Charlize began to discover and consolidate a new, more compassionate and empowered view of self and others.

Session 15

At beginning of Session 15, the therapist asked Charlize what remained to be addressed in the remaining therapy sessions, and she decided to focus on new perceptions of her mother and the importance of her being able to assert her own boundaries with her mother. Charlize described a recent situation in which she had stepped back and observed her mother, which confirmed a new awareness of her mother's limited relational capacities while, at the same time, acknowledging that she had and did deserve better emotional and physical care from a mother. In essence, she no longer second-guessed her negative perceptions of her mother's capacity to care for others or the importance of needs for emotionally bonding, security, and trust with another.

To strengthen the coconstruction of an emergent, new self-narrative (Discovery Storytelling), her therapist encouraged Charlize to imagine speaking to her mother, from her new perspective on self and others, in the context of a final EE dialogue.

Client: You say you care about me, but I see you taking money from me when I don't have much to give, turning tears off and on to get what you want, depending on Grandmother's income, choosing not to work.

Therapist: How do you feel watching her?

Client:	Manipulated, used, angry. I'm not your game piece, your bank, your grocery store.
Therapist:	Angry.
Client:	Yes, angry, if you want a relationship with me, that's fine, but respect what I say . . . I'm not going to be your mother, sacrifice me and my kids' needs for you . . . I see now it wouldn't have mattered what I did as a child. She would have been the same [new view of self and other].
Therapist:	How do you feel knowing that?
Client:	Sad, I wasted a lot of time, giving up on hopes that we bond, that she will change. But I am happy I am the person I am, not a weak person or like her. I endured a lot and I did not become like her. I care about people, not just myself. I care about my children and how they feel. I am going to be the best person I can be. I am strong because of the past.

The dialogue involved the first clear expression of anger and assertion of boundaries with no collapse into fear (Degree of Resolution Scale [DRS] Level 3; Singh, 1994). This is Discovery Storytelling and is indicative of a new coherent narrative concerning self and mother.

Session 16

The final session consisted of mutual feedback and engagement in a reflective, coconstructive elaboration of Charlize's experiences of change and the articulation of a new more empowered and agentic self-narrative, helpful and hindering aspects of therapy, and directions for the future. Her therapist asked her to think back to the beginning of therapy, as compared with now, and to reflect on what she had discovered about herself, what was working for her now, and equally important, her understanding of how those important changes had happened. Her therapist's open-ended questions engaged a process-guiding inquiry into the coelaboration of Charlize's self-narrative change (Discovery Storytelling), focusing on how that had happened and how it was different from the maladaptive assumptions and outcomes of her Same Old Storytelling. She described herself as having been angry, confused, lashing out at her husband, very insecure, focused on other people's needs versus her own, wishy-washy, and indecisive before she entered therapy. She also thought that her primary relational concerns stemmed solely from the sexual abuse, and she had not realized how much her mother's emotional neglect had so deeply harmed and impacted her sense of trust and security in others.

Her therapist also asked Charlize where she stood regarding the key issues that had been the primary focus of their therapy sessions together. In terms of sexual abuse, she stated, "I realize now I can't be with my daughter 24/7, but I can ensure an open relationship so if anyone does touch her inappropriately she will tell me." This clearly represented a shift in the grip of the maladaptive Same Old Story relational patterns in her current relationships. In terms of her mother, Charlize stated, "I have more understanding of the reality versus what I hoped for. I feel more in control of my own life versus focused on her needs, I know her personality, it's so clear now, I see the potential for manipulation and can set boundaries with her. I know I will never have a close relationship with her; well, maybe it's possible, but I wouldn't put money on it. I suppose I always will have hope but it will not rule me. I will allow my mother to be an adult. I will no longer go through the old process of giving in, feeling hurt, and withdrawal." The emergence of a new view of self and others, in the context of Discovery Storytelling, is full resolution on the DRS Level 7, which includes accepting her mother as she is, letting go of expectations that her mother will meet her unmet needs for deep connection, and placing a greater focus on meeting her own needs. As demonstrated previously, this resolution is the foundation for an integrated, new self-narrative with new possibilities for more adaptive thoughts, feelings, and behaviors.

Charlize's therapist shared his reflections on the therapy process with her as well. He recalled that early on she had looked strong, competent on the outside, but he also saw how she struggled to disclose her deepest, darkest secrets and personal memories to him and to further explore and articulate the competing plotlines of her conflicting emotions, intentions, hopes and fears. The therapist said, "But you are psychologically minded, you can connect the dots yourself. For example, we spent one session on sexual abuse then you quickly moved on—Wow! I saw changes over time. We were peeling back the layers, getting to the core. You were able to fully utilize the process of self-exploration." He then asked her about her hopes for the future. Charlize replied, "I want to continue to chip away at expressing things with my mother, being more direct. Eventually she will know where I stand. And I will not make assumptions but will ask people how they feel also. I feel stronger, more in control, more brain space to focus on other things."

Conclusions

EFTT with Charlize resulted in a profound shift in her self-narrative. At the beginning of therapy, she described herself as someone who was angry, confused, lashing out at her husband, very insecure, and indecisive, and she blamed herself for not disclosing sexual abuse. She had limited awareness of her own feelings and needs and of the depth of the pain associated with her mother and her own inability to assert her boundaries for fear of rejection, always acquiescing to her mother's and, to some extent, her husband's demands. She felt like a powerless victim who had endured sexual abuse for years because of her mother's neglect and who had always felt manipulated, and "used" by her. At the same time, she was clinging to the hope that she would be able to "bond" with her mother. She felt sad, alone, and unloved by her mother and like an outsider in all her extended family relationships.

By Session 6, she had resolved the sexual abuse. By midtreatment, she felt closer to her husband and was able to trust and depend on him. At the end of therapy, she was emotionally aware of how she has been wounded by her mother, and she clearly saw and accepted that her mother was not capable of the kind of connection Charlize wanted. She was clear about her values, feelings, and needs. She wanted to have her mother in her life but was able to assert her boundaries with her. She saw herself as a strong woman, unlike her mother, who was capable of open and intimate relationships with her children and husband and able to fulfill her dreams and goals.

MARK

The last phase of EFTT began with further exploration of Mark's issues with self-confidence and more two-chair work with "Dr. No" (Competing Plotline Storytelling). Later sessions continued to focus on his past and current relationships with his father, mother, and wife. His narratives became increasingly experiential and reflective, with greater access to adaptive feelings and needs. At the end of therapy Mark reported several Unexpected Outcomes and Discoveries about himself and his relationships. In particular, his new narrative included a positive view of himself and a less hostile and more differentiated view of his parents as being incapable of change.

Session 17

At the beginning of Session 17, Mark reported the he was feeling good about changes he had made in his life and now wanted to focus more on the present and future to ensure that he would not fall into "old ruts." His therapist asked him to be specific about what he meant by "old ruts," to which he immediately responded, "feeling negative, selfish, withdrawn," a key maladaptive Same Old Story plotline. He then stated that he had realized recently that he no longer seemed to be haunted by issues with his mother—a clear marker of Unexpected Outcome Story. Aware of the therapeutic importance of this shift for Mark, his therapist then focused on experientially processing the emotional impact and meaning of his new story.

> *Therapist:* What does happen on the inside when you think of your parents?

Client: A little sad that they think I'm nuts, but I'm no longer angry. It's too bad that we can't be closer, but my family is screwed up, they can't change.

With the expression of this new adaptive emotion that challenged the reactive, angry, enraged plotline of the Same Old Story, a new Completing Plotline Story marker now emerged in the session. In response to hearing the adaptive emotion and needs for connection versus maladaptive fears, reactive anger, and withdrawal, his therapist then suggested a final imaginal confrontation (IC) to try to bring closure to his family concerns. She began the dialogue by first reevoking Mark's core childhood trauma memory of begging for his mother's forgiveness for hours: "What happens to you on the inside when you remember that incident? Is it different?" Mark's vocal quality was more modulated than in early sessions; he clearly held his mother accountable for harm and distance in their relationship and for the negative effects on himself and their relationship.

Therapist: Be specific about the most damaging effects.

Client: The negativity, constant criticism, I have no love for you. It makes me sad, but how can you raise children without love? This is what happens.

Therapist: How do you imagine she would respond to hearing what you have to say?

Client: What I want or what I believe would happen?

Therapist: Both.

Client: I want them to say I'm sorry, to acknowledge damage, but she would say "sorry" sarcastically, cry so hard, "we gave you everything," she would never back down, she is unbendable, a one-way street. I just can't connect with you. I feel sad that I have no feelings for you, that I don't have a mother I love.

Therapist: You really missed out.

Client: Yes, that's so important.

Therapist: Say more about how important that would be to have a mother you loved.

Client: Nice to have someone to talk to, to listen, they don't know me.

Therapist: They don't know you, their son. That's a huge loss, for both of you. ["Yes"] Anything else you want to say?

Client: You taught me a lesson in how not to raise my kids, but I'm not mad anymore, I'm over it, okay with it all. I'm just sorry you can't listen, it can't be different.

His therapist also encouraged Mark to assert his boundaries with his mother. When asked how he felt after the dialogue, he stated that he used to be all churned up after participating in an IC dialogue but this time he felt "peaceful, relaxed, I like it, I have a smile instead of a frown." This was a primary adaptive emotional response that created an Unexpected Outcome Story and new story plotline. In this final dialogue, Mark evidenced genuine acceptance and letting go of his longing and wishes for his parents to change, and he did not collapse into powerlessness and resignation or hard "f-you" and rejecting anger in the pseudoresolution that had been observed in previous IC interventions. It is important that there was a significant shift in his view of his mother. She was no longer "a monster" but rather someone rigid and incapable of hearing his perspective.

Session 18

Session 18 focused on understanding more fully the confusing feelings or "pressure" he felt to continue a relationship with his mother, despite his awareness that he did not love or respect her, and on his belief that she had done nothing to deserve his respect, "I'm just programmed." Picking up indicators of Mark's confusion and puzzlement about feeling caught between two very different emotional plotlines, his therapy proposed a two-chair dialogue to explore both sides of the Competing Plotlines in the therapy session. Mark initially attributed the pull toward his mother as "I kind of want revenge," to have a chance to prove that he was not "Mark, the asshole" that he thought they saw him as, so his mother wouldn't think he was "a selfish prick." The therapist encouraged further elaboration: "So it's to prove her wrong, kind of rub it in her face?" Mark agreed that he got satisfaction out of proving her wrong but also realized that he was staying in the relationship for his daughter as well as himself and that he did not want to act in petty and revengeful ways, like her. The therapist highlighted his values and standards to be a decent person, to do the right thing, thus supporting the coconstruction of a more coherent and positive self-narrative.

Sessions 19 and 20

Sessions 19 and 20 focused on identifying Unexpected Outcome Storytelling, helping Mark to elaborate, story, and reflectively explore new ways of being as new story outcomes had emerged over the course of therapy. He told a story about success with requesting more opportunities at work.

> Client: I was focused on what I wanted and it paid off. I got a pro-
> motion. Before I always felt negative, angry that I did not

achieve my potential, and had low confidence. I would not ask because I always expected the negative—Dr. No.

Therapist: It was gutsy, ballsy, to ask for what you wanted, and a vote of confidence, people respond to you differently [reinforcing his new Outcome Story].

His therapist also offered helpful, process-guided open questions to scaffold an inquiry into his own experience of achieving this important new outcome and heightening his sense of personal agency.

Therapist: What gets in your way about being positive?

Client: [reflective] Anger and expectations when things don't work out. I am not good at rolling with the punches, too controlling, demanding.

Therapist: How do you want to be?

Client: I want to let go of expectations of others, not be so angry, overanalytical, critical, and judgmental of others. It eats me up.

At the end of the session, she asked Mark how he felt about ending therapy. Mark said he would miss having someone to talk to, tell how he feels, someone who can listen and give feedback. Therapist: "That is a definite need that you have, you have been able to make use of that. Are there people in your life you can do that with?"

Session 20

At the beginning of Session 20, both client and therapist focus on reflectively processing the trauma narrative he wrote just before the session. Mark stated that as he wrote his trauma narrative, he had pictured his own kids getting the kind of treatment he did, never being told they were loved, getting strapped. He also stated that social norms have changed regarding how we treat and discipline children and acknowledged that his parents probably "didn't know any better." This indicated a more differentiated perspective of his parents and a shift in the Same Old Story (DRS Level 7) of blame and defensive anger.

Mark then disclosed a recent story about his son's birthday party, how he had been angry and "bent out of shape" with his son's behavior, but then realized he was wrong and apologized. This was a positive new interpersonal outcome and Unexpected Outcome Storytelling marker exemplar that directly challenged the negative expectations of his Same Old Story and critical view of self. To facilitate a heightened awareness of the significance of this new outcome, his therapist then asked him to reflect on and describe what was happening to him on the inside—emotionally—during the episode and to identify what had triggered his defensive angry outburst, in the first place. Mark stated, "I was feeling disrespected. But I realized I was overreacting. I went into the garage, felt bad, mad at myself. I realized this was another example of having unrealistic expectations of a teenage boy. I wanted to handle the situation better." His therapist highlighted his decision to handle his anger differently in this situation and then invited him to reflect further on the meaning, for him, that he was able to not only shift out of anger but to also apologize for his actions.

> *Therapist:* So you corrected your behavior. Are you satisfied with how you handled it?
>
> *Client:* I feel good that I admitted it. Before I couldn't take any criticism, admit I was wrong, but now I can stop and think about it [Discovery Storytelling].

In his thoughtful response, Mark identified a significant shift in his emotional reactions, in terms of a before-and-after contrast that signified the emergence of a new, more agentic and compassionate view of self and others. This is the hallmark of Discovery Storytelling markers and a significant indicatory of self-identity narrative change.

Mark then shared another recent story of positive change and new adaptive outcomes—Unexpected Storytelling—that challenged the negative plotlines of his previous, maladaptive Same Old Story. He revealed that he had been receptive and open to his brother's overtures to connect and that this was the first time anyone in his family had acknowledged that he was in therapy for childhood abuse and that he was having marital difficulties. Aware of the key importance of Mark's new capacity to not only show vulnerability to a family member but also allow and accept compassion and empathy in return—a new adaptive emotional/relational plotline—his therapist further highlighted how important it was for him to receive that validation from his brother. She empathically supported his new desire for openness and to feel connected to people he really cared about. Her empathically attuned, process-guided response contributed to a further articulation of Mark's new view of self, which was further validated in the context of a Discovery Storytelling mode when Mark responded that he was no longer the angry, spiteful, jealous person he had been before and how he was different from his parents. He provided, as narrative proof, a specific poignant story of his young daughter being upset before bed and that he, unlike his parent, could never let his little girl go to bed crying (Discovery Story). The therapist acknowledged, "This is so important, for her, and for you." Overall, Mark's empathically attuned therapist provided supportive, process-guiding responses that highlighted the disclosure of new story outcomes that directly challenged the negative Same Old Story plotlines and new views of self that included his most cherished desires for connection, strengths, values, and accomplishments, and she asked about his goals for the future. Mark stated that he had made positive personal changes that were important for himself and his children; he anticipated that his impending divorce from his wife would be tough, but he expressed confidence now that he would be able to handle it.

Conclusions

At the beginning of therapy, Mark was chronically angry, viewed himself as an "ugly person" like his mother, was unable to express his feelings and opinions, and was defensive and unable to admit his mistakes. He was full of hatred and negativity for how he was treated as a child. He was able to identify feelings, but his narrative quality was highly overcontrolled, with no emotional arousal, flat vocal quality, and facial expression. However, he used rich metaphors to describe his internal experience, which provided a window into his inner world. He also was highly motivated, ready to change (Transitional narratives indicating access to adaptive internal experience), and responsive to the therapist's questions and directives to attend to and explore his internal experience. Because Mark originally identified disrespect for women as a core problem, his therapy seems to represent a transformational relational experience with a female therapist.

Over the course of therapy, his storytelling was increasingly emotionally engaged. He expressed adaptive anger and sadness and reflected on associated meanings to construct a more coherent and adaptive self-narrative. At the end of therapy, Mark accepted his parents as being unable to change and his marriage as likely being beyond repair. He accepted responsibility in the latter situation. He also was more aware of and compassionate toward himself for the emotional pain he suffered as a child. He viewed himself as a decent and likeable man, a loving father, and a successful professional. He was more able to express his feelings and opinions, to admit and correct his mistakes. Mark was optimistic about the future, despite his likely divorce.

AFTERWORD: PROCESS-DIAGNOSIS AND MARKER-GUIDED INTERVENTION

One of the strengths and distinguishing features of emotion-focused therapy (EFT), in general, is the emphasis on process-outcome research involving the intensive analysis of dozens of videotaped therapy sessions to understand in-session change processes. Emotion-focused therapy for trauma (EFTT) developed from such an analysis of a subset of clients in a clinical trial who were dealing with childhood abuse. EFTT has been further refined through the analysis of therapy processes in two subsequent clinical trials. For example, research resulted in the development of a less evocative and less stressful reexperiencing procedure for helping clients to reprocess painful memories of childhood abuse. This type of process-outcome research means that clinicians and their clients can have confidence both in the efficacy of EFTT and in the in-session processes that are most beneficial. The latter is what is most relevant to clinical practice.

http://dx.doi.org/10.1037/0000041-014
Narrative Processes in Emotion-Focused Therapy for Trauma, by S. C. Paivio and L. E. Angus

A necessary feature of process-outcome research is the development and use of reliable measures to assess the quality of key in-session processes. Because higher quality client processes on these measures have been related to better outcome, these research tools also can act as "process maps" to guide effective intervention, moment by moment and session by session. One contribution of this book is the presentation of several empirically derived process maps that identify, for example, specific steps in the process of resolving "unfinished business" concerning perpetrators of abuse and neglect, intrapersonal struggles concerning fear of emotional experience and self-blame for the abuse, and narrative-emotion Problem, Transition, and Change Storytelling markers—and intervention strategies—to enhance trauma narrative coherence, productive emotional meaning making, and adaptive self-narrative change in productive EFTT sessions. Research-supported, video-based process maps are invaluable tools for enriched clinical training as they show how the identification of client process markers, emerging in the cut and thrust of actual therapy sessions, can effectively guide the implementation of specific therapeutic responses/interventions in productive EFTT sessions. Accordingly, an additional contribution of this book is the inclusion of detailed clinical examples and transcriptions of actual therapy sessions, as evidenced in the intensive case analyses of Charlize and Mark, to illustrate the implementation of EFTT intervention principles and marker-guided intervention strategies that effectively address a range of maladaptive emotions, Incoherent Storytelling, and Reflective processing difficulties in early-, middle-, and late-phase EFTT.

PAST, PRESENT, AND FUTURE

EFTT is based on more than 25 years of clinical psychotherapy research. EFTT moved the general model of EFT forward by applying it to a particular client group. In most previous manuscripts on EFT and EFTT, the importance of client narrative processes is acknowledged but remains in the background. This book moves an integrative focus on narrative and emotion processes to the foreground and, for the first time, makes explicit what therapists are implicitly responding to in client storytelling. A narrative-informed approach to EFTT integrates the narrative-emotion process (NEP) model with the model of resolution underlying EFTT. As such, this approach identifies steps in the process of resolving issues with perpetrators, in the phases of therapy, that are observed in the context of client trauma narrative disclosures and participation in key interventions.

In terms of clinical training and practice, the NEP Problem, Transition, and Change Storytelling markers were developed (a) to equip therapists with a systematic, process-diagnostic map to rapidly assess the quality and degree of narrative, emotional and meaning-making process indicators evidenced in client storytelling and then (b) to support the implementation of marker-guided, clinical interventions, on a moment-by-moment basis, for enriched EFTT case conceptualization, trauma narrative integration, emotional transformation, and self-narrative change. In so doing, the NEP model provides experienced EFT practitioners with a differentiated process map to identify Problem, Transition, and Change Storytelling markers and implement interventions that are related to increased disclosure of trauma memories, engaged emotional experiencing in the context of storytelling, as well as enriched emotional meaning making that not only supports the EFTT intervention model but also enriches treatment outcomes by facilitating client self-narrative coconstruction, especially in late-phase sessions.

For clinical practitioners new to EFTT, or practicing in narrative-based therapy approaches, NEP Storytelling markers equip therapists with a simplified, process-diagnostic map to quickly identify and assess a complex range of EFTT client process markers for enriched case conceptualization and implementation of marker-guided interventions. More specifically, the NEP Problem, Transition, and Change markers assess (a) level and kind of emotional expression (e.g., level of emotional arousal, adaptive versus maladaptive, level of emotional engagement with trauma material); (b) level and degree of self-reflective client processing and meaning exploration (e.g., capacity to focus on internal experiences, depth of experiencing); and (c) trauma narrative coherence, evidenced in client storytelling, during EFTT sessions. As such, key NEP markers provide novice EFTT therapists with a practical process map to rapidly assess and address problems in trauma narrative incoherence, emotional over- and underregulation, depth of experiential engagement, and readiness for change in early-phase EFTT sessions. Additionally, they support the implementation of EFTT tasks/interventions to access new adaptive emotional plotlines; facilitate trauma resolution; and support the development of a more agentic, empowered, and compassionate self-identity narrative, in mid- and late-phase EFFT sessions. In particular, NEP marker-guided responses are intended to help clients to access and integrate trauma memory narratives and painful emotions for enriched, reflective meaning making, emotional transformation, and self-narrative change, at each stage of therapy.

Finally, next steps in the elaboration of our integrative, process-diagnostic approach to working with both narrative and emotion processes in EFTT will include the development of video-based introductory and advanced-level training workshops that are designed to equip clinicians with enhanced empathy and process-diagnostic skills for the timely implementation of marker-guided strategies and effective EFTT treatment interventions. In turn, we hope to further evaluate these training initiatives in terms of client trajectories of change and overall treatment efficacy, for further refinement of our clinical models and the development of innovative process-diagnostic maps and marker-guided interventions. It is our hope that future clinicians and psychotherapy researchers might also be encouraged to engage in this collaborative dance of systematic observation and discovery, for enhanced practice innovation and effective treatment outcomes. This hope was the inspiration for our book.

APPENDIX: ABBREVIATED DEGREE OF RESOLUTION SCALE

Level 1: Stuck in the Same Old Story. Client is stuck in the "same old story" consisting of global negative views of significant others and maladaptive views of self and repeated patterns of maladaptive behavior.

Level 2: Emotional Reaction to Trauma Memories. An emotional reaction is evoked in response to recalling autobiographical trauma memories and imagining abusive or neglectful others in the imaginal confrontation (IC) or empathic exploration (EE) procedures. Initially the emotional reaction is typically undifferentiated global distress, hurt, blame, and complaint about the other, and collapse into resignation and hopelessness that things will ever change.

Level 3: Working Through Self-Related Difficulties. Clients' stories concerning self, perpetrators, and trauma memories typically are dominated by repeated collapse into fear/avoidance, self-doubt, guilt, shame, and self-blame. Their storytelling may also include internal struggles and conflicts, typically between a dominant maladaptive part and authentic "experiencing" self with healthy feelings and needs.

Level 4: Full Expression of Adaptive Emotion. Client narratives concerning perpetrators and traumatic events now contain clear and uninhibited expressions of adaptive anger at violation and sadness at losses and the associated meanings. Clients are able to identify unmet needs, but may not yet feel fully deserving of them.

Level 5: Increased Entitlement to Unmet Needs. Clients begin to feel increasingly entitled to having had their attachment needs met. Client self-narratives include views of self as having legitimate wants and needs, and they begin to hold abusive and neglectful others, rather than self, accountable for harm.

Level 6: More Adaptive Perceptions of Self and Other. The self is seen as more autonomous and powerful and perpetrators are seen in a more differentiated and realistic light. The client may forgive the other and/or clearly hold the other, rather than self, responsible for harm. Clients also begin to report experiencing new feelings and reactions in their current lives, for example, they are able to assert their boundaries with others.

Adapted from *Emotion-Focused Therapy for Complex Trauma: An Integrative Approach* (p. 301), by S. C. Paivio and A. Pascual-Leone, 2010, Washington, DC: American Psychological Association. Copyright 2010 by the American Psychological Association.

Level 7: Full Resolution. Clients have let go of expectations regarding the other, for example, that they will apologize or respond to unmet needs, and look to their own resources to meet existential or interpersonal needs. Clients may express a sense of relief and acceptance. They feel finished in terms of issues with the other and focus more on personal strengths.

GLOSSARY

adaptive emotion: immediate, biologically based, survival-oriented affective response.

alexithymia: difficulties identifying and labelling emotional experience, confusing feelings with bodily experience, external orientation.

emotional differentiation: the process by which a global emotional response is situated into its constituent parts in the context of a story.

emotion schemes: an internal structure that organizes current emotional responses in terms of past emotional experiences and lived stories.

emotion scripts: an emotionally based sequence that guides actions.

healthy resources: adaptive feelings, needs, perceptions, reactions, and behaviors.

lived stories: the subjective experience of a lived event that has yet to be externalized as a "told story."

macronarrative: the integration of personal stories to create a self-identity narrative.

maladaptive emotion: immediate affective response that have become dysfunctional in current situations because of past learning history.

mentalization: the sociocognitive capacity to think about oneself and others as psychological beings and to consider underlying mental states and motivations when interpreting behaviors.

micronarrative: individual personal stories disclosed in therapy sessions.

narrative-emotion change markers: client emotional and behavioral indicators of experienced change and the emergence of a more adaptive view of self and enhanced self-coherence.

narrative-emotion problem markers: client performance indicators of emotional avoidance, dysregulation, lack of narrative specificity, low coherence, and intrapersonal "stuckness."

narrative-emotion process markers: client performance indicators of underlying emotion, narrative, and meaning-making processes.

narrative-emotion transition markers: client performance indicators of enhanced personal meaning making, narrative coherence, emotional engagement, and readiness for change.

narrative scaffolding: the application of narrative schema for the organization of lived experiences.

personal storytelling: representing lived experiences as told stories that unfold along a linear timeline with beginnings, middles, and ends.

reflective functioning: used interchangeably with "mentalization."

self-identity narrative: the narrative organization of personal stories, over time, for the articulation of a coherent life story and view of self.

specific autobiographical memory (ABM): the organization of lived personal experiences as episodic, imagistic events that are remembered over time.

symbolizing: the articulation of felt or lived experiences in words or images.

REFERENCES

American Psychiatric Association. (2000). *Diagnostic and statistical manual of mental disorders* (4th ed., text rev.). Washington, DC: Author.

American Psychiatric Association. (2013). *Diagnostic and statistical manual of mental disorders* (5th ed.). Arlington, VA: Author.

American Psychological Association (Producer). (2013). *Emotion-focused therapy for trauma* [DVD]. Available from http://www.apa.org/pubs/videos/4310912.aspx

American Psychological Association (Producer). (2015). *Narrative processes in emotion-focused therapy for trauma* [DVD]. Available from http://www.apa.org/pubs/videos/4310940.aspx

Amir, N., Stafford, J., Freshman, M. S., & Foa, E. B. (1998). Relationship between trauma narratives and trauma pathology. *Journal of Traumatic Stress, 11*, 385–392. http://dx.doi.org/10.1023/A:1024415523495

Angus, L. (2012). Toward an integrative understanding of narrative and emotion processes in emotion-focused therapy of depression: Implications for theory, research and practice. *Psychotherapy Research, 22*, 367–380. http://dx.doi.org/10.1080/10503307. 2012.683988

Angus, L., Boritz, T., & Carpenter, N. (2013). Narrative, emotion and meaning making in psychotherapy: From theoretical concepts to empirical research findings. *Archives of Psychiatry and Psychotherapy, 32*, 329–338.

Angus, L., & Bouffard, B. (2004). The search for emotional meaning and self-coherence in the face of traumatic loss in childhood: A narrative process perspective. In J. Raskin & S. Bridges (Eds.), *Studies in meaning 2: Bridging the personal and social in constructivist psychology* (pp. 312–322). New York, NY: Pace University Press.

Angus, L., Gonçalves, M., Boritz, T., & Mendes, I. (in press). Narrative processes in emotion-focused therapy: Research findings and implications for practice. In L. S. Greenberg & R. N. Goldman (Eds.), *The handbook of emotion-focused therapy*. Washington, DC: American Psychological Association.

Angus, L., & Kagan, F. (2007). Empathic relational bonds and personal agency in psychotherapy: Implications for psychotherapy supervision, practice and research [Special section]. *Psychotherapy: Theory, Research, Practice, Training, 44*, 371–377. http://dx.doi.org/10.1037/0033-3204.44.4.371

Angus, L., Levitt, H., & Hardtke, K. (1999). The narrative processes coding system: Research applications and implications for psychotherapy practice. *Journal of Clinical Psychology, 55*, 1255–1270. http://dx.doi.org/10.1002/(SICI)1097-4679 (199910)55:10<1255::AID-JCLP7>3.0.CO;2-F

Angus, L., Lewin, J., Boritz, T., Bryntwick, E., Carpenter, N., Watson-Gaze, J., & Greenberg, L. (2012). Narrative processes coding system: A dialectical constructivist approach to assessing client change processes in emotion-focused therapy of depression. *Research in Psychotherapy: Psychopathology, Process and Outcome, 15*, 52–61.

Angus, L. E., & McLeod, J. (Eds.). (2004a). *The handbook of narrative and psycho-therapy: Practice, theory and research.* Thousand Oaks, CA: Sage. http://dx.doi.org/10.4135/9781412973496

Angus, L., & McLeod, J. (2004b). Self-multiplicity and narrative expression in psychotherapy. In H. J. M. Hermans & G. Dimaggio (Eds.), *The dialogical self in psychotherapy* (pp. 77–90). New York, NY: Brunner & Routledge. http://dx.doi.org/10.4324/9780203314616_chapter_5

Angus, L., Watson, J., Elliott, R., Schneider, K., & Timulak, L. (2015). Human-istic psychotherapy research 1990–2015: From methodological innovation to evidence-supported treatment outcomes and beyond [Special issue]. *Psycho-therapy Research, 25*, 330–347. http://dx.doi.org/10.1080/10503307.2014.989290

Angus, L. E., Boritz, T., Bryntwick, E., Carpenter, N., Macaulay, C., & Khattra, J. (2016). The Narrative-Emotion Process Coding System 2.0: A multi-methodological approach to identifying and assessing narrative-emotion process markers in psychotherapy. *Psychotherapy Research*, 1–17. Advance online publication. http://dx.doi.org/10.1080/10503307.2016.1238525

Angus, L. E., & Greenberg, L. S. (2011). *Working with narrative in emotion-focused therapy: Changing stories, healing lives.* Washington, DC: American Psychological Association. http://dx.doi.org/10.1037/12325-000

Angus, L. E., & Kagan, F. (2013). Assessing client self-narrative change in emotion-focused therapy of depression: An intensive single case analysis. *Psychotherapy: Theory, Research, & Practice, 50*, 525–534. http://dx.doi.org/10.1037/a0033358

Angus, L. E., Lewin, J., Bouffard, B., & Rotondi-Trevisan, D. (2004). "What's the story?" Working with narrative in experiential psychotherapy. In L. E. Angus & J. McLeod (Eds.), *Handbook of narrative and psychotherapy: Practice, theory, and research* (pp. 86–101). Thousand Oaks, CA: Sage. http://dx.doi.org/10.4135/9781412973496.d8

Angus Narrative-Emotion Marker Lab. (2015). *Narrative-Emotion Processes Coding System manual.* Unpublished manuscript, available from Lynne Angus, 108C BSB, York University, Toronto, Ontario, Canada, M4E 3N4.

Bateman, A., & Fonagy, P. (2013). Impact of clinical severity on outcomes of mentalisation-based treatment for borderline personality disorder. *The British Journal of Psychiatry, 203*, 221–227. http://dx.doi.org/10.1192/bjp.bp.112.121129

Baumeister, R. F., & Newman, L. S. (1994). How stories make sense of personal expe-riences: Motives that shape autobiographical narratives. *Personality and Social Psychology Bulletin, 20*, 676–690. http://dx.doi.org/10.1177/0146167294206006

Beaudreau, S. A. (2007). Are trauma narratives unique and do they predict psycho-logical adjustment? *Journal of Traumatic Stress, 20*, 353–357. http://dx.doi.org/10.1002/jts.20206

Bernstein, D., & Fink, L. (1998). *Manual for the childhood trauma questionnaire.* San Antonio, TX: The Psychological Corporation.

Bolger, E. A. (1999). Grounded theory analysis of emotional pain. *Psychotherapy Research, 9*, 342–362. http://dx.doi.org/10.1080/10503309912331332801

Boritz, T., Barnhart, R., Angus, L., & Constantino, M. J. (2016). Narrative flexibility in brief psychotherapy for depression. *Psychotherapy Research*, 1–11. Advance online publication. http://dx.doi.org/10.1080/10503307.2016.1152410

Boritz, T. Z., Angus, L., Monette, G., & Hollis-Walker, L. (2008). An empirical analysis of autobiographical memory specificity subtypes in brief emotion-focused and client-centered treatments of depression. *Psychotherapy Research, 18*, 584–593. http://dx.doi.org/10.1080/10503300802123245

Boritz, T. Z., Angus, L., Monette, G., Hollis-Walker, L., & Warwar, S. (2011). Narrative and emotion integration in psychotherapy: Investigating the relationship between autobiographical memory specificity and expressed emotional arousal in brief emotion-focused and client-centred treatments of depression. *Psychotherapy Research, 21*, 16–26. http://dx.doi.org/10.1080/10503307.2010.504240

Boritz, T. Z., Bryntwick, E., Angus, L., Greenberg, L. S., & Constantino, M. J. (2014). Narrative and emotion process in psychotherapy: An empirical test of the Narrative-Emotion Process Coding System (NEPCS). *Psychotherapy Research, 24*, 594–607. http://dx.doi.org/10.1080/10503307.2013.851426

Bowlby, J. (1988). *A secure base: Clinical applications of attachment theory.* London, England: Routledge.

Bowlby, J. (1997). *Attachment and loss.* London, England: Pimlico. (Original work published 1969)

Briere, J., & Scott, C. (2006). *Principles of trauma therapy.* London, England: Sage.

Brody, L. R., & Park, S. H. (2004). Narratives, mindfulness, and the implicit audience. *Clinical Psychology: Science and Practice, 11*, 147–154. http://dx.doi.org/10.1093/clipsy.bph065

Bruner, J. (1986). *Actual minds, possible worlds.* Cambridge, MA: Harvard University Press.

Bruner, J. (1991). *Acts of meaning.* Cambridge, MA: Harvard University Press.

Bruner, J. (2004). The narrative creation of self. In L. E. Angus & J. McLeod (Eds.), *The handbook of narrative and psychotherapy: Practice, theory, and research* (pp. 32–14). Thousand Oaks, CA: Sage. http://dx.doi.org/10.4135/9781412973496.d3

Bryntwick, E., Angus, L., Paivio, S., Carpenter, N., & Macaulay, C. (2014, July). *Investigating narrative and emotion integration in emotion-focused therapy for complex trauma: A process-outcome analysis.* Panel discussion at the 45th annual International Meeting for the Society for Psychotherapy Research, Copenhagen, Denmark.

Bucci, W. (1995). The power of the narrative: A multiple code account. In J. W. Pennebaker (Ed.), *Emotion, disclosure, and health* (pp. 93–122). Washington, DC: American Psychological Association. http://dx.doi.org/10.1037/10182-005

Bustamante, V., Mellman, T. A., David, D., & Fins, A. I. (2001). Cognitive functioning and the early development of PTSD. *Journal of Traumatic Stress, 14,* 791–797. http://dx.doi.org/10.1023/A:1013050423901

Carpenter, N., Angus, L., Paivio, S., & Bryntwick, E. (2016). Narrative and emotion integration processes in emotion-focused therapy for complex trauma: An exploratory process-outcome analysis. *Person-Centered and Experiential Psychotherapy, 15,* 67–94. http://dx.doi.org/10.1080/14779757.2015.1132756

Cawson, P., Wattam, C., Brooker, S., & Kelly, G. (2000). Childhood maltreatment in the United Kingdom: A study of the prevalence of abuse and neglect. *NSPCC Inform: The Online Child Protection Resource.* Retrieved from http://www.nspcc.org.uk/inform

Chagigiorgis, H. (2009). *The contributions of emotional engagement with trauma material to outcome in two versions of emotion focused therapy for trauma.* Unpublished doctoral dissertation, University of Windsor, Windsor, Ontario, Canada.

Chard, K. M. (2005). An evaluation of cognitive processing therapy for the treatment of posttraumatic stress disorder related to childhood sexual abuse. *Journal of Consulting and Clinical Psychology, 73,* 965–971. http://dx.doi.org/10.1037/0022-006X.73.5.965

Cloitre, M., Koenen, K. C., Cohen, L. R., & Han, H. (2002). Skills training in affective and interpersonal regulation followed by exposure: A phase-based treatment for PTSD related to childhood abuse. *Journal of Consulting and Clinical Psychology, 70,* 1067–1074. http://dx.doi.org/10.1037/0022-006X.70.5.1067

Conway, M. A., & Pleydell-Pearce, C. W. (2000). The construction of autobiographical memories in the self-memory system. *Psychological Review, 107,* 261–288. http://dx.doi.org/10.1037/0033-295X.107.2.261

Courtois, C., & Ford, J. (2013). *Treatment of complex trauma: A sequenced relationship-based approach.* New York, NY: Guilford Press.

Cunha, C., Mendes, I., Ribeiro, A. P., Angus, L., Greenberg, L. S., & Gonçalves, M. M. (2016). Self-narrative reconstruction in emotion-focused therapy: A preliminary task analysis. *Psychotherapy Research,* 1–18. Advance online publication. http://dx.doi.org/10.1080/10503307.2016.1158429

Daiute, C., & Nelson, K. (1997). Making sense of the sense-making function of narrative evaluation. In G. W. Bamberg (Ed.), Oral versions of personal experience: Three decades of narrative analysis [Special issue]. *Journal of Narrative and Life History, 7*(1–4), 207–215.

Damasio, A. R. (1999). *The feeling of what happens: Body and emotion in the making of consciousness.* New York, NY: Harcourt.

Daniel, S. I. F. (2011). Adult attachment insecurity and narrative processes in psychotherapy: An exploratory study. *Clinical Psychology & Psychotherapy, 18,* 498–511. http://dx.doi.org/10.1002/cpp.704

Dimaggio, G., & Semerari, A. (2004). Disorganized narratives: The psychological condition and its treatment. In L. E. Angus & J. McLeod (Eds.), *Handbook of* narrative and psychotherapy: Practice, theory and research (pp. 263–282). Thousand Oaks, CA: Sage. http://dx.doi.org/10.4135/9781412973496.d20

Elliott, R., Watson, J. C., Goldman, R. N., & Greenberg, L. S. (2004). *Learning emotion-focused therapy: The process-experiential approach to change.* Washington, DC: American Psychological Association. http://dx.doi.org/10.1037/10725-000

Enosh, G., & Buchbinder, E. (2005). Strategies of distancing from emotional experience: Making memories of domestic violence. *Qualitative Social Work: Research and Practice, 4,* 9–32. http://dx.doi.org/10.1177/1473325005050197

Ensink, K., Berthelot, N., Bernazzani, O., Normandin, L., & Fonagy, P. (2014). Another step closer to measuring the ghosts in the nursery: Preliminary validation of the Trauma Reflective Functioning Scale. *Frontiers in Psychology, 5.* https://dx.doi.org/10.3389/fpsyg.2014.01471

Etzion-Carasso, A., & Oppenheim, D. (2000). Open mother–pre-schooler communication: Relations with early secure attachment. *Attachment & Human Development, 2,* 347–370. http://dx.doi.org/10.1080/14616730010007914

Feldman, C., Bruner, J., Kalmar, D., & Renderer, B. (1993). Plot, plight, and dramatism: Interpretation at three ages. In W. Overton & D. Palermo (Eds.), *Jean Piaget Symposium Series: Vol. 21. The nature and ontogenesis of meaning* (pp. 310–365). New York, NY: Psychology Press.

Fergusson, D. M., Horwood, L. J., & Lynskey, M. T. (1996). Childhood sexual abuse and psychiatric disorders in young adulthood: II. Psychiatric outcomes of child sexual abuse. *Journal of the American Academy of Child Adolescent Psychiatry, 35,* 1365–1374.

Finkelhor, D. (1994). The international epidemiology of child sexual abuse. *Child Abuse & Neglect, 18,* 409–417. http://dx.doi.org/10.1016/0145-2134(94)90026-4

Fivush, R. (2012). Subjective perspective and personal timeline in the development of autobiographical memory. In D. Berntsen & D. C. Rubin (Eds.), *Understanding autobiographical memory: Theories and approaches* (pp. 226–245). Cambridge, England: Cambridge University Press. http://dx.doi.org/10.1017/CBO9781139021937.017

Foa, E. B., Huppert, J. D., & Cahill, S. P. (2006). Emotional processing theory: An update. In B. O. Rothbaum (Ed.), *Pathological anxiety: Emotional processing in etiology and treatment* (pp. 3–24). New York, NY: Guilford Press.

Foa, E. B., Keane, T. M., Friedman, M. J., & Cohen, J. A. (Eds.). (2009). *Effective treatments for PTSD: Practice guidelines for the International Society for Traumatic Stress Studies* (2nd ed.). New York, NY: Guilford Press.

Foa, E. B., Molnar, C., & Cashman, L. (1995). Change in rape narratives during exposure therapy for posttraumatic stress disorder. *Journal of Traumatic Stress, 8,* 675–690. http://dx.doi.org/10.1002/jts.2490080409

Fonagy, P., Gergely, G., Jurist, E., & Target, M. (2002). *Affect regulation, mentalization, and the development of the self.* New York, NY: Other Press.

Fonagy, P., Steele, M., Steele, H., Leigh, T., Kennedy, R., Mattoon, G., & Target, M. (1995). Attachment, the reflective self, and borderline states: The predictive specificity of the Adult Attachment Interview and pathological emotional development. In S. Goldberg, R. Muir, & J. Kerr (Eds.), *Attachment theory: Social, developmental, and clinical perspectives* (pp. 223–279). Hillsdale, NJ: Analytic Press.

Fonagy, P., Steele, M., Steele, H., Moran, G. S., & Higgitt, A. C. (1991). The capacity for understanding mental states: The reflective self in parent and child and its significance for security of attachment. *Infant Mental Health Journal, 12*, 201–218. http://dx.doi.org/10.1002/1097-0355(199123)12:3<201::AID-IMHJ2280120307>3.0.CO;2-7

Fonagy, P., & Target, M. (2005). Bridging the transmission gap: An end to an important mystery of attachment research? *Attachment & Human Development, 7*, 333–343. http://dx.doi.org/10.1080/14616730500269278

Ford, J. D. (2005). Treatment implications of altered affect regulation and information processing following child maltreatment. *Psychiatric Annals, 35*, 410–419.

Freer, B. D., Whitt-Woosley, A., & Sprang, G. (2010). Narrative coherence and the trauma experience: An exploratory mixed-method analysis. *Violence and Victims, 25*, 742–754. http://dx.doi.org/10.1891/0886-6708.25.6.742

Friedlander, M. L., Angus, L., Wright, S. T., Günther, C., Austin, C. L., Kangos, K., . . . Khattra, J. (2016). "If those tears could talk, what would they say?" Multi-method analysis of a corrective experience in brief dynamic therapy. *Psychotherapy Research*, 1–18. Advance online publication. http://dx.doi.org/10.1080/10503307.2016.1184350

Gendlin, E. T. (1997). *Focusing-oriented psychotherapy: A manual of the experiential method*. New York, NY: Guilford Press.

George, C., Kaplan, M., & Main, M. (1985). *Adult Attachment Interview*. Berkeley: University of California.

Goldman, R., & Greenberg, L. (1997). Case formulation in experiential therapy. In T. D. Eells (Ed.), *Handbook of psychotherapy case formulation* (pp. 402–429). New York, NY: Guilford Press.

Goldman, R. N., Greenberg, L. S., & Pos, A. E. (2005). Depth of emotional experience and outcome. *Psychotherapy Research, 15*, 248–260. http://dx.doi.org/10.1080/10503300512331385188

Gonçalves, M., Mendes, I., Ribeiro, A., Angus, L., & Greenberg, L. (2010). Innovative moments and change in emotion-focused therapy: The case of Lisa. *Journal of Constructivist Psychology, 23*, 267–294. http://dx.doi.org/10.1080/10720537.2010.489758

Gonçalves, M. M., & Stiles, W. B. (2011). Narrative and psychotherapy: Introduction to the special section. *Psychotherapy Research, 21*, 1–3. http://dx.doi.org/10.1080/10503307.2010.534510

Gottman, J. M. (1997). *Raising an emotionally intelligent child: The heart of parenting*. New York, NY: Simon & Schuster.

Gottman, J. M., Coan, J., Carrere, S., & Swanson, C. (1998). Predicting marital happiness and stability from newlywed interactions. *Journal of Marriage and Family, 60,* 5–22. http://dx.doi.org/10.2307/353438

Greenberg, L. S. (2002). *Emotion-focused therapy: Coaching clients to work through their feelings.* Washington, DC: American Psychological Association. http://dx.doi.org/10.1037/10447-000

Greenberg, L. S. (2011). *Emotion-focused therapy.* Washington, DC: American Psychological Association.

Greenberg, L. S., & Angus, L. E. (2004). The contributions of emotion processes to narrative change in psychotherapy: A dialectical constructivist approach. In L. E. Angus & J. McLeod (Eds.), *The handbook of narrative and psychotherapy: Practice, theory, and research* (pp. 330–349). Thousand Oaks, CA: Sage. http://dx.doi.org/10.4135/9781412973496.d25

Greenberg, L. S., Auszra, L., & Herrmann, I. R. (2007). The relationship among emotional productivity, emotional arousal and outcome in experiential therapy of depression. *Psychotherapy Research, 17,* 482–493. http://dx.doi.org/10.1080/10503300600977800

Greenberg, L. S., & Bolger, E. (2001). An emotion-focused approach to the over-regulation of emotion and emotional pain. *Journal of Clinical Psychology, 57,* 197–211. http://dx.doi.org/10.1002/1097-4679(200102)57:2<197::AID-JCLP6>3.0.CO;2-O

Greenberg, L. S., & Foerster, F. S. (1996). Task analysis exemplified: The process of resolving unfinished business. *Journal of Consulting and Clinical Psychology, 64,* 439–446. http://dx.doi.org/10.1037/0022-006X.64.3.439

Greenberg, L. S., & Hirscheimer, K. (1994, February). *Relating degree of resolution of unfinished business to outcome.* Paper presented at the meeting of the North American Society of Psychotherapy Research, Santa Fe, NM.

Greenberg, L. S., & Malcolm, W. (2002). Resolving unfinished business: Relating process to outcome. *Journal of Consulting and Clinical Psychology, 70,* 406–416. http://dx.doi.org/10.1037/0022-006X.70.2.406

Greenberg, L. S., & Paivio, S. C. (1997). *Working with emotions in psychotherapy.* New York, NY: Guilford Press.

Greenberg, L. S., & Pascual-Leone, J. (1997). Emotion in the creation of personal meaning. In M. J. Power & C. R. Brewin (Eds.), *The transformation of meaning in psychological therapies: Integrating theory and practice* (pp. 157–173). Hoboken, NJ: Wiley.

Greenberg, L. S., Rice, L. N., & Elliott, R. K. (1993). *Facilitating emotional change: The moment-by-moment process.* New York, NY: Guilford Press.

Greenberg, L. S., & Safran, J. D. (1987). *Emotion in psychotherapy: Affect, cognition and the process of change.* New York, NY: Guilford Press.

Grewal, D. D., Brackett, M., & Salovey, P. (2006). Emotional intelligence and the self-regulation of affect. In D. K. Snyder, J. A. Simpson, & J. N. Hughes (Eds.),

Emotion regulation in couples and families (pp. 37–55). Washington, DC: American Psychological Association. http://dx.doi.org/10.1037/11468-002

Habermas, T., & Bluck, S. (2000). Getting a life: The emergence of the life story in adolescence. *Psychological Bulletin, 126,* 748–769. http://dx.doi.org/10.1037/0033-2909.126.5.748

Hager, D. L. (1992). Chaos and growth. *Psychotherapy: Theory, Research, Practice, Training, 29,* 378–384. http://dx.doi.org/10.1037/h0088539

Hall, I. E. (2012). *Therapist relationship and technical skills in two versions of emotion focused trauma therapy.* Unpublished doctoral dissertation, University of Windsor, Windsor, Ontario, Canada.

Halligan, S. L., Michael, T., Clark, D. M., & Ehlers, A. (2003). Posttraumatic stress disorder following assault: The role of cognitive processing, trauma memory, and appraisals. *Journal of Consulting and Clinical Psychology, 71,* 419–431. http://dx.doi.org/10.1037/0022-006X.71.3.419

Hardt, J., & Rutter, M. (2004). Validity of adult retrospective reports of adverse childhood experiences: Review of the evidence. *Journal of Child Psychology and Psychiatry, 45,* 260–273. http://dx.doi.org/10.1111/j.1469-7610.2004.00218.x

Hayes, S. C., Wilson, K. G., Gifford, E. V., Follette, V. M., & Strosahl, K. (1996). Experimental avoidance and behavioral disorders: A functional dimensional approach to diagnosis and treatment. *Journal of Consulting and Clinical Psychology, 64,* 1152–1168. http://dx.doi.org/10.1037/0022-006X.64.6.1152

Herman, J. L. (1992). Complex PTSD: A syndrome in survivors of prolonged and repeated trauma. *Journal of Traumatic Stress, 5,* 377–391. http://dx.doi.org/10.1002/jts.2490050305

Holmes, J. (2001). *The search for the secure base: Attachment theory and psychotherapy.* London, England: Routledge.

Holowaty, K. A. M., & Paivio, S. C. (2012). Characteristics of client-identified helpful events in emotion-focused therapy for child abuse trauma. *Psychotherapy Research, 22,* 56–66. http://dx.doi.org/10.1080/10503307.2011.622727

Howard, G. S. (1991). Culture tales. A narrative approach to thinking, cross-cultural psychology, and psychotherapy. *American Psychologist, 46,* 187–197. http://dx.doi.org/10.1037/0003-066X.46.3.187

Ingram, R. E., & Price, J. M. (Eds.). (2010). *Vulnerability to psychopathology: Risk across the lifespan* (2nd ed.). New York, NY: Guilford Press.

Izard, C. E. (2002). Translating emotion theory and research into preventive interventions. *Psychological Bulletin, 128,* 796–824. http://dx.doi.org/10.1037/0033-2909.128.5.796

Jelinek, L., Stockbauer, C., Randjbar, S., Kellner, M., Ehring, T., & Moritz, S. (2010). Characteristics and organization of the worst moment of trauma memories in posttraumatic stress disorder. *Behaviour Research and Therapy, 48,* 680–685. http://dx.doi.org/10.1016/j.brat.2010.03.014

Khayyat-Abuaita, U. (2015). *Changes in the quality of emotional processing in trauma narratives as predictor of outcome in emotion-focused therapy for complex trauma.* Unpublished doctoral dissertation, University of Windsor, Windsor, Ontario, Canada.

Klein, M. H., Mathieu-Coughlan, P., & Kiesler, D. J. (1986). The Experiencing Scales. In L. S. Greenberg & W. M. Pinsof (Eds.), *The psychotherapeutic process: A research handbook* (pp. 21–71). New York, NY: Guilford Press.

Koren-Karie, N., Oppenheim, D., Haimovich, Z., & Etzion-Carasso, A. (2003). Dialogues of seven-year-olds with their mothers about emotional events: Development of a typology. In R. N. Emde, D. P. Wolfe, & D. Oppenheim (Eds.), *Revealing the inner worlds of young children: The MacArthur Story Stem Battery and parent-child narratives* (pp. 338–354). New York, NY: Oxford University Press.

Laible, D., & Panfile, T. (2009). Mother–child reminiscing in the context of secure attachment relationships: Lesson in understanding and coping with negative emotions. In J. A. Quas & R. Fivush (Eds.), *Emotion and memory in development: Biological, cognitive, and social considerations* (pp. 166–195). New York, NY: Oxford University Press. http://dx.doi.org/10.1093/acprof:oso/9780195326932.003.0007

Lane, R., Ryan, L., Nadel, L., & Greenberg, L. (2015). Memory reconsolidation, emotional arousal and the process of change in psychotherapy: New insights from brain science. *Behavioral and Brain Sciences, 38,* 1–64. http://dx.doi.org/10.1017/S0140525X14000041

Lanius, R. A., Williamson, P. C., Densmore, M., Boksman, K., Neufeld, R. W., Gati, J. S., & Menon, R. S. (2004). The nature of traumatic memories: A 45-TfMRI functional connectivity analysis. *The American Journal of Psychiatry, 161,* 36–44. http://dx.doi.org/10.1176/appi.ajp.161.1.36

Leahy, R. L., Tirch, D., & Napolitano, L. A. (2011). *Emotion regulation in psychotherapy: A practitioner's guide.* New York, NY: Guilford Press.

LeDoux, J. (1996). *The emotional brain: The mysterious underpinnings of emotional life.* New York, NY: Simon & Schuster.

Levy, K. N., Meehan, K. B., Kelly, K. M., Reynoso, J. S., Weber, M., Clarkin, J. F., & Kernberg, O. F. (2006). Change in attachment patterns and reflective function in a randomized control trial of transference-focused psychotherapy for borderline personality disorder. *Journal of Consulting and Clinical Psychology, 74,* 1027–1040. http://dx.doi.org/10.1037/0022-006X.74.6.1027

Linehan, M. M. (1993). *Cognitive-behavioral treatment of borderline personality disorder.* New York, NY: Guilford Press.

Linehan, M. M. (1997). Validation and psychotherapy. In A. C. Bohart & L. S. Greenberg (Eds.), *Empathy reconsidered: New directions in psychotherapy* (pp. 353–392). Washington, DC: American Psychological Association. http://dx.doi.org/10.1037/10226-016

Luborsky, L., & Crits-Christoph, P. (1990). *Understanding transference: The CCRT method.* New York, NY: Basic Books.

Macaulay, C., Angus, L., Carpenter, N., Bryntwick, E., & Khattra, J. (2016). *The developmental and interpersonal basis of narrative self-coherence: Rationale for a narrative-emotion integration processes (NE-P) model of psychotherapeutic change.* Manuscript submitted for publication.

Macaulay, C., Angus, L., Khattra, J., Westra, H., & Ip, J. (2017). Client retrospective accounts of corrective experiences in motivational interviewing integrated with cognitive behavioral therapy for generalized anxiety disorder. *Journal of Clinical Psychology: In Session, 73*(2).

Machado, P. P. P., Beutler, L. E., & Greenberg, L. S. (1999). Emotion recognition in psychotherapy: Impact of therapist level of experience and emotional awareness. *Journal of Clinical Psychology, 55,* 39–57. http://dx.doi.org/10.1002/(SICI)1097-4679(199901)55:1<39::AID-JCLP4>3.0.CO;2-V

MacMillan, H. L., Tanaka, M., Duku, E., Vaillancourt, T., & Boyle, M. H. (2013). Child physical and sexual abuse in a community sample of young adults: Results from the Ontario Child Health Study. *Child Abuse & Neglect, 37,* 14–21. http://dx.doi.org/10.1016/j.chiabu.2012.06.005

Main, M. (1991). Metacognitive knowledge, metacognitive monitoring, and singular (coherent) vs. multiple (incoherent) model of attachment: Findings and directions for future research. In C. M. Parkes, J. Stevenson-Hinde, & P. Marris (Eds.), *Attachment across the life cycle* (pp. 127–159). London, England: Routledge.

Main, M., & Goldwyn, R. (1984). Predicting rejection of her infant from mother's representation of her own experience: Implications for the abused-abusing intergenerational cycle [Special issue]. *Child Abuse & Neglect, 8,* 203–217. http://dx.doi.org/10.1016/0145-2134(84)90009-7

Margola, D., Facchin, F., Molgora, S., & Revenson, T. A. (2010). Cognitive and emotional processing through writing among adolescents who experienced the death of a classmate. *Psychological Trauma: Theory, Research, Practice, and Policy, 2,* 250–260. http://dx.doi.org/10.1037/a0019891

Matos, M., Santos, A., Gonçalves, M., & Martins, C. (2009). Innovative moments and change in narrative therapy. *Psychotherapy Research, 19,* 68–80. http://dx.doi.org/10.1080/10503300802430657

McAdams, D. P. (1993). *The stories we live by: Personal myths and the making of the self.* New York, NY: William Morrow.

McAdams, D. P., & Janis, L. (2004). Narrative identity and narrative therapy. In L. E. Angus & J. McLeod (Eds.), *Handbook of narrative and psychotherapy: Practice, theory, and research* (pp. 158–173). Thousand Oaks, CA: Sage. http://dx.doi.org/10.4135/9781412973496.d13

McKee, R. (1997). *Story: Substance, structure, style and the principles of screenwriting.* New York, NY: HarperCollins.

McLeod, J. (2004). Social constructionism, narrative and psychotherapy. In L. E. Angus & J. McLeod (Eds.), *Handbook of narrative and psychotherapy: Practice, theory, and research* (pp. 350–365). Thousand Oaks, CA: Sage. http://dx.doi.org/10.4135/9781412973496.d26

Meins, E., Fernyhough, C., Fradley, E., & Tuckey, M. (2001). Rethinking maternal sensitivity: Mothers' comments on infants' mental processes predict security of attachment at 12 months. *Journal of Child Psychology and Psychiatry, 42,* 637–648. http://dx.doi.org/10.1111/1469-7610.00759

Mendes, I., Ribeiro, A. P., Angus, L., Greenberg, L. S., Sousa, I., & Gonçalves, M. M. (2010). Narrative change in emotion-focused therapy: How is change constructed through the lens of the innovative moments coding system? *Psychotherapy Research, 20,* 692–701. http://dx.doi.org/10.1080/10503307.2010.514960

Mendes, I., Ribeiro, A. P., Angus, L., Greenberg, L. S., Sousa, I., & Gonçalves, M. M. (2011). Narrative change in emotion-focused psychotherapy: A study on the evolution of reflection and protest innovative moments. *Psychotherapy Research, 21,* 304–315. http://dx.doi.org/10.1080/10503307.2011.565489

Mergenthaler, E. (2008). Resonating minds: A school-independent theoretical conception and its empirical application to psychotherapeutic processes. *Psychotherapy Research, 18,* 109–126. http://dx.doi.org/10.1080/10503300701883741

Mlotek, A. E. (2015). *The contributions of therapist empathy during session one to client emotional engagement and outcome in emotion-focused therapy for complex trauma.* Unpublished master's thesis, University of Windsor, Windsor, Ontario, Canada.

Mundorf, E. S. (2013). *Childhood abuse survivors' experience of self over the course of emotion-focused therapy for trauma: A qualitative analysis.* Unpublished doctoral dissertation, University of Windsor, Windsor, Ontario, Canada.

Mundorf, E. S., & Paivio, S. C. (2011). Narrative quality and disturbance pre- and post-emotion-focused therapy for child abuse trauma. *Journal of Traumatic Stress, 24,* 643–650. http://dx.doi.org/10.1002/jts.20707

Najavits, L. M. (2002). *Seeking safety: A treatment manual for PTSD and substance abuse.* New York, NY: Guilford Press.

Neimeyer, R. A. (1995). Client generated narratives in psychotherapy. In R. A. Neimeyer & M. J. Mahoney (Eds.), *Constructivism in psychotherapy* (pp. 231–246). Washington, DC: American Psychological Association. http://dx.doi.org/10.1037/10170-010

Neimeyer, R. A. (Ed.). (2001). *Meaning reconstruction and the experience of loss.* Washington, DC: American Psychological Association. http://dx.doi.org/10.1037/10397-000

Nelson, K. (1996). *Language in cognitive development: The emergence of the mediated mind.* Cambridge, England: Cambridge University Press. http://dx.doi.org/10.1017/CBO9781139174619

Nelson, K., & Fivush, R. (2004). The emergence of autobiographical memory: A social cultural developmental theory. *Psychological Review, 111,* 486–511. http://dx.doi.org/10.1037/0033-295X.111.2.486

Newman, E., Riggs, D. S., & Roth, S. (1997). Thematic resolution, PTSD, and complex PTSD: The relationship between meaning and trauma-related diagnoses. *Journal of Traumatic Stress, 10,* 197–213. http://dx.doi.org/10.1002/jts.2490100204

Novaco, R. W. (2007). Anger dysregulation. In T. A. Cavell & K. T. (Eds.), *Anger, aggression and interventions for interpersonal violence* (pp. 3–54). Mahwah, NJ: Erlbaum.

Nussbaum, S. (2014). *Change in emotional processes in client self-narratives in emotion-focused therapy for trauma.* Unpublished master's thesis, University of Windsor, Windsor, Ontario, Canada.

O'Kearney, R., & Perrott, K. (2006). Trauma narratives in posttraumatic stress disorder: A review. *Journal of Traumatic Stress, 19,* 81–93.

Paivio, S. C. (2013). Essential processes in emotion-focused therapy. *Psychotherapy: Theory, Research, & Practice, 50,* 341–345. http://dx.doi.org/10.1037/a0032810

Paivio, S. C., & Carriere, M. (2007). Contributions of emotion-focused therapy to the understanding and treatment of anger and aggression. In T. A. Cavell & K. T. Malcolm (Eds.), *Anger, aggression, and interventions for interpersonal violence* (pp. 143–164). Mahwah, NJ: Erlbaum.

Paivio, S. C., & Cramer, K. M. (2004). Factor structure and reliability of the Childhood Trauma Questionnaire in a Canadian undergraduate student sample. *Child Abuse & Neglect, 28,* 889–904. http://dx.doi.org/10.1016/j.chiabu.2004.01.011

Paivio, S. C., & Greenberg, L. S. (1995). Resolving "unfinished business": Efficacy of experiential therapy using empty-chair dialogue. *Journal of Consulting and Clinical Psychology, 63,* 419–425. http://dx.doi.org/10.1037/0022-006X.63.3.419

Paivio, S. C., Hall, I. E., Holowaty, K. A. M., Jellis, J. B., & Tran, N. (2001). Imaginal confrontation for resolving child abuse issues. *Psychotherapy Research, 11,* 433–453. http://dx.doi.org/10.1093/ptr/11.4.433

Paivio, S. C., Holowaty, K. A. M., & Hall, I. E. (2004). The influence of therapist adherence and competence on client reprocessing of child abuse memories. *Psychotherapy: Theory, Research, Practice, Training, 41,* 56–68. http://dx.doi.org/10.1037/0033-3204.41.1.56

Paivio, S. C., Jarry, J. L., Chagigiorgis, H., Hall, I., & Ralston, M. (2010). Efficacy of two versions of emotion-focused therapy for resolving child abuse trauma. *Psychotherapy Research, 20,* 353–366. http://dx.doi.org/10.1080/10503300903505274

Paivio, S. C., & Laurent, C. (2001). Empathy and emotion regulation: Reprocessing memories of childhood abuse. *Journal of Clinical Psychology, 57,* 213–226. http://dx.doi.org/10.1002/1097-4679(200102)57:2<213::AID-JCLP7>3.0.CO;2-B

Paivio, S. C., & McCulloch, C. R. (2004). Alexithymia as a mediator between childhood trauma and self-injurious behaviors. *Child Abuse & Neglect, 28,* 339–354. http://dx.doi.org/10.1016/j.chiabu.2003.11.018

Paivio, S. C., & Nieuwenhuis, J. A. (2001). Efficacy of emotion focused therapy for adult survivors of child abuse: A preliminary study. *Journal of Traumatic Stress, 14,* 115–133. http://dx.doi.org/10.1023/A:1007891716593

Paivio, S. C., & Pascual-Leone, A. (2010). *Emotion-focused therapy for complex trauma: An integrative approach.* Washington, DC: American Psychological Association. http://dx.doi.org/10.1037/12077-000

Paivio, S. C., & Patterson, L. A. (1999). Alliance development in therapy for resolving child abuse issues. *Psychotherapy: Theory, Research, Practice, Training, 36,* 343–354. http://dx.doi.org/10.1037/h0087843

Paivio, S. C., & Shimp, L. N. (1998). Affective change processes in therapy for PTSD stemming from childhood abuse. *Journal of Psychotherapy Integration, 8,* 211–229. http://dx.doi.org/10.1023/A:1023265103791

Pascual-Leone, J. (1987). Organismic processes for neo-Piagetian theories: A dialectical causal account of cognitive development. *International Journal of Psychology, 22,* 531–570. http://dx.doi.org/10.1080/00207598708246795

Pascual-Leone, J. (1990a). An essay on wisdom: Toward organismic processes that make it possible. In R. J. Sternberg (Ed.), *Wisdom: Its nature, origins, and development* (pp. 244–278). New York, NY: Cambridge University Press. http://dx.doi.org/ 10.1017/CBO9781139173704.013

Pascual-Leone, J. (1990b). Reflections on life-span intelligence, consciousness and ego development. In C. Alexander & E. Langer (Eds.), *Higher stages of human development: Perspectives on adult growth* (pp. 258–285). New York, NY: Oxford University Press.

Pascual-Leone, J. (1991). Emotions, development, and psychotherapy: A dialectical–constructivist perspective. In J. D. Safran & L. S. Greenberg (Eds.), *Emotion, psychotherapy, and change* (pp. 302–335). New York, NY: Guilford Press.

Pelcovitz, D., Kaplan, S. J., DeRosa, R. R., Mandel, F. S., & Salzinger, S. (2000). Psychiatric disorders in adolescents exposed to domestic violence and physical abuse. *American Journal of Orthopsychiatry, 70,* 360–369.

Pennebaker, J. W., & Seagal, J. D. (1999). Forming a story: The health benefits of narrative. *Journal of Clinical Psychology, 55,* 1243–1254. http://dx.doi.org/10.1002/ (SICI)1097-4679(199910)55:10<1243::AID-JCLP6>3.0.CO;2-N

Pilkington, B., & Kremer, J. (1995). A review of the epidemiological research on child sexual abuse: Clinical samples. *Child Abuse Review, 4,* 191–205. http://dx.doi.org/ 10.1002/car.2380040306

Polkinghorne, D. (2004). Narrative therapy and postmodernism. In L. E. Angus & J. McLeod (Eds.), *Handbook of narrative and psychotherapy: Practice, theory, and research* (pp. 52–68). Thousand Oaks, CA: Sage. http://dx.doi.org/10.4135/ 9781412973496.d5

Pos, A. E., Greenberg, L. S., Goldman, R. N., & Korman, L. M. (2003). Emotional processing during experiential treatment of depression. *Journal of Consulting and Clinical Psychology, 71,* 1007–1016. http://dx.doi.org/10.1037/0022-006X.71.6.1007

Pynoos, R. (1996). Children exposed to catastrophic violence and disaster. In C. R. Pfeffer (Ed.), *Intense stress and mental disturbance in children* (pp. 181–208). Washington, DC: American Psychiatric Press.

Ralston, M. B. (2006). *Imaginal confrontation versus evocative empathy in emotion focused trauma therapy.* Unpublished doctoral dissertation, University of Windsor, Windsor, Ontario, Canada.

Robichaud, L. K. (2004). *Depth of experiencing as a client prognostic variable in emotion-focused therapy for adult survivors of childhood abuse.* Unpublished master's thesis, University of Windsor, Windsor, Ontario, Canada.

Rubin, D. C., Feldman, M. E., & Beckham, J. C. (2004). Reliving, emotions, and fragmentation in the autobiographical memories of veterans diagnosed with PTSD. *Applied Cognitive Psychology, 18*, 17–35. http://dx.doi.org/10.1002/acp.950

Saarni, C. (1999). *The development of emotional competence*. New York, NY: Guilford Press.

Sarbin, T. (1986). *Narrative psychology: The storied nature of human conduct*. New York, NY: Praeger.

Schank, R. (2000). *Tell me a story: Narrative and intelligence*. Evanston, IL: Northwestern University Press.

Scher, C. D., Forde, D. R., McQuaid, J. R., & Stein, M. B. (2004). Prevalence and demographic correlates of childhood maltreatment in an adult community sample. *Child Abuse & Neglect, 28*, 167–180. http://dx.doi.org/10.1016/j.chiabu.2003.09.012

Schore, A. N. (2003). *Affect dysregulation and disorders of the self*. New York, NY: Norton.

Scoboria, A., Ford, J., Hsio-ju, L., & Frisman, L. (2006, May). *Exploratory and confirmatory factor analysis of the Structured Interview for Disorders of Extreme Stress*. Paper presented at the Society for the Exploration of Psychotherapy Integration, Los Angeles, California.

Scott, M. J., & Stradling, S. G. (1997). Client compliance with exposure treatments for posttraumatic stress disorder. *Journal of Traumatic Stress, 10*, 523–526. http://dx.doi.org/10.1002/jts.2490100315

Seedat, S., Nyamai, C., Njenga, F., Vythilingum, B., & Stein, D. J. (2004). Trauma exposure and post-traumatic stress symptoms in urban African schools: Survey in Cape Town and Nairobi. *British Journal of Psychiatry, 184*, 169–175.

Shaver, P. R., & Mikulincer, M. (2007). Adult attachment strategies and the regulation of emotion. In J. J. Gross (Ed.), *Handbook of emotion regulation* (pp. 446–465). New York, NY: Guilford Press.

Siegel, D. J. (2003). An interpersonal neurobiology of psychotherapy: The developing mind and the resolution of trauma. In M. F. Solomon & D. J. Siegel (Eds.), *Healing trauma: Attachment, mind, body, and brain* (pp. 1–54). New York, NY: Norton.

Singer, J. A., & Blagov, P. S. (2004). Self-defining memories, narrative identity, and psychotherapy: A conceptual model, empirical investigation, and case report. In L. E. Angus & J. McLeod (Eds.), *Handbook of narrative and psychotherapy: Practice, theory, and research* (pp. 228–246). Thousand Oaks, CA: Sage. http://dx.doi.org/10.4135/9781412973496.d18

Singer, J. A., & Salovey, P. (1993). *The remembered self: Emotion and memory in personality*. New York, NY: Free Press.

Singh, M. (1994). *Validation of a measure of session outcome in the resolution of unfinished business*. Unpublished doctoral dissertation, York University, Toronto, Ontario, Canada.

Slade, A., Grienenberger, J., Bernbach, E., Levy, D., & Locker, A. (2005). Maternal reflective functioning, attachment, and the transmission gap: A preliminary study. *Attachment & Human Development, 7*, 283–298. http://dx.doi.org/10.1080/14616730500245880

Sonkin, D. (2005). Attachment theory and psychotherapy. *The California Therapist, 17*, 68–77.

Spence, D. (1982). *Narrative truth and historical truth: Meaning and interpretation in psychoanalysis.* New York, NY: Norton.

Sroufe, L. A. (2005). Attachment and development: A prospective, longitudinal study from birth to adulthood. *Attachment & Human Development, 7*, 349–367. http://dx.doi.org/10.1080/14616730500365928

Stern, D. (1985). *The interpersonal world of the infant.* New York, NY: Basic Books.

Stoltenborgh, M., Bakermans-Kranenburg, M. J., Alink, L. R. A., & van IJzendoorn, M. H. (2012). The universality of childhood emotional abuse: A meta-analysis of worldwide prevalence. *Journal of Aggression, Maltreatment & Trauma, 21*, 870–890. http://dx.doi.org/10.1080/10926771.2012.708014

Stoltenborgh, M., Bakermans-Kranenburg, M. J., van IJzendoorn, M. H., & Alink, L. R. A. (2013). Cultural-geographical differences in the occurrence of child physical abuse? A meta-analysis of global prevalence. *International Journal of Psychology, 48*, 81–94. http://dx.doi.org/10.1080/00207594.2012.697165

Stoltenborgh, M., van IJzendoorn, M. H., Euser, E. M., & Bakermans-Kranenburg, M. J. (2011). A global perspective on child sexual abuse: Meta-analysis of prevalence around the world. *Child Maltreatment, 16*, 79–101.

Tadeski, R. G., Park, C. L., & Calhoun, L. G. (1998). *Posttraumatic growth: Positive changes in the aftermath of crisis.* Mahwah, NJ: Erlbaum.

Taylor, G. J., Bagby, R. M., & Parker, J. D. A. (1997). *Disorders of affect regulation: Alexithymia in medical and psychiatric illness.* Cambridge, England: Cambridge University Press. http://dx.doi.org/10.1017/CBO9780511526831

Teasdale, J. D. (1999). Metacognition, mindfulness and the modification of mood disorders. *Clinical Psychology & Psychotherapy, 6*, 146–155. http://dx.doi.org/10.1002/(SICI)1099-0879(199905)6:2<146::AID-CPP195>3.0.CO;2-E

Thorne, A., & McLean, K. C. (2002). Gendered reminiscence practices and self-definition in late adolescence. *Sex Roles, 46*, 267–277. http://dx.doi.org/10.1023/A:1020261211979

Thorne, A., & McLean, K. C. (2003). Telling traumatic events in adolescence: A study of master narrative positioning. In R. Fivush & C. Haden (Eds.), *Connecting culture and memory: The development of an autobiographical self* (pp. 169–185). Mahwah, NJ: Erlbaum.

Toth, S. L., Rogosch, F. A., & Cicchetti, D. (2008). Attachment theory-informed intervention and reflective functioning in depressed mothers. In H. Steele & M. Steele (Eds.), *The Adult Attachment Interview in clinical context* (pp. 154–172). New York, NY: Guilford Press.

Trevarthen, C., & Hubley, P. (1987). Secondary intersubjectivity: Confidence, confiding, and acts of meaning in the first year. In A. Lock (Ed.), *Action, gesture, and symbol* (pp. 183–239). New York, NY: Academic Press.

Tromp, S., Koss, M. P., Figueredo, A. J., & Tharan, M. (1995). Are rape memories different? A comparison of rape, other unpleasant and pleasant memories among employed women [Special issue]. *Journal of Traumatic Stress, 8*, 607–627.

Turner, A. (2001). *The relationships among childhood maltreatment, alexithymia, social avoidance, and social support.* Unpublished master's thesis, University of Windsor, Windsor, Ontario, Canada.

Tuval-Mashiach, R., Freedman, S., Bargai, N., Boker, R., Hadar, H., & Shalev, A. Y. (2004). Coping with trauma: Narrative and cognitive perspectives. *Psychiatry: Interpersonal and Biological Processes, 67*, 280–293. http://dx.doi.org/10.1521/psyc.67.3.280.48977

Uddo, M., Vasterling, J. J., Brailey, K., & Sutker, P. B. (1993). Memory and attention in combat-related post-traumatic stress disorder (PTSD). *Journal of Psychopathology and Behavioral Assessment, 15*, 43–52. http://dx.doi.org/10.1007/BF00964322

van der Kolk, B. A., Hopper, J. W., & Osterman, J. E. (2001). Exploring the nature of traumatic memory: Combining clinical knowledge with laboratory methods. *Journal of Aggression, Maltreatment & Trauma, 4*, 9–31. http://dx.doi.org/10.1300/J146v04n02_02

van der Kolk, B. A., & McFarlane, A. C. (1996). The black hole of trauma. In B. A. van der Kolk, A. C. McFarlane, & L. W. Weisaeth (Eds.), *Traumatic stress: The effects of overwhelming experience on mind, body, and society* (pp. 3–23). New York, NY: Guilford Press.

White, M. (2004). Folk psychology and narrative practices. In L. E. Angus & J. McLeod (Eds.), *The handbook of narrative and psychotherapy: Practice, theory, and research* (pp. 15–52). Thousand Oaks, CA: Sage.

White, M. (2007). *Maps of narrative practice.* New York, NY: Norton.

White, M., & Epston, D. (1990). *Narrative means to therapeutic ends.* New York, NY: Norton.

Wigren, J. (1994). Narrative completion in the treatment of trauma. *Psychotherapy: Theory, Research, Practice, Training, 31*, 415–423.

Williams, J. M., Barnhofer, T., Crane, C., Herman, D., Raes, F., Watkins, E., & Dalgleish, T. (2007). Autobiographical memory specificity and emotional disorder. *Psychological Bulletin, 133*, 122–148. http://dx.doi.org/10.1037/0033-2909.133.1.122

Wolfe, D. (2007). Understanding anger: Key concepts from the field of domestic violence and child abuse. In T. Cavell & K. Malcolm (Eds.), *Anger, aggression and interpersonal violence* (pp. 393–402). Mahwah, NJ: Erlbaum.

INDEX

Psychoeducation, 30
Psychotherapy research, 51, 58
PTSD. *See* Posttraumatic stress disorder

Ralston, M. B., 85, 140
Re-experiencing procedures, 138–143.
    See also Empathic exploration;
    Imaginal confrontation
Re-experiencing symptoms
    tasks for working through, 34, 36
    types of, 16–17
Reflective functioning (RF)
    and client storytelling, 46–48
    corrective effects of, 99
    defined, 249
Reflective Story markers
    and empathy, 98
    interventions with, 117, 119
    in middle phase of therapy, 172–176,
        187–190
    overview, 60–62, 90, 92–93
    and self-related difficulties, 110
    and symbolization of meaning, 103
    therapist encouragement for use of,
        99–100
Reflective storytelling, 67
Reflexive narrative mode, 50
Reflexivity, 56, 67
Relational difficulties
    as long-term effect of trauma, 22
    in narrative-informed approach to
        EFTT, 68–71
Relational structure, 66
Relief, 211
Renderer, B., 40
Repetitive storytelling, 66–67
Resolution. *See* Model of resolution
Revenson, T. A., 23
RF. *See* Reflective functioning
Riggs, D. S., 24
Role play. *See* Imaginal confrontation;
    Two-chair dialogues
Roth, S., 24
Rotondi-Trevisan, D., 48

Sadness
    adaptive functions of, 29, 81–82
    differentiation of, 127
    and emotional transformation, 67–68
    function of, 20
    intervention with, 107–108

Safe haven (attachment), 44–45
Safety, 28, 98–99
Same Old Story markers
    on Degree of Resolution Scale, 247
    in early phase of therapy, 125,
        128–130, 134, 136–137, 143
    and empathy, 98
    identifying elements of, 109
    interventions with, 113, 114
    in late phase of therapy, 210,
        211–213, 215, 224
    in middle phase of therapy, 168–169,
        176, 179, 182
    overview, 60–62, 90, 91
    therapist responses to, 101
Santos, A., 213
Scaffolding, narrative, 55, 118, 172,
    249
Schank, R., 48
Scher, C. D., 14
Secondary emotions
    maladaptive. *See* Maladaptive
        emotions
    types of, 30
Secure attachment
    and client storytelling, 46
    and narrative processing, 19
    and reflective functioning, 47
Secure base (attachment), 45
Self-awareness, 132–133
Self-coherence, 42–44
Self-confidence, 22, 34
Self-criticism, 81–82
Self-doubt, 179
Self-esteem issues, 22
Selfhood
    dialectical construction of, 56
    emergence of, 72
    narrative senses of, 41
    origins of, 44
Self-identity narrative, 57–58
    coconstruction of new, 168, 228
    compassionate, 210, 245
    defined, 249
    emergence of, 18, 20, 147
    emotionally-integrated, 60, 65, 95
    omissions in, 217
Self-incoherence
    and complex trauma, 49–52
    and overgeneral autobiographical
        memory, 49

ABOUT THE AUTHORS

Sandra C. Paivio, PhD, CPsych, is currently a consultant at the York University Psychology Clinic, where she provides individual psychotherapy, graduate training, and supervision. She is professor emeritus in the Psychology Department at the University of Windsor, and has more than 20 years of clinical experience. She is one of the developers of emotion-focused therapy, particularly applied to complex trauma (EFTT), and has conducted clinical trials evaluating efficacy and processes of change in EFTT. Dr. Paivio is the author of numerous publications on trauma and psychotherapy, including *Working With Emotions in Psychotherapy* (with Leslie S. Greenberg), *Emotion-Focused Therapy for Complex Trauma: An Integrative Approach* (with Antonio Pascual-Leone), and she is featured in two American Psychological Association (APA) videos illustrating EFTT. Dr. Paivio has presented numerous workshops nationally and internationally and provided intensive graduate student and professional training in EFT and EFT specifically for trauma. She also is an invited member of the APA (Division 56, Trauma Psychology) working group developing best practice guidelines for complex trauma and received a Lifetime Achievement Award from the Trauma Section of the Canadian Psychological Association (2014). Dr. Paivio maintains a part-time private practice in Toronto, Ontario, Canada.

Lynne E. Angus, PhD, CPsych, is a professor of psychology at York University in Toronto, Ontario, Canada, and a clinical supervisor and therapist at the York University Psychology Clinic. Dr. Angus practices, supervises, and conducts psychotherapy research addressing the contributions of narrative and emotion processes for clinically significant change, particularly in the context of emotion-focused therapy. Over the past 25 years, she has published more than 90 publications addressing the unique contributions of metaphor, narrative, emotion, and meaning-making processes to productive client change, and has conducted numerous training workshops addressing implications for effective therapy practice. She coauthored *Working With Narrative in Emotion-Focused Therapy: Changing Stories, Healing Lives* (with Leslie S. Greenberg), and was featured in an APA therapy DVD with Sandra C. Paivio, *Narrative Processes in Emotion-Focused Therapy for Trauma*. Dr. Angus was the senior coeditor of *The Handbook of Narrative and Psychotherapy: Practice, Theory, and Research* and was also coeditor of *Bringing Psychotherapy Research to Life: Understanding Change Through the Work of Leading Clinical Researchers*. She is a past president of both the International Society for Psychotherapy Research and the North American Chapter, Society for Psychotherapy Research.